The African City

This unique book tries in a short format to give the reader a comprehensive picture of cities in Africa from early origins to the present. It is comprehensive both in terms of time coverage, from before the Pharaohs to the present moment, and in that it tries to consider cities from the entire continent, not just sub-Saharan Africa. Apart from factual information and rich description material culled from many sources, it looks at many issues, from why urban life emerged in the first place to how present-day African cities cope in difficult times. Instead of seeing towns and cities as somehow extraneous to the real Africa, it views them as an inherent part of developing Africa – indigenous, colonial, and post-colonial – and emphasizes the extent to which the future of African society and African culture will likely be played out mostly in cities. Different positions and debates amongst scholars on African cities receive considerable attention. The book is written to appeal to students of history but equally to geographers, planners, sociologists, and development specialists interested in urban problems.

Bill Freund is Professor of Economic History and Development Studies at the University of KwaZulu-Natal. He is the author of many books, including *The African Worker* (Cambridge University Press, 1995).

New Approaches to African History

Series Editor
Martin Klein, *University of Toronto*

New Approaches to African History is designed to introduce students to current findings and new ideas in African history. Although each book treats a particular case and is able to stand alone, the format allows the studies to be used as modules in general courses on African history and world history. The cases represent a wide range of topics. Each volume summarizes the state of knowledge on a particular subject for a student who is new to the field. However, the aim is not merely to present views of the literature, it is also to introduce debates on historiographical or substantive issues. As such, a particular volume may argue for a particular point of view. The aim of the series is to stimulate debate, to challenge students and general readers. The series is not committed to any particular school of thought.

Other books in the series:

Africa Since 1940, by Frederick Cooper
Muslim Societies in African History, by David Robinson
Reversing Sail: A History of the African Diaspora, by Michael Gomez

The African City

A History

Bill Freund
University of KwaZulu-Natal

CAMBRIDGE
UNIVERSITY PRESS

CAMBRIDGE UNIVERSITY PRESS
Cambridge, New York, Melbourne, Madrid, Cape Town, Singapore, São Paulo

Cambridge University Press
32 Avenue of the Americas, New York, NY 10013-2473, USA

www.cambridge.org
Information on this title: www.cambridge.org/9780521821094

First published 2007

Printed in the United States of America

A catalog record for this publication is available from the British Library.

Library of Congress Cataloging in Publication Data

Freund, Bill.
The African city : a history / Bill Freund.
    p.   cm. – (New approaches to African history)
Includes bibliographical references and index.
ISBN-13: 978-0-521-82109-4 (hardback)
ISBN-10: 0-521-82109-6 (hardback)
ISBN-13: 978-0-521-52792-7 (pbk.)
ISBN-10: 0-521-52792-9 (pbk.)
1. Cities and towns – Africa – History.   2. Urbanization – Africa – History.
I. Title.   II. Series.
HT148.A2A3435   2007
307.76096–dc22   2006008554

ISBN   978-0-521-82109-4 hardback
ISBN   978-0-521-52792-7 paperback

Contents

Preface

Urbanisation is one of the most important social processes observed and written about over time. From a variety of beginnings, cities have evolved into sites where more and more complex activities take place. At a certain point historically, the city may look parasitic on the productive countryside, where the balance between human beings and nature is so much better sustained. However, further along the line the city itself becomes the logical home for multitudes of social and economic activities that are fundamental to the material life of mankind. And with that, the balance between city and countryside changes.

Cities attract friends and enemies. The city on the hill is a symbol of wisdom and balance, of the good life, and of democratic politics. The metropolis – Smoketown, Shackland – is the site of alienation and oppression where modernity becomes a prison for men and women. On the whole, this book will try to avoid these kinds of moral judgements, not that they may not lack validity within particular discourses and for particular individuals or types of individuals. Given the author's special interests, much attention will be paid to economic and social processes and where the city fits into them. The city evolves distinctive cultural forms, some of them largely appropriate only to urban life, and I shall try to do some justice to these cultural forms. It also becomes in need of a distinctive politics that fits the dense interstices of urban living. These will take a more important form as our narrative proceeds and urban politics acquires this distinctiveness.

This work is a synthesis not only of monographic work but of syntheses. There have been not only numerous excellent studies of

urban life and urban history situated in Africa, but even some excellent general works on some aspects of urban society. The ambition
here is to create a larger picture of African cities developed historically from the proverbial beginning. This is, I believe, a path that
has not been trodden. Why do it? One reason for this is that while
particular towns and cities that fit particular historical purposes and
political or economic ends may come and go, the urban tradition is
one of accretion and agglomeration, not one of entirely distinct stages.
Cities inevitably carry baggage from their individual and collective
pasts that have to be understood. Another reason is to confront the
rural bias that affects much African studies, particularly in the English
language scholarly tradition. Mahmood Mamdani has provided for us
a framework for colonial politics in Africa that divides rule between
the potentially democratic world of the citizen and the autocratic world
of the subject – and native authority (*Citizen and Subject*, Princeton:
Princeton University Press, 1996). On the whole, the city was the more
likely residence of the citizen and the concept of individual citizenship,
so standard in the colonial metropoles, potentially threatened the form
of colonial rule in Africa. Rural studies, peasant studies, have easily
represented themselves as the true Africa. By contrast, this book insists
not only that the urban has a historic place in Africa of some importance – even if it is not necessarily the home of citizen democracy –
but that this importance has grown and grown and that the future of
Africa is likely to be increasingly urban. African studies have to situate
themselves in part on an urban foundation. In the last two chapters,
I draw a distinction between modernist interpretations of the city and
postmodern approaches. I will have to admit to my prejudices being
very largely modernist myself, but I can see the strength of some post-
modern insights and try to bring those to bear on the discussion in
those chapters.

Africa is also a good place to study cities because African cities are
so varied. We can find one-industry towns as well as diverse urban
economies, fragile and nascent urban development traceable from the
historical record and the work of archaeologists as well as some of the
Third World metropolises that rightly exercise the minds of development experts. Nice as it might be to be an expert on everywhere, this
scholar has his special interests and areas in which he has a strong
background. In recent years, I have written quite a lot on the political economy of Durban, the South African city in which I live. This
has extended itself as well into participation in a comparative project

involving the French city of Marseilles and the Ivorian city of Abidjan. It enabled me to reacquaint myself with the magnetic appeal of the West African city. My memories include impressions of living in Zaria and Dar es Salaam as well as more fleeting time passed in many other cities from Cairo to Tananarive, from Asmara to Dakar.

In this book, I have tried to do justice to very different parts of the African continent in putting forward a continental portrait. With some misgiving about his own limitations, this has meant the author has discarded the usual idea of sub-Saharan Africa and integrated Africa north of the Sahara, notably Egypt, into this portrait. My hope is that this may help in the task of deracialising the way readers look at this enormous continent and stressing the human variety that can be found in historic and contemporary Africa. Having worked with French colleagues and plunged into the relevant literature in French, a literature which has long been much more sympathetic to the urban in Africa in general, I have tried frequently to use examples from Francophone countries and material written in French in order to make them more available to readers without French.

I need to thank especially Martin Klein for his faith in my ability to carry through this ambitious project as well as a number of anonymous readers whose criticism contained useful suggestions that allowed me to take this study forward. One of these who revealed her identity was Catherine Coquery-Vidrovitch. Although there are some differences in how we analyse African cities, there are many parallels in our thinking, manifest in her superb review article on African urban history for the 1991 *African Studies Review*. Indeed, had she completed her proposed two-volume study of African cities, this book would have had far less justification. I would like to thank also two distinguished urban scholars in South Africa, Alan Mabin and Sue Parnell, for wading through my first draft. I must thank also the reader for the final version of the manuscript whose concerns have pushed me towards a slightly more didactic text which will hopefully assist student readers particularly.

The initial phase of gathering ideas and working towards a proposal was made possible by my time as a Guest Researcher at the Nordic Africa Institute in Uppsala, Sweden, in 1999. Of the many helpful people there, I would like to single out the director of the then urban studies programme, my late and much missed Norwegian friend Mariken Vaa. The last phase has involved coming to the School of Oriental & African Studies of the University of London as a British Academy Visiting Professor, where I was the guest of Henry Bernstein and the Department of Development Studies. For this I must thank Henry, SOAS, and the Academy. I also have tried out parts of this book as seminar papers in a number of settings, notably the African Studies Centre at the University of Bayreuth (Germany); the annual meeting of the African Studies Association of Australasia and Oceania (at Perth, Australia); at WISER, the Witwatersrand Institute for Social and Economic Research at the University of the Witwatersrand in Johannesburg, South Africa; and at a conference held by the Netherlands Institute on War Documentation in Amsterdam. In the last case, the paper I gave will be published in a modified form in the Netherlands. I am very thankful in each case for the practical assistance provided. Thanks also to Tom Leighton for Egyptian references and to the Frankl-Bertrams for making research work in London seem like research done at home.

I would like especially to thank Helen Hills at Cambridge University Library for her help in obtaining the images that appear as Figures 1, 2, and 3; the assistance of Marie-Paule Blasini for her help in obtaining the image that appears as Figure 4; and Georges Gottleib, for his help in obtaining the image that appears as Figure 8. Thanks are also due to Dr. and Mrs. Sifrin and the University of the Witwatersrand in connection with Figures 8 and 9, the Gerard Sekoto reproductions; and to the Johannesburg Art Gallery for imaging these paintings.

Apart from the acknowledgements to photographers, I would like also to thank the following for help with regard to photographs: Eric Crahan, Olivier Graefe, Jeremy Grest, Rem Koolhaas, and Brigitte Lachartre. Thanks also to Frank Sokolic, my talented mapmaker, and to Mary Cadette, my very helpful project manager at Techbooks.

CHAPTER 1

Urban Life Emerges in Africa

In the preface and, by implication, in the title of this chapter, I have suggested that cities evolve; I accept an essentially evolutionary model in my analysis of what follows. It is possible to argue rather that there are or were uniquely African kinds of cities or towns, before the incorporation of Africa into world-systems with wide economic networks and defining urban cultural structures, as a cultural statement about Africanness. However, the assumption here is that there are several reasons why urban life emerges anywhere: environmental, ritual, political, and economic, all of which will be examined in more detail. This would be true for any major area in the world and up to a point may come together in very different and quite unique combinations. This volume will emphasise that the evolutionary model needs to be modified to an important extent by the incorporation of earlier elements into later urban development, just as forms of rural settlement may be carried into urban ways of living. Old cities are inevitably accretions with layers that survive from their past, cultural if not physical. The division of this African urban history into chapters that look at the impact of incorporation into the beginnings of a world-economy, at colonialism and at the post-colonial situation, tries to give character to evolutionary change, but it does not mean to suggest that there are no continuities from one phase to another.

Africa is an ideal setting for studying the beginnings of urbanisation. In many regions of the African continent, the rise of new towns belongs to the relatively recent historical record, while a considerable number of archaeological excavations have been aimed at trying to discern the nature of urban life in the past, at just how, when, and why it developed. This chapter considers the information available on the character of early urbanisation and highlights what we are able to surmise about towns and cities at different phases of their development. It will involve making some mighty leaps in terms of distance between times and places.

This chapter will not proceed chronologically; its first pages will move northwards in space and focus on different early *types* of urban settlements, settlements with little evidence of influence from outside Africa. Such types are far from being mutually exclusive, but the examples given are meant to highlight particular aspects more clearly. On a time frame, we will go back as far as five thousand years ago to the Old Kingdom of Egypt – but, where such settlements show little evidence of influence from the increasingly commercialised global networks in touch with the West, some of my examples are from a relatively recent date, including the first example I will be giving.

As one of the authors cited below, anthropologist John Peel, has written about the large Yoruba urban settlements of south-western Nigeria, particularly as they may have been before the nineteenth century, they often seem to defy simple categorisation on a rural-to-urban continuum. The link between urban places discussed has to be understood as *conceptual* rather than *linear* in order to do justice to the structure of ideas that follow in the next pages. Thus we will often interrogate why and to what extent these places are urban. We shall move through a number of descriptive sequences before taking stock by looking at the types of urban structures as a whole. It is important to stress that if they fail to meet certain contemporary criteria of what a city should be like, such settlements should not be dismissed but rather embraced with interest for their unique configurations and contribution to the cultural development of mankind.

In the second half of the chapter, the narrative will come closer to following a conventional order in time, and major outside influences assimilated into African experience – Greek, Punic, Roman, and Islamic, as well as earlier sub-global world-systems – will be taken on board. Here the urban becomes incontestable: the economy became more varied and involved intensified specialisation. Urban life had to be sustained by systematic agricultural surplus from outside in part determining urban-rural relationships. A definite and distinct urban culture within the system emerged. Whether by incorporation,

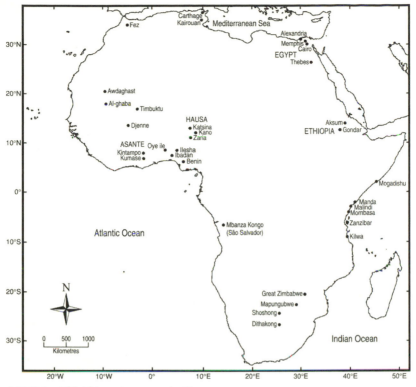

MAP 1. Old African towns and cities.

conquest, or other means of change, this did represent an evolutionary shift in North Africa in the first three cases and far more widely in
the fourth. The characteristic urban features of these systems will be
highlighted in the descriptions of the second half of the chapter.

We shall in fact begin at a fairly late point on the time frame. In
southern Africa – at the western edge of where Bantu-speaking agri-
culturalists settled in what is today Botswana – there have for several centuries been surprisingly large human agglomerations. Contemporary social scientists who specialise in the study of this area have
called them "agro-towns." These agro-towns may have contained ten
to twenty thousand people before the coming of colonial rule, although
the evidence also suggests that they expanded very substantially in the
context of the insecure and unstable conditions of the nineteenth century. Shoshong, capital of the Ngwato state in the nineteenth century,
may have attracted thirty thousand people, although they were rarely

all present in the town at once. Kanye, Serowe, and Molepolole in present-day Botswana are surviving examples of this phenomenon.

Europeans were astonished at the size of Dithakong, the most southerly such town. When they encountered it at the start of the nineteenth century, it was as large as the colonial capital of Cape Town. Although the agro-towns were invariably the core of important Tswana chiefships, it is striking to note that further to the east, in somewhat wetter country, closely related Sotho speakers showed little sign of taking to such large settlements. Nor did they exist in the time equivalent of the European Middle Ages when Tswana speakers apparently first settled in Botswana. It was only somewhat later, after a period of desiccation and retreat eastwards followed by resettlement after the year 1500, that this kind of unusual settlement pattern emerged.

There is no straightforward explanation for why this happened. The agro-towns are certainly emblematic of the power of chiefs gathering together a variety of people under their sway. In fact, the structure of the towns resembled a series of villages based on descent and affiliation to a chief or elder; a distinct feature was the space for the *kgotla*, a communal and ceremonial meeting ground that virtually defines what community means to the Tswana. But Tswana chiefs were not immeasurably powerful, nor was this the only way a chief in Africa could gain submission. Up to a point, defense may have been a factor in the gathering of large numbers of people. The sheer size of the agglomerated population in open country could represent a formidable deterrent to an invading band of some sort. Similarly, concentration was certainly related to ecological choices. Good water supplies, the presence of a remarkable hill, were typically features of the large settlement. In no way, however, could the Tswana economy be said to be so rich as to have supported urbanisation in the sense of a surplus that could sustain many non–food producers. Family members, and notably the women, had to scatter widely to farm and to gather foodstuffs. Young men spent most of their time living at cattle posts which were maintained at a long distance from the town, often on land which was too dry to support agriculture.

Concentration created problems and, as a result, until the changes of the nineteenth and twentieth centuries, which lent commercial and administrative purposes to towns that they had never before enjoyed, they died after a time. In the words of Neal Parsons, the size of Tswana towns accelerated the course of a cycle, exactly like that known to villages, where the town had to be moved and the population shifted, often with considerable frequency. Tswana urbanisation promoted a "cycle of depletion of local grasslands, cultivable soils, wood and water supplies."[1] In particular, Parsons believes that the efflorescence and subsequent disappearance of the Tswana town closely correlated to the depletion of wood resources in its vicinity. Thus Shoshong died to be replaced by Phalatswe – Old Palapye – at the close of the 1880s. Dithakong had long disappeared by then. The agro-town structure did not lend itself without outside stimulus to the emergence of economic activities that were specifically urban in character. However, we need to respect as one facet of human evolution this rare but not unique kind of preference for a herding and farming people to choose to live and develop their sense of community in settlements the size of large towns.

If we look for analogies in southern Africa, for a pattern with which to configure Tswana urbanisation, there is one possibility that stretches back much further in time. Over a period of some centuries, stone construction of an impressive nature took place at relatively permanent settlements in south-central Africa, mainly in modern Zimbabwe – which derives its modern name from what seems to be a Shona word for such settlements (madzimbahwe, chiefs' residences) – but extending into the territory of Botswana. Less architecturally impressive stone construction in fact was undertaken extensively all over the South African Highveld, continuing into recent times. Most of this construction is accompanied by the traces of relatively small settlements, villages, but not all. Some clearly mark fairly large communities. The oldest site associated with this pattern is at Mapungubwe, in the Limpopo Province of South Africa near to the river of that name. Mapungubwe is a hill site with some impressive graves and beautiful art objects that can be associated with the beginnings of a gold trade to the coast more than a thousand years ago. The residence of a royal family or clan atop the hill is a remarkable feature. But as an urban community it seems to have been quite small and limited.

Further north are the ruins of what we call Great Zimbabwe, not far from the modern town of Masvingo, Zimbabwe. Here there are esthetically awesome remains – a beautiful circular tower, high walls sometimes shaped to allow for step construction, ornate walling patterns

---

[1] Neil Parsons, "Settlement in East-Central Botswana c.1820–1900" in R. Renee Hitchcock & Mary Smith, eds., *Settlement in Botswana: The Historical Development of a Human Landscape* (Marshalltown: Heinemann, 1982), 120.

representing impressive man-hours of labour, construction above the valley site on a hill that earlier archaeologists dubbed the Acropolis, where daily requirements would have to have been brought laboriously by porters. There is much that we shall never know about these ruins, but there are some points concerning Zimbabwe on which scholars seem to agree. One is that the valley contained a dense community of mud- and wood-constructed homes – many plastered in their heyday – where people once lived. Up to fifteen thousand of them may have been resident at once on a site of seven hundred hectares.[2] David Beach has imagined this as "a great mass of packed huts that spread across the valley in between the marshes and up the hillsides on terraces . . . basically a mid thirteenth to fourteenth century construction."[3] The stone remains were certainly not houses. The walls, of little use for defense, may at most have served to block off activities, perhaps sacred activities, from the mass of the population.

We will never know exactly what purpose the different structures served. The archaeologist Tom Huffman has made a series of creative suggestions based on his study of the sacred iconography of Venda-speaking people who live south of the frontier in South Africa and who may maintain more of the older culture of Great Zimbabwe than the people who live closer to the ruins today. At the least, they suggest an added element we need to consider, the importance of the sacral: urban sites can serve as ideal placements for ceremonies and activities that link men to ancestors and to gods in a way that knits together a "community." The sacred element has clearly sometimes been of real significance in explaining the roots of urban agglomeration and may have been the main element here. If Huffman is right, sacred activities associated with a powerful chiefly dynasty, or dynasties, were more important than any economic impulse in bringing together this large community, which was comparable to the big Tswana agro-towns in size.

Historians feel confident that Great Zimbabwe was the centre of a state that traded gold with the Indian Ocean coast, and that it was a city in effect linked by an umbilical cord to Kilwa, which controlled this trade at its height, and which was the most impressive urban community that developed on the coast of East Africa before the coming

[2] Thomas Huffman, *Snakes and Crocodiles: Power and Symbolism in Ancient Zimbabwe* (Johannesburg: University of Witwatersrand Press, 1996), 125.
[3] D. N. Beach, *Zimbabwe Before 1900* (Gweru: Mambo Press, 1984), 25.

of Europeans. We shall look at Kilwa later in the chapter. But though there are traces of long-distance trade in the ruins of Great Zimbabwe (Indian beads, a Persian bowl, Chinese porcelain), they have an extraneous quality – shards of pottery and coins rather than the unveiling of a real merchant quarter or any site that indicates intensive commercial activity. The decline of this remarkable settlement may have to do with shifts in the gold trade, although this is not a settled point amongst scholars. Nor is it really clear how the gold trade impacted on the strengthening of political power in the region.

Scholars have generally concluded that the large population concentration at Great Zimbabwe, despite all the human effort that went into the moulding of its stones, was not sustainable after a time, just as with the Tswana agro-towns. The valley in which the ruins are situated seems to have become agriculturally barren through intensive cultivation and/or climate change. It was abandoned by around 1450, perhaps after two hundred years of settlement, and no community of any size was thereafter reestablished there. Whatever environmental reason there may have been for settling this site initially – if one existed – it was an evanescent one.

There are numerous other similar ruins in the region, notably further west in increasingly dry parts of Matabeleland and into northern Botswana, but the stonework there was not so extensive or impressive and the scale of settlement smaller. Beach suggests that they were cultural outliers, perhaps established by fragmenting branches of chiefly families, with less and less wealth or link to overseas trade. This seems even truer of the Shona chieftaincy capitals described by Portuguese visitors from the sixteenth century, generally further north. The Mutapa dynasty frequently built stockaded towns with little or no stoneworks and more emphasis on defense; this was the ruling power that profited from the gold trade in its later centuries of existence. Great Zimbabwe was perhaps a kind of urban experiment that failed rather than evolving along a path of greater complexity and sophistication. Perhaps the Tswana agro-town idea was influenced by this *type* of larger settlement in some way and represents its only later successor.

São Salvador and Gondar

Within a century or so of the end of Great Zimbabwe, contact with Europeans was a factor in the making of other impressive urban sites in the African interior. However, the urban character of these sites remained incomplete. One example was Mbanza Kongo, the capital of a large and powerful state south of the Congo River within modern Angola which traded – especially for slaves – with the Portuguese from the fifteenth century. The Portuguese were very interested in the Kongo kingdom as an ally and made determined efforts to assimilate it to a European model, in particular to Christianise it. The royal family patronised a literate Christian culture for generations, and willingly took on some forms of European statehood in the eyes of their trading partners. The capital, impressively sited on a mountainous plateau, attracted mainly retainers of the royal house but also became the site for a set of Christian buildings, constructed from stone under the direction of Europeans at first – but for some time with cadres of Africans who had mastered relevant building techniques – and housing monks and priests. It probably reached its apogee in the middle of the seventeenth century.

To Europeans, it was the passably noble city of São Salvador. Facing the plaza, accompanying a cathedral and palace, was a small walled town inhabited by the Portuguese. To Africans, Mbanza Kongo remained a place where narrow paths ran between walled compounds with enough space for livestock and garden farming but with room for agriculture as town and countryside merged into one another. Even the palace was not inhabited for very long; it was probably inconvenient and dirty compared to the typical large compound structure. Royal patronage remained so much the basis for economic activity that private property in particular locations seems never to have developed. There was little space for even rudimentary urban civil society, yet the aura of sacred power associated with this site long outlived the secular decline of the kingdom after the end of the seventeenth century, and the physical locale retained a cultural importance as a remnant of its urban glory long after the political significance of Mbanza Kongo had faded. "Mbanza" has long had, perhaps even before the creation of this town, an association with urbanity and civility in the Kikongo language, distinguishing it from village life. Yet beside the remarkable stone facades that spelt civilisation to Europeans, an African community with different associations had actually breathed life into São Salvador and made it a vital place shared by people. Thus the eighteenth-century city, which remained of considerable regional sacred and even political importance, with population concentrations at times as large as in the past, continued to be identified with the old stone buildings, even whilst they fell increasingly into ruins.

Thousands of kilometres from Mbanza Kongo, another Portuguese-influenced stone city was rising on the Ethiopian plateau – Gondar. The emperor Fasilidas, who reigned in the second quarter of the seventeenth century, despite the expulsion of the Jesuits and the restoration of Coptic Orthodoxy as the church of Ethiopia, was responsible for authorising the construction of palaces and churches at this town one hundred kilometres or so north of Lake Tana. By contrast with Mbanza Kongo, this construction process continued over several generations. This was an apparently flagrant departure from Ethiopian history, where no permanently constructed capital had existed for a thousand years.

The Ethiopian highlands have been the home of an indigenous class society of lords and peasants for many centuries; however, although trading settlements have undoubtedly existed for a very long time, urbanisation was a weak force. What happens if one does look back a further one thousand years from the time of Fasilidas? Parallel to the existence of the late Roman Empire, a kingdom which converted to Christianity and where a Semitic language ancestral to present linguistic uses was dominant, focussed on the city of Aksum. Aksum remained of great importance for many centuries and reemerged as a Christian centre and market town in medieval and later times. However, the archaeologist David Phillipson has recently concluded that whereas "Aksum was of a size and importance to merit the term 'city' . . . there is no evidence that Aksum was a city as that term is sometimes understood. Its structures, as presently known, comprised large buildings of unknown purpose, but clear elite associations, as well as funerary and other monuments, and religious buildings."[4] So far as we know, ordinary folk lived at some distance from this sacred core near to cultivable fields. Aksum lacked defensive walls. The commercial life of the Aksumite state must have been considerable (it minted coinage), but perhaps not much of it went on within this early African city; its political and sacred role doubtless reflected yet older Ethiopian traditions that have been discerned only vaguely so far by archaeologists.

---

[4] David Phillipson, "Aksumite Urbanism" in David Anderson & Richard Rathbone, eds., *Africa's Urban Past* (Oxford & Portsmouth, NH: James Currey & Heinemann, 2000), 61.

Thereafter, later Ethiopian rulers travelled constantly with their courts in order to keep control of their subjects; they did not try to contain unruly subordinates within a town's wall. Ethiopian Christianity focussed particularly on monasteries rather than urban cathedrals. Before Gondar was constructed, the court would often consist of hundreds of tents housing camp followers. Not only was this understood as a means for the court to impress its authority on key regions, it had as well an environmental logic. The weight of this kind of crude natural exploitation of foodstuffs, timber, and other products fell only seasonally on particular localities if the court moved about, and in absentia, the region was allowed to recover. Less impressive buildings by far marked the existence of regional market centres and towns which have attracted relatively little attention from historians of Ethiopia.

Gondar itself was important for its association with royalty and, through royalty, with the church, rather than for particularly significant commercial activities. A sacred iconography detailed this importance. Donald Crummey's recent study records no less than eleven important royal churches in the vicinity. He has also recently insisted that the change initiated by permanent construction in Gondar was less dramatic than meets the European eye. Seventeenth-century "Gondar was above all a winter residence, a place where the court, and its ever-widening circles of minions and dependents, passed the season of the rains."[5] The ambulant nature of the state continued after the rise of permanent construction in Gondar into the nineteenth century through a period of royal weakness. By the middle of the eighteenth century, the commercial pace of life was picking up and Gondar was acquiring more economic importance (unlike Mbanza Kongo). Surviving documentation indicates the growing frequency of house sales and purchases; wealthy people began to have a stake in the permanent prosperity of Gondar independent of the fate of the enfeebled royal dynasty. This pattern of commercialisation, which began to transform older population agglomerations everywhere in nineteenth-century Africa, if they survived its convulsions, will emerge more clearly in the following chapter. Gondar and Mbanza Kongo are in some respects another *type* of early town compared to south-central African agro-towns and the walled remains of Zimbabwe, although their respective evolutions diverged.

---

[5] Donald Crummey, *Land and Society in the Christian Kingdom of Ethiopia from the Thirteenth to the Twentieth Century* (Oxford: James Currey, 2000), 74.

Cities Develop in Egypt

The slow emergence of urbanism, of full-blown city life, is also to some degree observable at a yet much greater distance in time from us, in ancient Egypt. Through much of its very long history, particularly before the New Kingdom (1540–1070 BC), the Nile Valley knew population concentrations to some extent, but only extremely slowly were cities in the full sense of the word "invented." Indeed, for long, such concentrations, to the extent that we can guess from the size of the locations, may not have been much bigger than the urban sites we have been considering above elsewhere in Africa. Ancient Egypt lacked money; exchange took the form of distribution in kind. Domestic architecture, according to archaeologists, seems to have consisted to a very large extent on facilities for hoarding grain, for milling, and for brewing. There is thus an evident logic in the Egyptian domestication of the cat as a means of dealing with the scourge of rodents. Domestic architecture was normally constructed of mud and one storey high, ideally built around a courtyard. Given the difficulties of producing a surplus, it is likely that urban households normally required and had access to agricultural land nearby. And distribution in turn was handled by the temples in the name of the gods. Traders were generally economic agents who operated in the name of officials and/or temple priests.

With time, houses became grander. Large villas had columned halls while courtyards contained pools of water. Distinct spaces for cooking were established as kitchens and limited forms of furniture for storage and sitting were carved from wood. For the wealthy, bed rests were supplemented with wooden beds. The roof level was often used as pavilion space for relaxation as well as storage reached by stairways while Thebes contained houses of more than one storey. Small windows were carved into walls so as not to let in dust.

The great monuments of Egypt that define its renown are associated with worship and with a state intimately connected to worship, where the natural and supernatural were tightly linked. Much was directly produced in order to support the activities of the afterlife. Secular residences, even of the powerful, seem to have been smaller and their grandest spaces reserved for public ceremonials. Much of what we know about the lives of ordinary men and women comes from archaeological excavations of the homes of those who worked on

funerary projects and as servants of temples. Though Egyptian art is
full of images of the homely, the real separation of a private sphere of
life independent of the sacred was a very slow process. Thus urban
agglomerations probably largely emerged as, and long remained, the
homes of those tied to rituals of worship of the gods and the needs
of the afterlife. By the time of the New Kingdom, Memphis, built on
the site where the Nile parts into the many channels of the Delta,
had become an important shipbuilding and commercial centre, but at
least one-third of urban space was taken up by temple enclosures and
the like.

Yet Egyptian towns may have exhibited a high degree of planning,
reflecting their religious and bureaucratic character which made quite
an impression: "The first sights to be seen as you approached the city's
harbour in your river boat were the golden tips of hundreds of temple
flagpoles flashing like crystals in the distance; then, as you drew closer,
myriad linen pennants glittering against the purple cliffs."[6] The chief
officials of towns in Egypt were effectively chief priests, and the physical layout of urban space was certainly thought through carefully. In
the one example we know of – an ancient Egyptian city that has been
excavated relatively intact, Amarna – the key structural element was
a great temple-lined avenue; there is little evidence of interest, however, in the structure of residential areas. Early in the New Kingdom,
for instance, Thebes, the key urban settlement of Egypt and a place
of "spectacle and munificence,"[7] was entirely evacuated and levelled
in order to make space for new stone temples. The new – and still
unwalled – Thebes, called by Egyptians simply The City or something like Waset (Thebes was a name used by the Greeks), stretched
for perhaps fifteen kilometres along the Nile. The commercial life –
and far more privatised space – of the cities of Mesopotamia (contemporary Iraq) appears to have developed millennia in advance of the
parallel riverain civilisation of Egypt. Nor did Egyptian culture have
much space for the "urban" as a way of life; the good life was imagined to be one on a farm. Only very slowly did the economic world
of exchange and commodity production emerge within the cultural
carapace of Egyptian religion and the structures and people associated

[6] John Romer, *Ancient Lives: The Story of the Pharaoh's Tombmakers* (London: Weidenfeld
& Nicolson, 1984), 4.
[7] Barry Kemp, *Ancient Egypt: Anatomy of a Civilisation* (London & New York:
Routledge, 1989), 206.

with worship. There are thus important parallels between the history of urbanisation in Egypt and elsewhere in Africa if one allows for the uniquely lengthy time frame of that history.

Early West African Cities

Yet the early history of West Africa also allows us to consider many urban settlements over a span of as much as two thousand years. Oral tradition, surviving elements in more recent urban life, couple with the evidence provided by archaeology to suggest something about the life of such settlements. It is the latter discipline which permits us to write something about the ancient settlements near the modern town of Djenne, Mali. The old settlements of the river Niger are famously associated with the trans-Saharan trade in gold; we tend to assume that they are best thought of as arising in connection with commercial link-ages. The Jenne-Jeno site which has been explored by the McIntoshes, towards the northern edge of the belt of rain-fed cultivation in West Africa and convenient to the movements of caravans aiming at oases in the Sahara, would seem to fit this model perfectly. However, what has been found instead is that population concentration at this site two thousand years ago *preceded* the trans-Saharan trade and the arrival of the camel and seems primarily to have been a response to the particu-lar characteristics of the local environment, where desert, desert-edge plain, and river meet. Nor are there clear traces of any political or sacral authority to explain this concentration. There were perhaps twenty thousand people resident in Jenne-Jeno around the year AD 800 with clear signs of economic specialisation, but the site has left no traces of elite construction or political centralisation of any importance – no public buildings, monuments, or shrines. Gao, eventually the centre of the Songhay state and the site of the oldest dated epigraphic evi-dence in the Sahel, has revealed a somewhat parallel history. Similar sites, pre-Islamic, pre–international trade, for instance in the vicinity of Timbuktu, are suspected to exist as well.

It is from the 1060s that we have a description by an Arab geogra-pher, al-Bakri, of the capital city of a desert-edge West African state associated with the gold trade, a city called al-Ghaba, or "the grove," presumably from its association with a sacred grove. The larger urban entity (or ruler or state?) was known to the Arabs as Ghana. By the eleventh century, it had an Islamic component, but al-Ghaba was the

royal town at a distance from the commercial Muslim one in which
"houses are constructed of stone and acacia wood. The king has a
palace with conical huts [around], surrounded by a fence like a wall."
Around the traditional capital were compounds containing domed
structures, where local gods and ancestors were worshipped. This is a
very different picture than what the McIntoshes have given us in the
case of Djenne. Political authority in Ghana was effectively linked to
spiritual power, and both infused the capital. The site of the capital
of Ghana has been identified with ruins at Kumbi Saleh in southern
Mauritania – but frustratingly no traces have been uncovered of a pre-
Islamic or non-Islamic town there.

In other parts of West Africa, somewhat different patterns yet again
have been discerned. As we turn south and east towards the densely
peopled territory of present-day Nigeria, predilections towards urban
concentration go back far into the past. Moreover, the conventionally
urban elements have largely been in place for centuries. In the savanna
regions, the states that existed in the sixteenth century and later were all
associated with, indeed named for, their capital cities. Kano, the largest
of the northern Nigerian cities of today, can be associated particularly
with a sacred height, Dalla Hill, where powerful spirits were thought
to dwell. Dalla towers over the vicinity, a fertile and today extremely
densely settled area. Nearby are particularly rich sources of iron ore.
Much agricultural land was enclosed within the impressive outer walls
of Kano, which defended an economic world not yet distinct from the
countryside. Walling defined large territories around all the Hausa-
speaking cities of the central savanna of West Africa, in fact.

The *birni*, or city, as a distinct social unit is an old established (but
how old?) conceptual unit in the Hausa language quite distinct from
the village or town. For centuries, characteristically urban activities
have marked the *birane*. Kano, for instance, became a major commercial centre, a place of wealth whose ruler was a source of, and controller
of, wealth. Within the hierarchy of officials conventionally brought to
bear by urban-based authority were figures that were essentially urban
in function – associated with the good order of the town or the market.
Probably initially the supervision of the market was female, reflecting
feminine power over trade.

The formation of peoples, the spread of states and Islam, are intimately linked to the influence of the *birni*. For the historian Abdullahi
Smith, the *birni* must by definition have had walls. Political authority
and defense were a key defining attribute. The other characteristic is

the population mix: any *birni* will contain different quarters inhabited by different peoples. The *sarki*, or ruler, cannot be a tribal chieftain. By definition he will sustain authority over a mixture of peoples. Nigerian archaeology is not advanced enough to suggest when the *birane* emerged but the implication from Smith is that they had been evolving from the time of Ghana and the earliest urban or quasi-urban settlements around Djenne and Timbuktu, thus also equivalent to the European Middle Ages or even a bit earlier. The walls of Kano and Zaria (which enclose Kufena, an impressive stone ridge hill comparable to Dalla) go back to the fifteenth century and probably had even older foundations. It is impossible to say what the earliest urban agglomerations were like, but they long ago evolved conventional if distinct urban forms.

Further south in Nigeria nearer the savanna-forest border and even within the forest zone, an urban pattern has also prevailed for a very long time. It is, as in the savanna, not merely a question of capital towns, but of entire networks of towns and cities. The most remarkable pattern of all is associated with the Yoruba-speaking peoples of south-western Nigeria. A very large percentage of Yoruba speakers at the time of the British conquest were located in agglomerations, some of them, notably Ibadan with more than two hundred thousand inhabitants, very sizeable indeed. These cities were almost certainly far smaller and probably far less characterised by commercial and artisanal activity before the turmoil of the early nineteenth-century Yoruba civil wars and the rapid increase in commoditised trade thereafter, but they certainly existed – and were substantial.

Ibadan was organised around networks of compounds led by the heads of lineages who were in effect its landowners. Such compounds in modern times have contained forty to four hundred inhabitants, the largest number of whom in the nineteenth century were household pawns (indebted dependents) and slaves. As further north, particular urban quarters were associated with particular ethnic groups or particular forms of worship. By and large, the population, living in walled compounds, went out to work in the fields, where they often maintained temporary shelter. So there were limits to the urban character of these settlements. Yet by the nineteenth century they were the core site of Yoruba craft-guild production and maintained an intense commercial life. Markets lay at the heart of these large and remarkable towns – but intra-town trade was probably far more important even than regional commerce. And Yoruba towns became

the site of festivities, of sacred rituals that defined the town and
its inhabitants.

A. L. Mabogunje points also to the other central focus in the Yoruba,
or Nigerian town: political power. The layout of the town – its iconography – expressed a geography of power. Evidence of immense and
elaborate walling, if it does not still exist, can usually be traced even
now. Thus Oyo ile, the greatest political centre until the close of
the eighteenth century, was surrounded by walls which covered fifteen to twenty square miles. The British traveller Clapperton reported
the existence of seven separate markets in 1826. For the Yoruba, ile
Ife, indeed the site of remarkable thousand-year-old bronzes uncovered in colonial times, was the town that marked their origins as a
civilised people. Officialdom, as in Hausa towns, was called into being
to arrange the administration of the city and urban life itself. Ibadan,
a nineteenth-century creation, is a remarkable case: it had no single
ruler and obviously represented a federation of people from different
places who came together voluntarily and who considered each other as
equals. In this sense, it is a cosmopolitan city as Smith discussed for the
Hausa *birane*.

The British sociologist John Peel has provided us with a close look at
a less well-known Yoruba town, Ilesha, which contained a population
of twenty to twenty-five thousand people in the late nineteenth century,
a period of decline. Ilesha can be best defined as the centre of a state, a
political and sacral capital rich in royal graves and shrines, which contained a large range of quarters, generally dominated by major chiefly
households and often associated with particular lineages. A system of
titled offices linked political and administrative duties to membership
in the state. Through situation in such a quarter, individuals can be
accurately described as persons who belong in the city, as citizens. Of
course the majority of the population consisted of household dependents, certainly in the nineteenth century slaves being very numerous, who were not citizens. But Peel prefers to see the parallel as one
with a Greek *polis* of free citizens, rather than an aristocracy, controlling "slaves . . . junior males . . . strangers . . . subordinate communities,
to say nothing of women" – in fact thus revealing the same ambigu-
ity hidden in Greek urbanism and citizenship as concepts.[8] A study

[8] J. D. Y. Peel, *Ijeshas and Nigerians: The Incorporation of a Yoruba Kingdom, 1890s–1970s*
(Cambridge: Cambridge University Press, 1983), 45.

of town history reveals as well more than harmony; violent conflicts between quarters – the *ija igbooro* – punctuated town history.

Dominant households had practical obligations in terms of the care of their quarter of the town as well as ritual functions; sometimes they were associated with craft specialities. Everyone had access to fields which supported the life of the household and formed the basis of the economy – fields as far as twelve miles from the urban residence – and modest dwellings providing more temporary shelter among those fields in many cases. There were satellite towns that owed allegiance to Ilesha; some were just villages but others participated in an urban network in which they could under particular circumstances lose or gain further lustre. In Peel's view "'town' seems a curiously flat designation for what kind of entity it was, and the unhelpfulness of the 'rural-urban' continuum, to which Yoruba towns are a kind of affront, is more indicative of its inadequacy as a framework of cross-cultural comparison than that of the nature of a place like Ilesha."[9] Yet in some respects he sees Ilesha as having a very characteristically urban feel culturally and politically.

In the southern part of West Africa, other cities also call for some mention, often cities that particularly reflected the majesty of a state and created boundaries and suitable space for the residence of a sacred ruler. This too may reflect a very old pattern, although to date it is impossible to give their lineage or point of origins. There are some differences but probably far more similarities with the Yoruba town model, although large towns were nowhere else so characteristic of human settlement. Two examples are the city of Benin in south-central Nigeria, east of Yoruba country and, considerably further west, Kumase in what is today the republic of Ghana. Benin, little influenced by European styles, was memorably described by a Dutch traveller, Olfert Dapper, in 1668 as "big as the town of Haarlem [this in fact refers to the royal precinct only]" and characterised by wide thoroughfares and a vast royal precinct with beautifully wrought galleries and decorated, low-lying palaces. The great wall complex of Benin, of which some remains still stand, presents spatial puzzles to the archaeologist. The importance of the ruler's compound suggests the centrality of political life in organising and defining the town.

[9] Ibid., 31.

This can be said equally of Kumase, the seat of the Asantehene and central place of the Asante Confederacy, the dominant power during the eighteenth and nineteenth centuries through much of the modern republic of Ghana. Built on the slopes of a rocky ridge, in the early nineteenth century Kumase contained a permanent population of fifteen to twenty thousand people, the kind of figure we have repeatedly noted in African population centres over the centuries. However, the numbers would swell enormously at times of festivals and seasons when it is was important for courtiers to appear before the Asantehene and diminish dramatically when the Asantehene was absent for any time. Feeding even the smaller numbers, however, required an urban setting where much of the population farmed and spent time in surrounding villages in the vicinity of Kumase. Early European visitors have given graphic evidence of decorated courtyards and galleries that marked the sacred and political character of the city, rather as was the case in Benin. As in Benin, the public ways were very well cared for: "The streets are generally very broad and clean and ornamented, with many beautiful banyan trees, offering a grateful shade from the powerful rays of the sun."[10]

In his massive history of Asante, Ivor Wilks places the greatest weight by far on the political culture of the region in explaining the growth of Kumase. Asante was very active commercially in its heyday, trading gold and kola nuts over long distances. But commerce was not primarily handled in Kumase. And Kintampo, the great northern market town, which dealt with the northern trade, seems to have been a city of relatively ephemeral dwellings and little political weight. Kumase was a city, but one that depended very one-sidedly on the physical imposition and needs of a powerful king; it is difficult to understand otherwise as an urban space. Generally speaking, a variety of *types* of urban settlements evolved in West Africa with similarities and also significant differences, notably over time.

This survey has suggested some of the variety, the geographical spread and range over time of early urban growth in Africa. Urbanisation rested on several pillars. The first and most difficult to pin down clearly was environmental: the discovery of particular sites where

---

[10] From an account of 1848 cited by Ivor Wilks, *Asante in the Nineteenth Century: The Structure and Evolution of a Political Order* (Cambridge: Cambridge University Press, 1975), 381.

FIGURE 1. Kumase, the capital of Asante: street scene and palace.
Source: Dupuis, *Journal of a Residence in Ashantee* (1824). Courtesy of
Cambridge University Library.

economic possibilities suggested the importance of human concentration to cultivating populations as in Jenne-Jeno or the Kalahari agro-
towns. The second was sacred, the spiritual importance within many
African cultures for a common place of worship and awe, no doubt
tied in generally to the emergence of beliefs that transcended local
ancestor cults. This element was already important at Aksum or Great
Zimbabwe. The third lay in the rise of powerful states, often closely tied
to religious rituals. There probably also lies a fourth category where
urban and rural mesh in an original way and the walled compounded
town becomes inherent in the cultural definition of the whole society, as we find in what is today Ghana and Nigeria. From the time of
ancient Egypt, however, the political and the religious held economic
implications, even if the economy did not easily emerge as a separate
sphere of life. In the remainder of this chapter, we are going to suggest
that the importance in some times and places of involvement in large-
scale commercial activity and incorporation into long-distance trade
circuits, sometimes marked by direct colonisation from outside, lent a
major new element to the process of urbanisation. Of course, this will
be most obvious when we examine human settlement linked to trade

with the "world-economy," with the rising star of Europe, but before we turn to that in Chapter Two, we must consider urbanisation linked to earlier such influences before the modern era.

Alexandria and Carthage

The first region of Africa where such influences became very important was North Africa, and we can best understand their impact by concentrating on two remarkable cities: Alexandria and Carthage. These were truly great cities, classic as well as Classical cities, displaying all the features that have fascinated scholars about urban life. They were very large compared to the towns we have been examining, and supplying them must have transformed wide swathes of countryside in the interests of creating a viable market. They were cosmopolitan with complex economic activities, massive amounts of commerce and craft activities breathing life into their streets and alleyways. The public architecture of Alexandria was very famous in its day, massive and intended to be very permanent, although little of it survives. Alexandria was the site of the great Lighthouse of Pharos, 135 metres high, guiding ships to its harbour, the tallest construction in the late Classical world, as well as the Library which may have been the greatest repository of Classical learning extant and the Museum where scholars from many lands assembled. The population included many intellectuals among its different social strata and, no doubt, a large number of wage-earners or proletarians. It was certainly also a city of poverty as well as wealth. Estimates for a much smaller city, Hermepolis, whose records have survived for some of the Roman period, reveal that of the land owned by urban dwellers, some 78 percent was owned by 2 percent of individuals. Alexandria was probably characterised by much greater concentrations of wealth. Both Alexandria and Carthage had an essentially foreign origin and could not have existed without the growing integration of the North African littoral into a larger world economically. Phoenicia, Greece, Rome – these were all cultures that were fundamentally urban in their core – were the principal influences here.

Alexandria was founded after the death of Alexander the Great in the fourth century BC and was the capital of the Ptolemies, descended from a general of the conqueror, and later the provincial capital of Roman Egypt. First ruled as a city by a Senate, Alexandria lost autonomy early and a huge part of it was covered with palaces and state property, but it had a distinct municipal administration. Moreover, quarters, and notably distinct neighbourhoods (each was called an *amphodon*), had a leadership recognised by the Romans. This pattern would recur in Egypt and the Islamic world in later centuries up to the present. In addition, the Romans continued to favour the city by exempting all its citizens from the payment of standard taxes paid by other Egyptians; just as under the Ptolemies, the associations with Greekness already gave Alexandria prestige. Such associations were for centuries very important to the elite; popular culture was probably far more heterogeneous and influenced by older Egyptian strains of thought.

The city was organised according to a plan which divided distinct quarters – Alpha to Epsilon – by wide avenues and contained excellent examples of all the public facilities admired in the Greek urban world, a stadium, a hippodrome (with factions in some way equivalent to modern sports team followings), a theatre, a market, and many temples. Many of these facilities were municipal and a source of revenue for the local state which also charged market taxes. Particularly in the second century AD, Alexandria was reconstructed along more Roman lines and "the urban elite incorporated Rome into the ritual life of the city and transformed the cityscape to give [it] a more Classical aspect."[11] The port was characterised by grandiose architecture, while a massive system of cisterns, some still extant, provided water via a freshwater canal. There were smaller settlements in the surrounds, which must have been involved in the task of supplying this ancient megalopolis, as well as seaside resorts.

Excavations at the small Delta city of Oxyrhynchus reveal that in Roman times and after, no less than ninety economically distinct guilds were present. Alexandria must have known far more. This immense urban world of perhaps two hundred thousand people contained an important quarter of native Egyptians, but it was a city of foreigners, above all Greeks, and also a very large number of Greek speaking Jews in the Delta quarter. Indeed there are records of expulsions of "superfluous" Egyptians to the countryside. The Old Testament was first translated into Greek in Alexandria, and it was a major growth point for early Christianity as well as for the formation of post-Temple Judaism in the Diaspora – that Greek word first applied in Alexandria

---

[11] Richard Alston, *The City in Roman and Byzantine Egypt* (New York & London: Routledge, 2002), 247.

to the exile of the Jews. The status of the numerous Jewish population was a major political issue. They were excluded from such institutions as the gymnasia which marked the definition of Greekness and from which emanated politically powerful clubs. Violent conflict between Jews and Greeks – which seem to have been caused by these claims, led to the segregation of Jews in Delta in AD 38. It was a feature of early Roman Alexandria until the major revolt of the Jews was put down in AD 115, after which the Jewish community lost most of its political significance. In fact, Alexandria had a history of factional violence, sometimes related to issues such as food prices but usually with a strongly political bias.

The power of Greekness in Alexandria paralleled the gradual decline and involution of ancient Egyptian culture which survived longest in the countryside. For centuries before the Ptolemies, Egypt had become more and more subject to foreign invaders from Asia or from the Nile Valley in what is today the Sudan, increasingly placed into a commercialised Mediterranean nexus that incorporated the valley as a source of agricultural wealth with trade extending deep into the African interior. The Greeks came to Egypt not only as traders but as settlers and had already established a number of cities in the Nile Delta. In fact, they seem generally to have established themselves in new urban communities rather than those which had been important under the pharaohs. Further east in Cyrenaica (eastern Libya), Greeks also became settlers in Africa and founded city-states which ruled a native population not without tension. The rise of cosmopolitan Alexandria can be contrasted with a rural Egypt where an inward-looking village culture dominated by the priests retained a core of practices from the older civilisation. The form Egyptian Christianity would take, characterised by the preeminence of monasteries and hermits, would build on this remnant culture before the advent of Islam. Christianity affected the structure of urban life as churches acquired importance, however, and resulted in a comeback for the Coptic form of Egyptian vis-à-vis the Greek language. But Alexandria's apogee was the phase of cultural cosmopolitanism; its capacity to diffuse culture through the valley of the Nile was extremely limited. With the rise of Islamic Cairo, Alexandria went into relative decline. Although Mediterranean linkages retained some significance, the core of political and economic life lay in the Nile Valley again rather than in the Mediterranean, and so it would remain until the nineteenth century.

Carthage has origins that go back somewhat further. This great city was founded by Phoenicians, the Lebanese of the ancient world, who combined commerce with settlement and had the western Mediterranean as their chosen field of expansion, from perhaps as early as 800 BC. Carthage, which retained strong filial ties to the cities of Phoenicia – the name was a Greek transliteration for the words for new city – and continued to revere their gods in human and other forms of sacrifice, was the dynamic centre of this expansion. It generated satellite cities and trading entrepôts from modern Tunisia westwards, in Spain and the islands of the western Mediterranean as well as on the African continent. From Carthage, the Punic language as well as Semitic religious forms spread through western North Africa, and both retained their importance long after the Romans destroyed Carthage in 146 BC. Carthage too was very large, a city that current scholarship estimates had a population of one hundred thousand people (perhaps peaking at twice that figure at the time of its destruction), with a powerfully commercial vocation and a large range of economic specialisation. The heart of its trade consisted of natural products such as wine and olive oil. From the fifth century BC, it began to issue coins. Carthage held multistoried buildings and developed a system of aqueducts and tanks to supply residents with water. Its government was dominated by a Senate or Council, but there was a far more representative general assembly as well as the continual threat to popular governance from power plays by overweening generals, just as in Rome. Indeed as in Rome, the Greek influence on Carthage was very strong in décor and architecture as well as civic life. However, and in this sense typical of some other Semitic speaking cultures, there was a strong bias against lifelike images in Carthaginian culture; it has left few remnants of any artistic interest. The religion of Carthage was focussed on civic power and loyalty, by contrast to the ancient Egyptian context whereby temple worship had overridden any other urban purpose. At first, Carthage was a kind of island city, linked to a network of trading towns throughout the western Mediterranean with relatively little contact in depth with the African population. However, with time, Carthage evoked imitations in the capitals of Berber-speaking rulers further west while ruling directly a "native" population – who spoke Punic and tried to absorb elements of its culture.

After the Roman conquest, a typically Roman network of cities arose in this part of Africa. These cities had the features of imperial towns everywhere – fora, market facilities, aqueducts, temples, public gathering places, gymnasia, baths, libraries, cemeteries, stadia, and so forth, while at least low-lying and fertile parts of the region were incorporated into an empire that defined good order and the civilised life as urban. Most of these provincial centres went into sharp decline or disappeared with the decline of Roman authority after the fourth century.

Islamic Cities

From the continental point of view, impressive as was this new development from the perspective of constructing an urban history, it looks with our distant perspective like a first stage, which was followed by one far longer and more far-reaching, involving the influence of a new religion – Islam. Islam had broad cultural implications. It is a religion in which trade could flourish: it provided a banner whereby traders could safely reach distant shores and establish links of intellectual community and trust through faith. It is also a religion where urban society is admired and held up as a model for the good life. Islamic travellers almost invariably frame their accounts with a description of the piety and good morals – or otherwise – of the townsmen. For ibn Battuta visiting Kilwa in the fourteenth century, for example, the piety of the ruler, the state of learning, the condition of the mosques – these were the most important features of all on which to comment. Of course, Islam has appealed to peasants and to nomadic people as well as to urban dwellers, but the right course for Islamic observance was ideally centred in the city through an orderly regime that upheld its precepts.

The Islamisation of North Africa in the seventh century would lead to the emergence of both transformed and entirely new cities such as Kairouan in present-day Tunisia, spearhead of the conversion of the region, and of course the City Victorious, Cairo, built where the Nile Delta begins, not far from the site of ancient Memphis which now disappeared from history. Cairo was a sensational success as a commercial city after its initial foundation as essentially a military establishment. Here ibn Battuta writing in 1325 could only reach for superlatives – "mistress of broad provinces and fruitful lands, boundless in the profusion of its people, peerless in hearth and splendour, she is the crossroads of travellers, the sojourn of the weak and the powerful".[12] Still André Raymond believes that the frequently bruited figures of up to 500,000 for the population of Islamic Cairo are too large; he has

---

[12] André Raymond, *Cairo: City of History* (Cambridge, MA & Cairo: Harvard University Press and American University of Cairo Press, 2001), 120.

suggested also, contrary to the traditional view of decline over time, that Cairo continued to grow throughout the period of Mamluk and then Turkish rule, reaching a peak at the end of the eighteenth century of perhaps 250,000 people and thus comparable to the very biggest cities on the shores of the Mediterranean in other continents. It was certainly much the largest African city and for very long larger than any in Europe of the day. However, with the spread of Islam over many centuries, Muslim cities developed as well in other parts of Africa, such as Harar on the edge of the Ethiopian highlands.

Particularly distinctive were the trading towns of the East African coast, typically located on off-shore islands for security. The coast was brought into international trading routes by the favourable nature of the monsoons, allowing dhows to travel relatively easily in the right season between Africa, Arabia, the shores of India, and beyond. In Roman times at the latest, connections began with the ports of the Red Sea and, via Egypt, with the Mediterranean. But in fact archaeological evidence for urban life on the coast begins only in the Islamic era from about the eighth or ninth centuries. The oldest inscription that survives is from an otherwise unknown town on the island of Zanzibar dated to 1107, although Islamic remains from Manda off the Kenya coast are believed to date back several centuries earlier. If the commercial life of these towns was first based on trade in ivory and other wild products of Africa, it also involved the export from Africa of enough slaves to engender a revolt in what is today Iraq by the ninth century, and thereafter the gold trade became more important. The dominant city in this regard was Kilwa, in present-day Tanzania. Its written history was recorded in the sixteenth century. Kilwa boasted a fine palace, called today Husuni Kubwa, which enclosed a life of luxury, Islamic learning that won the approbation of travellers, and an economic location where craft activity (production of cotton cloth) joined with commerce. It is the one attested coastal city that minted its own coinage, reflecting the state's capacity to regulate commercial activity. The multidomed Friday Mosque was extended four times over in size during Kilwa's expansive years. The good state of preservation of its ruins gives us an excellent opportunity to imagine what it was like in the fourteenth and fifteenth centuries, when it particularly flourished.

The heyday of Kilwa can be linked chronologically to the heyday of Great Zimbabwe which historians assume controlled in some form the supply of gold, which arrived by caravan on the coast. Neville Chittick places its maximum population as upward of eleven thousand, small compared to the most sizeable cities in North Africa. It held much stone construction with an architectural style that Chittick describes as unique to the coast. Fifteenth-century Kilwa was certainly Swahili speaking, although no doubt its inhabitants often liked to trace paternal ancestry to Arabia, Persia, and elsewhere. Swahili evolved as a Bantu language influenced by Arabic from perhaps the tenth century and sustained both a sacred and secular literature. It was spoken up the coast as far as Mogadishu. Under the Arabised surface of coastal culture, references from travellers, more than the finds of archaeologists, suggest that earlier cultural forms had not died out by the fifteenth century. Thus in less wealthy towns than Kilwa, construction in wattle and daub predominated, just as it did for poorer houses in Kilwa. Descriptions of men with tattoos and other hints suggest a cultural heterogeneity about which the ruins are silent. Further north from Kilwa, Malindi and Mombasa and other towns developed on the coast of present-day Kenya where the gold trade cannot have been a factor. Despite their wealth, the impact of Kilwa and other entrepôt towns on the hinterland was small until the rise of a new kind of ivory caravan trade feeding into international capitalist circuits in the nineteenth century under the hegemony of Zanzibar.

In West Africa, long before the time of Zanzibar, Islam went hand in hand with the growth of trans-Saharan commerce and acquired increasingly deep local roots. The result was both the transformation, partially through accretion, of existing towns such as Kano or Djenne which acquired accoutrements typical of the Islamic town models but also no doubt long retained features of pre-Islamic urbanism.

What do we really mean by the Islamic city? We have the possibility of a normative model implied for one example – the Moroccan city of Fez as it was under the Marinid dynasty of the fourteenth century – in the classic monograph of the French scholar Roger le Tourneau. Le Tourneau saw the *madina* as having certain characteristic features wherever located in the Muslim world; however, he also stresses the distinctiveness of the particular – the "ways of Fez." Already many centuries ago there was a strong consciousness by its inhabitants of being part of the city, sharply marked off from the countryside, and of the city having a distinctive identifiable culture within the larger terrain of Morocco. Perhaps two common elements to Muslim cities that need to be stressed because they are so general are, first of all, the requirement that the state endow the Muslim religion with suitable facilities for worship, for study, and for the rites of passage in life.

In Fez, this meant the construction of mosques, some of a very high esthetic standard, it meant *madrasas* or schools that could perform more than elementary Koranic teaching and sustain intellectual and juridical activity within the confines of the permissible, and it meant such facilities as cemeteries and bath houses. Mosques could have a more harmonious relation with the state or could operate as the critical voice for a section of the urban population effectively.

Second, Fez had a complex and important economic life. While Fez households often possessed gardens outside the city, these were not really sites of agricultural production; it was characteristic that food was brought to the gardens from home when the family sought to eat there. Instead, food was purchased and in part processed, collectively and commercially. Fez had great markets and depended on a commercialised agriculture in the surrounding countryside for its staple foodstuffs. As a result of its historical evolution, in fact, Fez consisted of two physically distinct cities, one dominated by the palace, the military, and the state (*Fez Jdid*), and the other, older Fez – the "city of the people of Fez" – all the more given over to production and commerce. A multitude of crafts were characteristic of Fez, organised through guilds that controlled access and training, not dissimilar to older European practises. They were as much social as professional in character. By contrast to Europe, however, guilds did not come together to try to govern the city; this was seen as infringement on the good management of the state as a whole. The most common trade, weaving, took place in some five hundred workshops. Some of the craft production of Fez had wide currency in Morocco and, to a limited extent, beyond, and some depended on supplies from further afield (specialised textiles from Europe, gold from West Africa).

Fez had no real system of self-rule comparable to the Classical Mediterranean cities. Nonetheless regulation of good order was a major duty of the state. There was a governor who maintained order and controlled policing, a *cadi* who served as judge and religious administrator and a *muhtasib* who presided over the city's morals – dealing with petty disputes, regulating weights and measures, and so forth. At a level closer to the ground were quarter notables who mediated with state officials. A key feature in the administration of Fez was the excellent water supply of the city available for cooking, bathing, industrial purposes, and the disposal of waste; its maintenance was central to the entire functioning of Fez. By contrast, le Tourneau believed that the removal of other waste was a severe problem the state failed to resolve.

Islamic Cairo also consisted in early centuries of two distinct cities: the fortress established by the state, Fustat, and the commercial hive of al-Qahira, from which the city eventually took its name. Fustat was originally established in 642 as a camp city following the Arab conquest of Egypt, whereas al-Qahira, founded in 969, was the commercial city that arose in the following centuries. It was Saladin in the twelfth century who initiated the process of constructing a great wall around both cities that cemented their integration, an integration which superseded original Islamic ideas about urban function. By then Cairo had become the site of great libraries, beautiful mosques, stunning ceremonial performances, and a repository of decorative arts. Moreover, although Egypt, unlike Morocco, retains to this day a native Christian population, the majority was by this time Islamised, which also eased the integration of the city. Christians and Jews in Egypt became largely confined to distinct quarters where their notables administered local justice concerning the squabbles of everyday life.

Great commercial avenues ran the length of the city, parallel to the Nile, but these gave way to narrow and winding neighbourhood streets, in turn linked to a network of almost impenetrable alleys and blind entrances. These little neighbourhoods, fiercely defended by youths if they felt a threat from outsiders, were the heart of urban life. "What is striking in these neighbourhoods is that people feel more or less at home and at ease with each other. They like the animation and the colour of the narrow streets; they enjoy the tiny shops and this life in an ant-hill. One would also say this is necessary for their happiness." So said a medieval description.[13] The *hara* or neighbourhood was frequently entered only by passing a gate; it would contain a modest place of worship and a small market. Tiny shops sold cooked food which frequently was purchased rather than cooked in crowded dwellings.

If the homes of the wealthy contained some outside adornment in the forms of carved doors and the like, in general, comfort and affluence focussed on inner courtyards and halls obscured entirely from the public. The density of urban life was such, however, that by the twelfth century, many people of middling wealth were living in apartment blocks that stretched up to seven floors. In the Mamluk period during

---

[13] Gaston Wiet, *Cairo: City of Art and Commerce* (Norman: University of Oklahoma Press, 1964), 82.

FIGURE 2. Cairo: a major artery in the old city. *Source:* David Roberts, *Holy Land, Syria, Idumea, Arabia, Egypt and Nubia,* vol. 6 (1842). Courtesy of Cambridge University Library.

the forteenth and fifteenth centuries, we have even more impressive constructions: enormous inns or caravanserais occupying whole city blocks with connected apartment complexes on the upper floors. Cairo was remarkable for its diverse and complex social institutions such as al-Azhar, the mosque complex that served as a large and international theological university, or the *maristan* (hospital) of Qalawun which dated from the thirteenth century. This hospital, partitioned by sex of patients, could feed and clean the bedding of very large numbers, and there were physicians whose work was tied to the hospital. Some four thousand patients a day are said to have been brought there. The structure was linked to a *madrasa* and to a mausoleum that survives to the present.

Cairo did not have slums in the way they are understood by modern urbanists. This was a city where most of the poor were incorporated into more affluent households as servants and slaves. However, if later evidence can be extrapolated backwards, the urban periphery housed migrants and poor people who at least in later times resided in crowded courtyard complexes owned by landlords. Le Tourneau sees such migrants, also to be found in Fez, as potential new entrants to the city with reasonable possibilities for incorporation into the commercial and handicraft worlds over time.

Cities such as Fez and Cairo were prey to terrible plagues from time to time, although none created such devastation as to knock out growth for any long period of time so far as is known. Water was a key issue for Cairo. The city fountains were a fundamental amenity for the population. Wheeled traffic was not permitted in the city, where the carriage of trade goods as well as water was dependent on a huge supply of donkeys. Donkeys were for rent everywhere, unsurprising given the size of the city. Perhaps fifteen thousand were sent twice a day from the river to provide water for the city. Observing the Nilometer, which measured the height of the river as it altered seasonally, was an important activity. Both Fustat and al-Qahira were constructed well east of the river which tended to shift its channel further eastwards over time, creating large challenges in terms of water supply. Waste collection was also a major worry. Occasionally huge clean-ups of the main streets took place, but there was no systematic system to deal with garbage. Householders were supposed to light candles through the night to encourage safety; in fact, generally Cairo had a reputation for low rates of crime. Neighbourhood streets were not in any event much frequented by strangers after dark and the *hara* was often closed off then.

Cairo had a structure of municipal authority responsible to the state which became more complex with time. Yet under the surface, perhaps because Islam had no real space for municipal initiative and autonomy, the tendency for a differentiated and wealthy urban population to try to regulate their own affairs and exclude the state as much as possible can be found in various locales. According to Stambouli and Zghal, there was a general tension in Islamic North African cities between the desire for urban autonomy and dependence on the state, which in turn preyed on urban wealth as best it could. The North African city's real wealth came from commerce – the trans-Saharan gold trade before the seventeenth century in some cases, trans-Mediterranean commerce which made Tunis wealthy, for example, and pirate incursions against Christian vessels in general. Stambouli and Zghal place more emphasis than le Tourneau on the power of guilds as well as the importance of brotherhoods joining Muslim men together. They also stress the presence of poor people, usually of little account to the well-to-do merchants, artisans, and religious leadership, but not inconsequential.

At the same time, internal divisions within cities were often seminal. Islamic cities often contained quarters defined in ethnic or employment-specific terms which may reflect or exploit deep cultural divides. Smith has pointed out for the cities of present-day Northern Nigeria that the juxtaposition of ethnic quarters helped define and motivate urban life. By the fifteenth century, the most dramatically different subcommunity of Fez were the Jews who were later removed, apparently after a history of disputes, from the old city to the royal city where they lived in a ghetto or *mellah* and were associated with particular trades, such as working in precious metals as well as some forms of commerce. But early Fez (founded in the ninth century) had in fact consisted of two very distinct, rival wards, one associated with Kairouan looking east and the other with al-Andalus, Spain, looking north. Relations between the two were often tense and could lead to violence. This basic division was eliminated by unification in the eleventh century; however, although certain broad avenues connected the major parts of Fez, it was otherwise difficult to progress along the narrow roads built only for pedestrians and sleek mules. Neighbourhoods were sharply demarcated and remained important cultural subdivisions. Even the connecting avenues were shut off after dark and at other times. Festivals and organised fights between youths were structured in terms of particular quarters that maintained acute forms of rivalry.

These social forms echo Cairo but are equally the most important feature that the American anthropologist Horace Miner reported
for Timbuktu, in desert-edge present-day Mali, when he researched
this city on the eve of World War II, a time when it apparently preserved many older features. A three-way ethnic split (mediated of
course by French imperial rule) characterised social life, even though
all three groups were Muslims. His account contains a fascinating
description of a traditional form of football, where rivalries between
the groups were given legitimate but often violent expression. Intermarriage (as opposed to commercial sex relations) between the groups
was infrequent, although one of them owed its original formation to
unions between North African, Moroccan soldiers and West African
(Songhay) women and was thus defined.

Archaeological evidence of town life in the Saharan oasis of
Awdaghast (located in contemporary Mauritania) suggests that very
early (by the twelfth century), the *madina* model had taken over far
to the south. However, deeper in West Africa, cities such as Kano,
Katsina, and Zaria contained elements of older urban social life as
well as Muslim influences, at least before the further transformation
in a more classic Islamic direction after the religious wars of the early
nineteenth century. These wars aimed specifically at eliminating pagan
elements from the life of the community while containing a radical element of opposition to arbitrary government that really transcended the
issue of pagan survivals.

A first stage of interaction in West Africa must have often involved
the construction of separate Muslim towns, where foreign Muslims
especially were housed, as is reported already in the case of eleventh-
century Ghana. Later, more unified towns with some generalised Muslim adherence emerged. Mosques such as the magnificent mud-brick
mosque of Djenne were constructed, Islamic learning found a base,
and the state accepted many Muslim forms, but inside (and to a much
greater extent, outside) the city walls, other and older belief forms and
structures remained strong before 1800. When Kano was threatened
with devastation by the power of Kwararafa, a non-Muslim state far
to the south, in the late seventeenth century, the defenders turned to
"Chibiri and Bundun", spirits of old.[14] The *Dirki*, a Koran used as an
object linked to animal sacrifice, remained a holy object for far longer

---

[14] R. A. Adeleye, "Hausaland and Bornu" in J. F. Ade Ajayi & Michael Crowder,
History of West Africa, I (London & New York: Longmans & Columbia University
Press, 1972), 511.

to the Kanawa. Katsina, much nearer the Sahara, was by contrast the buzzing centre of quarters of Muslims from all over the central Sudan and beyond – Tuareg, Arabs, and so forth. Like Timbuktu, it could pride itself more on orthodoxy.

Taxing the markets, sometimes to the point of raising bitter resentment, was a major source of royal wealth. When Clapperton visited Kano in 1826, he could record the presence of a major market that functioned seven days a week, in which stallholders paid revenue to the administrator, "regulated with the greatest fairness."[15] There were massive amounts of foodstuffs, including grain, beans, and meat, but the custom of farming within the walls remained pivotal. The nineteenth century would certainly witness another, both wider and deeper, layer of Islam added to urban culture in West Africa.

Where African towns were deeply influenced by Islam, these features seem to recur repeatedly – internal ethnic and other divisions defining specific quarters that took able statecraft to tie together, a distinctive urban cultural ethic, a genuinely urban economy which could be separated from the state(although when the state itself was so transparently based on commercial activity, as in the towns of the East African littoral, another element needs to be added – the palace of Husuni Kubwa at Kilwa adjoins commercial facilities and space for warehousing conspicuously), and the imprint of Islam architecturally, albeit with many variations over time and space.

In the earlier parts of this chapter, we have examined the growth of urban agglomeration in many regions, often very gradual or reversible, where the emergence of large settlements contained both urban and non-urban elements in which the divide between town and countryside did not work as it is conventionally imagined by urban sociologists. This section of the chapter has thus brought a new element to the fore – the distinct separation of town and countryside with an unprecedentedly autonomous urban sphere, in a way that represents an evolution or accretion of fundamental importance in African urban history.

Selected Readings

Much of the material in this chapter comes from fragmentary accounts in wider histories. There are some excellent relevant chapters, however,

---

[15] In Thomas Hodgkin, *Nigerian Perspectives: An Historical Anthology* (London: Oxford University Press, 2nd edition, 1975), 287.

in David Anderson & Richard Rathbone, eds., *Africa's Urban Past* (Oxford & Portsmouth, NH: James Currey & Heinemann, 2000) including McIntosh on the Middle Niger, Thornton on Mbanza Kongo, and Phillipson on Aksum. Catherine Coquery-Vidrovitch, *Histoire des villes d'Afrique noire dès origines à la colonisation* (Paris: Albin Michel, 1993) is rich in ideas. An earlier study to consult is Richard Hull, *African Cities and Towns Before the European Conquest* (New York: W.W. Norton, 1976).

On Great Zimbabwe and its context, see D. N. Beach, *Zimbabwe Before 1900* (Gweru: Mambo Press, 1984); P. S. Garlake, *Life at Great Zimbabwe* (Gweru: Mambo Press, 1984); Martin Hall, *The Changing Past: Farmers, Kings and Traders in Southern Africa 200– 1860* (Cape Town & Johannesburg: David Philip, 1987), and Thomas Huffman, *Snakes and Crocodiles: Power and Symbolism in Ancient Zimbabwe* (Johannesburg: Witwatersrand University Press, 1996). On the Botswana agro-towns I am especially indebted to Neil Parsons, "Settlement in East-Central Botswana c. 1820–1900" in R. Renee Hitchcock & Mary Smith, eds., *Settlement in Botswana; The Historical Development of a Human Landscape* (Marshalltown: Heinemann, 1982).

Yoruba urbanism is dealt with in a classic article by William Bascom, "Urbanization among the Yoruba," *Africa*, XL, 1955. Later work includes the rich material in Peter Lloyd, A. L. Mabogunje, & B. Awe, *The City of Ibadan* (Cambridge: Cambridge University Press, 1967), Robert Smith, *Kingdoms of the Yoruba* (London: Methuen, 1969); Robin Law, "Towards a History of Urbanization in Pre-colonial Yorubaland" in Christopher Fyfe, ed., *African Historical Demography* (Edinburgh: University of Edinburgh Centre for African Studies, 1971); J. D. Y Peel, *Ijeshas and Nigerians; The Incorporation of a Yoruba Kingdom, 1890s–1970s* (Cambridge: Cambridge University Press, 1983), and Ruth Watson, *'Civil Disorder is the Disease of Ibadan': Chieftaincy and Civic Culture in a Yoruba City* (London, Ibadan, & Athens, OH: James Currey, Heinemann & Ohio University Press, 2003). Compare with Ivor Wilks' striking descriptions of urban life in Asante in *Asante in the Nineteenth Century: The Structure and Evolution of a Political Order* (Cambridge: Cambridge University Press, 1975). On Ethiopia, Ronald Horvath, "The Wandering Capitals of Ethiopia," *Journal of African History*, X(2), 1969, 205–20 can be updated with Donald Crummey, *Land and Society in the Christian Kingdom of Ethiopia from the Thirteenth to the Twentieth Centuries* (Oxford: James Currey, 2000).

My sources for ancient Egypt include Guillemette Ardreu, *Egypt in the Era of the Pyramids* (London: John Murray, 1997); Barry Kemp, *Ancient Egypt: Anatomy of a Civilization* (London & New York: Routledge: 1989), Elizabeth Riefstahl, *Thebes in the Time of Amenhotep III* (Norman: University of Oklahoma Press, 1964); John Romer, *Ancient Lives: The Story of the Pharaoh's Tombmakers* (London: Weidenfeld & Nicolson, 1984), and Dorothy Thompson, *Memphis under the Ptolemies* (Princeton: Princeton University Press, 1988).

For the era of Carthage and Alexandria, I have used for Carthage Gilbert and Colette Charles-Picard, *Daily Life in Carthage at the Time of Hannibal* (London: George Allen & Unwin, 1961), and Serge Lancel, *Carthage* (Paris: Fayard, 1992) and for Alexandria, Richard Alston's splendid *The City in Roman and Byzantine Egypt* (New York & London: Routledge, 2002), Michel Chauveau, *Egypt in the Age of Cleopatra* (Ithaca: Cornell University Press, 2000), Jean-Yves Empereur, *Alexandria, Past, Present and Future* (London: Thames & Hudson, 2002), P.M. Fraser, *Ptolemaic Alexandria* (Oxford: Clarendon Press, 1972), and Richard Todd, *Popular Violence and Internal Security in Hellenistic Alexandria* (Berkeley: University of California Press, 1963). R. C. C. Law's "North Africa in the Period of Phoenician and Greek Colonization c.800 to 323 BC" and "North Africa in the Hellenistic and Roman Periods 323 BC to AD 305" (both in J. D. Fage, ed., *Cambridge History of Africa*, II [Cambridge: Cambridge University Press, 1978] 107–47 and 148–209, respectively) cover both cities in short discussions and are probably more accessible to many African and Africanist readers than the classicist references.

For Islamic cities in Mediterranean Africa, a classic statement in English can be found in F. Stambouli & A. Zghal, "Urban Life in Pre-colonial North Africa," *British Journal of Sociology*, XXVIII, 1976, 1–20. Roger le Tourneau, *Fez in the Age of the Marinides* (Norman: University of Oklahoma Press, 1961) has been used extensively. See also Mohamed Chérif, *Ceuta aux époques almodhade et mérinide* (Paris: L'Harmattan: 1996) for a smaller Moroccan city. There are some remarkable books on old Cairo, such as Wladyslaw Kubiak, *al Fustat; its Foundation and Early Urban Development* (Warsaw: Warsaw University Press, 1982), Max Rodenbeck, *Cairo: the City Victorious* (London: Picador, 1998), Gaston Wiet, *Cairo: City of Art and Commerce* (Norman: University of Oklahoma, 1964), Janet Abu Lughod, *Cairo: One Thousand Years of the City Victorious* (Princeton: Princeton University Press, 1971), and, above all, André Raymond, *Cairo:*

City of History (Cambridge, MA: Harvard University Press & Cairo: American University in Cairo Press, 2001).

On the East African coast standard sources must include Neville Chittick, "The East Coast, Madagascar and the Indian Ocean" in Roland Oliver, ed., *Cambridge History of East Africa*, III (Cambridge: Cambridge University Press, 1977), 183–231, and John Sutton, *A Thousand Years of East Africa* (Nairobi: British Institute in Eastern Africa, 1990). In the Sahel, equivalents would be H. J. Fisher, "The Eastern Maghrib and the Central Sudan", in Oliver, as above, 232–330, and Nehemiah Levtzion, "The Early States of the Western Sudan" in J. D. Ajayi & Michael Crowder, eds., *History of West Africa*, I (London & New York: Longmans & Columbia University Press, 1972), 120–57. For a much later anthropological perspective, Horace Miner, *The Primitive City of Timbuctoo* (New York: Doubleday, 1953) is interesting. See also E. Ann McDougall, "The View from Awdaghast: War, Trade and Social Change in the Sahara from the Eighth to the Sixteenth Centuries," *Journal of African History*, XXVI, (1985). On the central savanna see H. F. C. Smith, "The Early States of the Central Sudan" in Ajayi & Crowder, as above, 158–201, and [as Abdullahi Smith] "Some Considerations Relating to the Formation of States in Hausaland" in *A Little New Light: Selected Historical Writings* (Zaria: Abdullahi Smith Centre for Historical Research, 1987), 59–79.

CHAPTER 2

African Cities and the Emergence
of a World Trading Economy

This chapter tries to explore in greater depth the impact of the waves of commercial penetration with their primary impetus in Europe which impacted in Africa from the fifteenth century onwards. In the previous chapter, we observed essentially commercial forms of urbanisation that can be linked to diffusion and incorporation. The influence of Greek, Punic, and then Roman urbanism in northern Africa was followed by the far more widely diffused Islamic impact. The Islamic impact, constantly reinforced with wide-ranging commercial linkages like the others, provided as well a model, or set of models, for the good society with a strong urban element. From early in the sixteenth century, Ottoman Turkish dominance was established in North Africa representing some significant changes; Morocco alone remained a sovereign state. However, the Islamic urban tradition was very well established and only altered to some extent. Thus we are here dealing with continuation rather than a total break. Contacts with European merchant capital and consequent responses largely represented the addition of a different layer of urban activity and urban life, although sometimes they did take place in regions of Africa where such contacts had little precedent.

It may be useful to map out the terrain of this chapter chronologically. From the fifteenth century and well into the seventeenth, the dominant European country in contact with Africa was Portugal. European commercial and political interests in Africa were variable and open-ended during this phase. Harsh and violent encounters were juxtaposed with meetings that took place on a relatively equal and respectful basis. There was little that one could call "colonial" in the sense of the establishment of political control. A striking feature was the emergence of new social strata, particularly on the West African littoral, who could act as intermediaries between what remained a potent African world on the one hand and the European visitors and traders on the other. Towns arising in this period housed these people and others who had become misfits in the wider society for one reason or another. Much of their population consisted of slaves, albeit slaves engaged in very diverse activities not necessarily lacking in social status.

Then from the early seventeenth century on for two centuries, Euro-African commerce was dominated by the slave trade, which had already been in the process of becoming more and more significant. During this phase, Portuguese trading hegemony gave way to the growing role of competitors, notably Britain and France. Some writers at least would see the period of slave trade dominance, when in many regions European knowledge about Africa actually regressed, as one marked by some new features in the form of possibilities for urban growth, to which we shall come. There were, however, certain exceptions to the typical pattern of Euro-African contact, such as the establishment of a genuine colonial system in what is today South Africa, based in this period to a large extent on the *importation* of slaves from Asia and many other parts of Africa. On the North African coast, cities were filled for some periods of time with thousands of European captives who would never return to Christian lands as well as slaves brought across the Sahara.

Finally, in the course of the nineteenth century, the slave trade became illegal and gradually disappeared giving way to a "legitimate" trade, while Barbary piracy was suppressed. Africa began to export commodities to the West on a much wider basis while purchasing industrially produced goods in return. At the same time, much of the political action was produced by ambitious African states able to use new weaponry to form large empires on the continent; much of Africa was in fact "partitioned" between such states as Egypt, Zanzibar, and a succession of Islamic *jihad* states in the West African savanna such as the different components of the Sokoto caliphate (in present-day Nigeria, Niger, and Cameroun). During this period there continued to be little direct colonial expansion by Europe except in the far south of Africa and in Algeria. This was in retrospect a transitional era to the colonial one, in which intensified commercial contacts brought

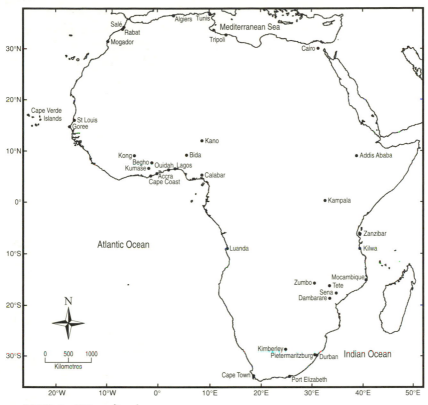

MAP 2. Cities of trade.

substantial change in many areas. Finally, there is the phase of rapid, outright imperial conquest in the late nineteenth century. But the creation of the real colonial city awaited imperial onslaught. It will be the subject of the next chapter.

If we try to establish a history of African urbanisation in this long and uneven phase, we are going to need to establish a few general points first. Perhaps the initial point that needs to be made is that there was no regular progression on a developmental ladder that saw towns becoming bigger and better. Many African towns lost, and kept losing, their significance while others disappeared entirely into the bush. Towns that live by commerce and by rulers who depend on commerce cannot survive the removal or disappearance of that commerce, whether the disappearance is caused by warfare, by changing commercial demands, or the shift in trade routes that are often possible. Thus the kind of urbanisation which had developed before 1500 in present-day Zimbabwe virtually disappeared, although a new, rather fragile kind of urban settlement, called by the Portuguese *feiras* [or fairs] with the implication of short-term periodic activity, emerged in response to the gold trade that continued to link the coast with the interior of south-central Africa.

They were not entirely temporary, however. One of these settlements, Dambarare, discovered by accident, has been excavated. There was indeed a transiency to Dambarare described as "a pathetic cluster of mud . . . huts within a wooden stockade" at the end of its existence in the very late seventeenth century.[1] However, the Portuguese presence was marked by the fort, by a moat, and by the existence of a small Catholic church. There may be a second church still to be unearthed according to some commentators. In the graveyard, presumably consecrated remains of European men and African men and women have been found by archaeologists. Nearby there are traces of attempts at gold mining. This is a very different kind of urban site than that of Great Zimbabwe. The only trace of the sacral comes from the Catholic side, and the commercial vocation of the settlement stands out dramatically. Thus much of the urban change of these centuries was markedly ephemeral.

Second, it is possible to note in other areas new waves of commercialisation that brought only a new layer of urban development and size whilst older patterns remained very significant, apparently completely dominant unless one searches beneath the surface.

North African cities actually changed fairly substantially from the sixteenth century onwards when Ottoman Turkish power controlled the coast eastwards of Morocco. Algiers emerged as an important city, especially with the arrival of many Muslim refugees from Spain after the Christian *reconquista*. According to one estimate, it contained no less than 85,000 people at its peak in 1600 of whom perhaps 25,000 were Christian European slaves (a figure which later diminished substantially).[2] These trends also affected Salé, Rabat, and Mogador (Essaouira) in Morocco. Tunis, the port near the site of ancient Carthage, overtook Kairouan, the cultural and military desert-edge centre in the interior of what is today Tunisia and Tripoli became a

---

[1] H. Ellert, *Rivers of Gold* (Gweru: Mambo Press, 1993), 56.
[2] Farouk Benatia, *Alger: agrégat ou cite? l'intégration citadine de 1919 à 1979* (Reghaia: SNED, 1980), 23.

significant centre. Tunis may have held a population of as much as 120,000 in the middle of the eighteenth century.

Cairo was no longer a fully independent political centre but its commercial life continued to buzz. Whatever one might say about the constitutional arrangements of the Janissaries and Ottoman agents from the sixteenth through the eighteenth centuries, the city was generally well run in terms of crime control; basic commodities, notably bread, ran short only relatively rarely and the city continued to have an increasingly complex local administration. Current research, based on careful consideration of the physical space filled in different periods, suggests that, contrary to the long-held view that it gradually shrank in size, Cairo actually grew, peaking in size with perhaps 250,000 inhabitants at the time of the arrival of Napoleon's army in 1798. In fact, its growth was slow and unsteady over the following half-century or thereabouts. During the Ottoman period, merchants played an important role in the physical evolution of the city as they constructed warehouses and mosques considered suitable for their own class, took to apartment living so that they could be close to their places of work, and converted much property from public or religious to private ownership in order to suit their needs. Much of the new wealth in seventeenth- and eighteenth-century Cairo can be linked first to the growing trade in spices and then to the fondness developing for coffee in the Middle East and, to a lesser extent, Europe. The Ottomans controlled the Yemeni source of coffee and Cairo was the great centre of transhipment. Scholars researching estates from the eighteenth century found that the wealthiest identifiable individual was a coffee merchant, approximately fifty thousand times richer than the man who left the smallest estate, a poor vegetable seller.[3] In this commercial entrepôt, there were also very large numbers of day-workers and street traders as well as armies of servants and slaves.

This pattern – change, overall growth, commercialisation – certainly stands as the gist of the literature on the commercialised towns of the West African savanna. It is likely that older forms, for example those which expressed pre-Islamic beliefs, were obliterated or forgotten in many cases where the wave of movements that aimed at creating truly Muslim societies won widespread support and became politically

[3] André Raymond, *Cairo: City of History* (Cambridge, MA: Harvard University Press and Cairo: American University Press, 2001), 207.

dominant. This was especially the case from the early nineteenth century where *jihads* overtook the populous and economically developed central savanna region located mainly in modern-day Nigeria.

In Kano, the greatest of all nineteenth-century artisanal and commercial centres, European travellers marvelled at the fine organisation of the market and the equitable relation between the state and commerce, whereas much trade was actually carried out within the houses of merchants. Hundreds of North Africans maintained homes, often with local wives, in Kano, and were the critical agents connecting the city to international commerce on a very broad scale. Although visitors noted the presence of European commodities available for sale, largely deriving from the trans-Saharan trade, they do not give the sense of a commercial world that has been transformed by European contacts; superficially, continuity with earlier times was apparent. However, "Kano people are reputed throughout the country for their astuteness in trade, their culture and worldly wisdom."[4] As the author noted, this repute itself was part of an aura which promoted the city's interests. The German traveller Karl Staudinger estimated Kano to have a population of sixty to eighty thousand in the late nineteenth century and to contain some five thousand foreigners during the height of the commercial season in winter. He describes some of the many commercial elements in the Kano economy, such as trade in guns, in horses, in ivory and ostrich feathers and in salt. He may have exaggerated the importance of the international trade across the Sahara to the city, but its growth through the nineteenth century was certainly a marked feature that fitted developments throughout the continent, introducing subtle changes.

One incident Staudinger reports sheds light on an aspect of Kano life. He was at one point assaulted with stones from a house in a largely Arab neighbourhood. On complaint to the authorities, the matter was taken very seriously and perpetrators punished. Staudinger writes about this in terms of the dignity of the nineteenth-century European, but it might better be taken as a sign of the importance in Kano given to the protection and good relations with foreigners of any sort of commercial bent. There is much less sense here of ancient residential quarters with considerable real autonomy from the life of the state and forms of self-government. The quarters of Kano, often associated with

---

[4] Karl Staudinger, *In the Heart of the Hausa States* (Athens, OH: Ohio University Press Monographs in International Studies, Africa Series 56, 1990), 229.

one or another ethnic character, were perhaps far more open to the control of the state in this commercial haven in preconquest days than was true of old North African cities.

For a clearer sense of change, a particularly good example would be the nineteenth-century island city of Zanzibar on the east African coast. Zanzibar arose as a city from the impulse of the Omani rulers who wished to establish a safe headquarters for their African trading empire. But culturally it was very much the continuation, indeed the apex, of the old coastal urban tradition that we have observed in the previous chapter. Some of the ancient coastal towns faded away as no doubt had been true in earlier epochs. The Portuguese attacked and for periods ruled most of the East African coast and, in so doing, ruined some old towns. Kilwa faded into insignificance to reemerge as a place of importance selling slaves, largely to the French, in the eighteenth century.

We have no records of large towns on Zanzibar island before the nineteenth century. The peninsula on which the town of Zanzibar would emerge was essentially just a locale for a fishing village until the end of the eighteenth century, but thereafter, and under the rule of the Omani sultans who relocated their capital from Arabia, Zanzibar grew to an unprecedented size. In the early nineteenth century, estimates tend to fall into the range typical of the larger African urban communities we have observed in the previous chapter, ten to fifteen thousand people. However, mid-nineteenth-century estimates go upwards from forty thousand and fifty thousand and reach even higher figures by the eve of colonial conquest in 1890. Its commercial character was readily apparent. Sheriff writes about the bulk of the largely enslaved labouring population of the town that "the servile working class . . . was largely connected to the commercial economy of the entrepôt and was involved in cleaning, preparing and transporting commodities."[5] The scale of Zanzibar allowed for a densely urban character and the display of a wide range of wealth and ethnic diversity. To begin with, fishing settlements on the shore consisted of wattle-and-daub construction and were architecturally very simple. But in the first half of the nineteenth century, this gave way to the construction of large numbers of stone houses in what is still known as Stone Town. These dwellings, constructed on narrow streets, often rose to three and four stories and

[5] Abdul Sheriff, *Slaves, Spices and Ivory in Zanzibar* (London: James Currey, 1987), 150.

were constructed around inner courtyards. The carved wooden door-
ways, similar to equivalent decorative features in Arabia and India,
have become an international hallmark of Zanzibar. Those Arabs who
owned plantations tended to prefer to live on them, but they still maintained town houses.

As the city expanded, Zanzibar's wattle-and-daub houses did not
disappear. Instead, they got expelled from the centre to the urban
periphery and across the little bridge that marked the entry to the
popular quarter of Ngambo. Here, thanks to the work of Garth Myers,
we know that the poorer Zanzibaris lived a life structured in terms of
belonging to well-organised urban subcommunities, sometimes with
an ethnic character and certainly with a specific way of speaking Swahili
that marked off the new urbanism. Affiliation to particular mosques
often defined particular social networks. The commercial nature of
Omani society was coupled with a strong cultural preference for outward austerity, at least in religious practise. Most mosques lacked
minarets entirely. This was not a city whose many mosques dominated
the skyline; religious practises hardly overshadowed the commercial
lifeblood of the city. The Zanzibar economy was dependent on the use
of slave labour, but the town itself, through the intensity of its commercial life, bored away at the simple master-slave dichotomy. Many
slaves were actually hired out by masters and lived off their own earnings. There were slaves who purchased and owned other slaves and as
such lived fairly independently. An important mark of the cash nexus
and its growing dominance was that land tenure, initially in the hands
of the wealthy and well-connected and directly acquired via the state,
tended to become commercialised: sales and rentals of urban land
become highly significant before colonial rule. This critical feature of
urban life could be discerned also in nineteenth-century Kano and
other strong commercial centres in Islamic West Africa. By the time of
British annexation in 1890, Zanzibar began to boast its first buildings
with lifts and other European-style improvements. These did not really
transform the city; instead they were accretions to what was beginning
to be a very complex organism. By the late nineteenth century, moreover, an urban popular culture distinct from that of the countryside
is identifiable with hindsight. This is less likely to have been the case
in all African towns which were being affected by commercial contacts, but new commercial influences were certainly felt in such diverse
and apparently totally indigenous settings as Kampala, capital of the

large kingdom of Buganda near the shores of Lake Victoria Nyanza as well as the more strategically sited Tswana agro-towns on the edge of the Kalahari.

Sheriff and others bring up as well for Zanzibar the theme of urban exploitation of the countryside. This is a partial reflection of the much starker division between town and country that began to exist for some urban situations, although it must have been a striking feature in Mediterranean Africa back for many centuries. Michael Mason, examining the *jihad* emirate of Nupe near the Niger above its confluence with the Benue, sees the capital city of Bida, as well as a number of predecessor towns, as essentially the headquarters of a predatory class of exploiters. The victims were the peasantry who suffered raids as well as more systematic extraction through various means of taxation. He describes this succession of towns as in effect "military camps superimposed on rural economic structures."[6] Bida was perhaps the largest city within the broader Sokoto Caliphate apart from Kano. Like its predecessor, Raba, it was particularly convenient for north-south trade. In general, Nupe, on the confluence of the Benue and Niger Rivers and not far from where the savanna and forest environments came into contact, was an extremely stimulating locale for water and land trade. Bida had a great reputation for textile production and was famous for the manufacture of glass. Craft production in Bida was certainly linked to trade and to production circuits that involved the peasantry very directly. Rural and small-town households were not necessarily confined to farming pursuits but instead were often the source of important market activities. A successful state, initially highly militarised and predatory – and also extremely ascetic with regard to worldly goods – created conditions for a multiplicity of economic activities to flourish and for wealth to build up. As a result, the city was both parasite/predator and stimulus/incentive to economic growth.

The centres of nineteenth-century states were particularly characterised by this kind of mixture, precisely because their economies were fuelled to an important extent by the rapid growth of commerce, even if they were not quite as conspicuously commercial as Zanzibar. To move outside the Islamic sphere, one can note that in the early phase of the

[6] Michael Mason, *The Foundations of the Bida Kingdom* (Zaria: Ahmadu Bello University, 1981), 57.

period covered in this chapter, the emperors in Ethiopia made Gondar
into a kind of permanent capital with large stone structures constructed
on the European model. Yet this did not stop the court from moving
around and Gondar from dramatically gaining and losing population in
the course of the passage of seasons. From the mid-eighteenth century,
the Ethiopian monarchy went through a period of decline and indeed
dissolution for a century, but thereafter an emphatic revival occurred.
The expansive, predatory, but also increasingly solid Ethiopian state
fastened on a new and permanent capital on the plateau of Shewa
around 1890 at Addis Ababa under the authority of Emperor Minilik.
This too was essentially a military camp in a period of intense mil-
itarisation. The city developed through the grant of land to various
officials and aristocrats, but as it took on a variety of state functions,
a railway was constructed. Commercial life intensified and a community of hangers-on and dependents of noblemen evolved a variegated
urban space that provided a growing market outlet. Bahru Zewde has
suggested that whereas the availability of firewood had always presented problems to the permanence of urban settlement in Ethiopia
on a large scale, the introduction of the Australian eucalyptus was
instrumental in the permanence of Addis Ababa. The new city particularly attracted people of low status and ethnic groups without a
strong position in Ethiopian society, which has been termed a "vast
non-industrial urban complex of heterogeneous ethnic groups" characterised by a high degree of transience.[7]

Beyond the question of urban rise and decline and the intensification of commerce affecting existing towns in Africa, the third point
to emphasise is the emergence at least in some parts of the African
continent of *networks* of towns in response to the demands of trade.
Kano was, amongst other things, part of a spatially grand network that
centred on Cairo: there were contemporary maps which made this
point in linear fashion. J.-F. Boutillier characterised the rise of Bouna,
located in the northern part of the contemporary Ivory Coast, through
networking. Bouna was a place where goods were traded. For instance,
the cowrie shells – acquired ultimately from the West African coast –
were traded for gold, still important in the market linkages of the Niger-
Senegal headlands region. For Boutillier, perhaps a bit schematically,

---

[7] W. A. Shack, "Urban Ethnicity and the Cultural Process of Urbanization in
Ethiopia" in Aidan Southall, ed., *Urban Sociology* (London: Oxford University Press,
1973), 260.

such trading towns were where the transhipment and exchange of goods emanating from particular environmental zones took place. Their existence could be understood only through the relationship of particular towns to other towns. Such networks involved direct trade, credit, the systems involved in relating to states through customs dues of all sorts, shipping and transport arrangements, as well as final sales. The network centre would contain all or the majority of such functions.

This is not to say that Bouna was purely commercial. It was also the centre of a small kingdom known as Koulango. For Koulango people, the difference between Bouna and its hinterland was not so great: their ritual life embraced the whole land, and townsmen continued to farm extensively. But there were also certain individuals, the *diatigi*, who hosted itinerant traders, and the links between landlord and guest were critical to the maintenance of the trade networks. At the same time there were great trading families who lived in Bouna but who had connections to traders by the same name in other related towns. Thus the important Ouattara clan had close links to the better-known town of Kong, also in the contemporary Ivorian savanna. There were traditions that linked this family back to Begho or Bighu, the first known trading community in what is today Ghana, whose emergence reflected the discovery and exploitation of gold in the Ghanaian forests by the fifteenth century. The interlinkage between trader and those based on the land was critical for successful governance. Integrative town festivals were enjoyed by the whole population. Bouna was not like the earliest West African trading communities which held two separate towns for Muslim merchants and natives, one part of a commercial far-flung archipelago and the other integrated with a unique hinterland outside its walls. There was an important element of integration in Bouna, but it continued to display an observable duality.

Kong was a more purely commercial centre despite its five mosques. Life in the nineteenth century very much centred on the market, characterised by big shade trees and dotted with temporary stands owned by travelling merchants. Beyond the market "the streets [were] tortuous and narrow. On a few small squares there [were] fig trees, a date palm or a *bombax* crowned with grasshopper nests."[8] Indigo dye pits were a prominent feature and beyond the established alleys stretched

---

[8] Louis Binger, *Du Niger au Golfe de Guinée par le pays de Kong et le Mosi*, I (Paris: Hachette, n.d.), 297, my translation.

enclosed gardens. Dyeing, the manufacture of clothing, and the cooking of food for sale were often engaged in by slaves while women sold
items such as kola nuts (and the poorest, firewood). Dances and music
at the time of night markets created an atmosphere of leisure that
appealed to the urban community which prided itself on its polite
manners. And, as an emporium town required, there was good order
maintained by a form of police who could hold individuals overnight
for bad behaviour. The carriage of guns and other weaponry in city
streets was not permitted. This picture, drawn by Louis Binger on the
eve of conquest, was that of a model savanna town, in this case very
much a Muslim island in a pagan sea, which perhaps occupied the
next highest rung after Bouna on this urban hierarchy.

Another urban network is identified and mapped out for a yet-earlier
period than that studied by Boutillier in the work of Ray Kea. Kea
believes that an active interrelated set of urban communities could be
found in the sixteenth and seventeenth centuries in Ghana itself, typically located a short distance inland from the Atlantic shore. If urban
life had given rise to Begho, stimulated by the rise of a caravan trade
to the savanna linking to desert crossings, it was greatly intensified by
the diversified but largely gold-based commerce that began to cross
the Atlantic and link what the Europeans called the Gold Coast by
sea. He cites the Dutch traveller de Marees:

> The towns which lie towards the interior of the country [that is, five to
> fifteen miles from the coast] are richer in goods and gold than the border
> [that is, coastal] towns, and have more houses and are more populous
> than the sea side towns; they also have wealthier merchants who con-
> duct more trade than those in the coastal towns whose inhabitants are
> the interpreters, boatmen, pilots, officials, fishermen and slaves of the
> inhabitants of the interior towns.[9]

Few Europeans visited these inland settlements, yet a gold-based economy led to commercialisation that stimulated crafts and commodity
production generally.

Kea's view contrasts with writers such as Mason who emphasize
urban parasitism or predation; these are urban communities characterised by a wide range of economic activities that have much to offer

---

[9] Quoted in Ray Kea, *Settlements, Trade and Polities in the Seventeenth-Century Gold Coast*
(Baltimore & London: Johns Hopkins University Press, 1982), 23.

FIGURE 3. Kong: characters in a street scene. *Source: Binger, Du Niger au Golfe du Guinée* (1892). Courtesy of Cambridge University Library.

in exchange with rural households. Such towns were typically the capitals of small states, states that were sometimes linked into confederacies. Thus the original Accra, Great Accra, was located inland some distance from the sea where the modern city of Accra is located, on the plains above. However, Kea sheds most light on Assin (Akani), an essentially non-monarchical polity which was particularly vibrant before the late seventeenth century. He thinks that perhaps as much as ten per cent of the regional population of what Europeans called the "Gold Coast" was urban during this period.

Kea believes that the slave trade, as it became more dominant, had a striking and largely negative effect on this urban system. Slaving and the associated gun trade gave first Denkyira and then the Asante Confederacy overwhelming power which lasted through most of the nineteenth century. Kumase, the capital of Asante and a city characterised by the households of the great Asante officials and representatives, took over a dominant position while many smaller centres declined. The Ga-speaking coastal communities that came together to form modern Accra were an exception: here again there was a kind of clustering of urban activity in an era of violence and concern about

security. Otherwise, craft activity tended to shift back into rural areas
and the urban population may have declined.

Somewhat parallel trends emerge from a recent detailed study
of Ouidah, one of the largest West African coastal towns. Ouidah,
conquered by the kingdom of Dahomey in 1727, was thereafter administered as a subordinate town entirely given over to commerce in the
heyday of the slave trade. Located close to the lagoon system just inland
from the coast, Ouidah was well located for holding and concentrating
slaves; perhaps one million eventually passed through its streets. Most
of its population consisted of slaves as well. The town probably had
more of the character of a multifaceted culture, where a palace and
places of worship were significant, when it was the heart of a small
independent state. Under Dahomean rule it was rather nondescript,
dominated by a market with the population clustered in quarters that
surrounded the three European forts where they worked. These forts
were more for trading than defence purposes; they were constructed
of mud with thatched roofs, although they were the sole buildings
in town of over one storey or with window openings. With time,
Ouidah became dominated by families associated with the slave trade,
sometimes of partly European descent, who achieved some autonomy
from Dahomey in their commercial dealings and prided themselves on
their understanding of the ways of those with whom they did business.

The divide between urban and rural life in southern West Africa can
be exaggerated. We have noted that the Koulango Kingdom had little
problem incorporating an urban component into its cultural configura-
tion. This is much clearer in a wide stretch of West Africa. Throughout
this area, the town-country divide long ago became a continuum measured in political and cultural as well as economic terms. It is true that
where large states formed, such as Benin, Dahomey, and Asante, the
capital cities retained a particularly important feel as sacral and political centres with commercial activities sometimes focussed elsewhere.
Thus Kintampo and Salaga were the nineteenth-century focal points
for Asante's very important commerce to the north with the savanna
regions of the subcontinent.

However, a very typical form was that of the city-state where the
urban and rural blended. Town-dwelling households retained rural
homes. This is very well known as a Yoruba cultural characteristic, as we have noted in Chapter One, but it is equally true for Ga
people in the region of Accra, for example. The Ga towns are the
sites of characteristic and important community rituals; they have a

"moral basis" for existence beyond their strategic or economic importance.[10] The political structure of towns reflected hierarchies based
on descent groups and military structures. Thus, when commercial
life became more significant, Ga culture was easily able to adjust itself
to a larger urban component. It is indicative that Ga towns had a
stable sex ratio, with more resident women than men; they were not
temporary magnets for migrants. Before trade with Europe became
significant, fishing and salt making were probably the major economic activities other than farming in coastal settlements; this easily
expanded to accommodate commerce. Great Accra declined in significance in favour of coastal communities where forms of money were
most available. In the slave-trade era, this gave way to greater concentration, with the three settlements that would form the basis of the
modern city of Accra – Dutch, British, and Danish, respectively –
growing to a population of perhaps fifteen thousand or so in the
nineteenth century.

However, a remarkable feature of the West African coast was the
emergence of communities that originated entirely from trade with
Europe, including some that we could call colonial, although until
the middle of the nineteenth century, that word is virtually entirely
inappropriate to West Africa (outside a few coastal settlements such
as St. Louis, Gorée, and Cape Coast) and, even after, remains very
marginal for another generation. The Gold Coast itself was the site of
two dozen European forts, some of them very close to one another,
which maintained themselves through playing on the rivalry of African
rulers or, more typically, accepting their protection. The first of these,
Elmina, founded by the Portuguese in the late fifteenth century and
whose castle is thus really an example of medieval European construction, was at the same time an often-thriving commercial centre
with an important daily market and a variegated population. In slave-
trade days, however, a few centres, notably Ouidah, Accra, and Cape
Coast, concentrated trade while problems of violence and security were
endemic. Relations with the powerful states of Dahomey and Asante
governed urban life.

John Parker, historian of Accra, highlights the extent to which an
older elite based on established links to political authority was in time
joined by a distinctive second elite which was frequently of racially

---

[10] John Parker, *Making the Town: Ga State and Society in Early Colonial Accra* (Oxford,
Portsmouth & Cape Town: James Currey, Heinemann & David Philip, 2000), 48.

mixed origin, often bearing a European surname and increasingly exposed to European education. In Accra, the Danish Lutheran church first provided this kind of formation through most of the eighteenth century; otherwise, the option was to send sons and daughters directly to Europe, an increasingly important practice. The history of this elite, with its remarkable ability to adapt to both European and African customs and politics, cannot be separated from the life of the towns, although often the African linkages were deep enough to provide real purchase on the social life of the interior. Far to the north-west and up the coast, the most important group of people who fitted this rubric were women, who were referred to in corrupted Portuguese as *signares*. In Muslim Senegambia, they were the only notably African Christians who traded and operated as dynamic economic actors on their own behalf. In the oldest French settlement of the region, St. Louis, a characteristic feature of social life was the *fanal*. The *fanal* was originally an ornamental decoration on a ship, an insignia that figured in town festivities in European ocean ports. In St. Louis from the seventeenth century, it was adapted into a festival of lanterns intended to honour and celebrate the *signares* on Christmas Eve. The lanterns accompanied the ladies on their way to Mass.[11]

An important coastal island town that developed late in the slaving period to the east of the Gold Coast was Lagos. Thriving on the slave trade and dominated by a Yoruba political hierarchy, early nineteenth-century Lagos faced inland where its source of wealth lay. It was a typical Yoruba town divided into politically structured quarters and characterised by multipurpose household compounds. Unusually, it fell under colonial control early as a means of trying to stem the slave trade. Made a British protectorate in 1851, it was proclaimed a colony a decade later, with its political rulers decisively subordinated to a new order. In 1866, Lagos was a city of approximately twenty-five thousand people. With the flourishing of new forms of commerce as well as profiting from being an administrative centre, this figure tripled by the eve of World War I. There emerged in Lagos a new kind of elite that profited and acquired status from living in what was taken to be a European manner, its origins very diverse and sometimes lowly. This was signalled by mode of dress, furnishing, and architecture and

---

[11] This festival has since become transformed through various mutations and, amongst other things, taken over by twentieth-century St. Louisien politicians.

perhaps above all by the forms of marriage in which a property-owning bourgeoisie emerged. At the same time, the development of a commercialised postslavery "legitimate trade" economy, which linked Lagos to the interior and in which Europeans did not intervene very effectively, permitted some people of standing to continue to breathe vitality into older social forms. Thus, as Kristin Mann shows, some women accepted polygamy and continued to do business on their own account while others tried to fit themselves to the roles of Victorian mistresses of households. In fact, as colonial racism became more intense, the appeal of African cultural revival grew before the end of the century.

Part of the reason why the possibilities of wealth remained so real in Lagos was the entrenchment of private property. Spatially encouraged by the city shifting its affluent gaze south to the sea rather than inland, culturally encouraged by the predilections of colonial rule, private landownership that could be inherited became more significant, and property values became considerable. This formed a basis of rentier capital even when African merchants became marginalized and their slaves set free. Wealthy families constructed very large houses and continued to live off their rental earnings. The British economic historian A. G. Hopkins has shown the progress of this development through the murky records of complex lawsuits. Lagos' bastard character, so typical of the hybrid cultural roots of coastal urban life, continued to harbour different forms of authority and identity at all class levels, just as did that of Accra, annexed by the British in 1874.

By contrast, St. Louis de Sénégal was a pure European creation, the first in West Africa, located on a narrow, sandy island with a poor water supply close to the mouth of the Senegal River, which runs as the frontier between modern Senegal and Mauritania. Also founded by the French in the seventeenth century was Gorée on an even smaller island – today a short ride by ferry from central Dakar. The only logic to these towns was security, as they had to be supplied for almost everything from outside. Even today Gorée's visitors can view the dark room in the castle giving on the ocean side that linked the settlement with the sea, evoking the gloom of the Atlantic slave trade – the quintessence of its reason for existence.

Initially it was not feasible for Europeans to conceptualise "African" towns as lived by their inhabitants, although descriptive literature sometimes did some justice to what they saw. In the substantial number of surviving drawings of early St. Louis, the dominant feature is always the fort, and the fort itself is depicted almost emblematically with the emphasis on those elements that linked it to current European military technology. How people lived around the fort and what adaptations they made to it (and vice versa) were for long not seen as being of the least significance, according to the fascinating studies of Alain Sinou. Apparently the fort dominated an exotic environment in a familiar way. In reality, European fortifications were very difficult to keep clean and were highly unsuitable to the tropical climate with their minimal ventilation. When one couples this with the general problems of health for Europeans resident on the West African coast, the picture is very different than what the iconography suggests. And certainly few Africans can have found life inside the fortifications – with its emphasis on defence, on the authority of the commander, and with much of the space designated for the practices of an alien church – very congenial.

The evidence of maps, pictures, and then photographs therefore is one of a very gradual process of indigenisation and adaptation, which took place only over generations. Gradually it became possible for map-makers to sketch in and admit to the existence of far more impermanent structures around the fort where basic economic activities could take place and where a population could exist in more comfort. It is thought that many, if not most, of the Frenchmen (there were also periods of occupation by other powers) came to live outside the perimeter created by the wall, partly to their economic advantage and partly to cohabit with the only women who were available in the neighbourhood. Impermanent dwellings of thatch and mud were often more shaded and comfortable as well, and maps acknowledged by the early nineteenth century that there was more to these towns than fortification.

In St. Louis by the early nineteenth century, however, a stronger colonial impulse, governed by real French authority, had begun to be felt. By 1800 there were perhaps already one thousand resident Europeans. Thus, it gradually turned into a colonial town – with a fine governor's mansion, the construction of substantial places of worship, and the removal of soldiers to purpose-built barracks. The surrounding town, which spread first through the island but eventually to the mainland Tongue of Barbary, was laid out with straight streets and the possibility of European-style town planning, and second stories began to be added to houses of increasing solidity, especially the homes of Christian residents and those who bore names indicating mixed origins.

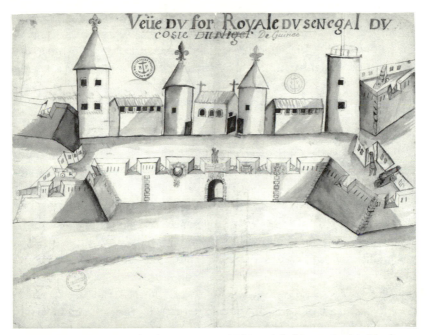

FIGURE 4. St. Louis, the fort: no sign of African inhabitants in this idealized view. *Source:* Courtesy of the Centre des Archives d'Outre-Mer, Aix en Provence, France.

By 1828 there were two hundred brick houses and by 1838 well over three hundred, of which more than two-thirds had a second storey.

West African house construction has historically focussed on walled compounds that surrounded courtyards and contained a variety of structures aimed at different uses. In such compounds, a considerable and varied population structured around a hierarchy of power could be found. Through the nineteenth century, simplified versions of such compounds began to give way, or to merge with European house models, to create a new and distinctive house architecture. In part this was a process of adaptation, but the role of the coastal urban populations of mixed origins was absolutely critical here. Room sizes grew and ceilings were raised while ground floors became surrounded with verandas. Often, because the ground was itself considered rather suspect in nature, the floor was lifted well above it. Upper floors were constructed when possible and balconies made available. Decorative material reflected eclectic adaptations of African and European styles. From what is today Ghana to Nigeria, a large role was played here by the so-called Brazilians, West Africans enslaved and brought to Brazil, where they learnt forms of carpentry and Latin American style, who eventually achieved emancipation and returned to run businesses in West Africa. They brought their sense of style and craftsmanship to the growing urban communities. The wealth of Lagos makes it an especially important location for such buildings to this day. In the busiest parts of the town, it was typical for ground floor space to be devoted directly to trade and business while family life took place upstairs. Astonishingly, wealthy individuals, for instance in the Niger Delta towns such as Calabar, actually ordered entire homes purpose-built in Britain and shipped for reassembly in West Africa by the late nineteenth century. However, even these were typical of the new emphasis on air circulation and shade.

West Africa in particular saw the vernacular adaptation of a colonial form of life that developed in India – the bungalow. With the onset of colonialism, the white form of the bungalow habitation and neighbourhood would flourish – large separate properties, very low population densities, snake fences, mosquito nets, and ample sporting facilities. Architectural adaptations on the one hand influenced the increasingly important and emblematic way of life of an emerging African elite and, on the other, would be an effective weapon for intensified racial segregation and separation from Africa as a dominant European presence established itself. Thus, an urban style emerged over time in coastal West Africa, which went together with developments in trade, politics, language, and belief systems, and it intrigued and influenced town dwellers far away from the coast. In the interstices of imperialism, it represented a model that would spread through the colonies acquired by Britain, France, and the other European authorities.

For a more distinctively European-generated urban development on the African continent and its environs before the nineteenth century, one can look into the history of cities and towns created by the Portuguese. The Portuguese settlement on Mozambique Island dates back to the first years of the sixteenth century. Once again, as with Goreé or St. Louis, we need to picture a small offshore island used as a strongpoint in the furtherance of trade. Mozambique, however, also served critically as a refreshment station on the great sea route between Portugal and Asia. As with West African examples, it was dependent on supplies from the immediate vicinity. There was water on the island, but the supply was insufficient and food came from the nearby mainland. However, Mozambique was from early on developed as a real city. The fort of São Sebastião, finished in 1583, was one

FIGURE 5. Ibo, northern Mozambique: ruins suggest the past. *Source:* Michel Loye; used by permission.

of the most impressive defensive structures built anywhere by Europeans beyond their own waters. Although there was no cathedral, an array of ecclesiastical buildings, notably Jesuit and Dominican headquarters, were constructed. Charitable and municipal institutions on the metropolitan model were also created. There was a prison and a fine public square. Even in decline, the urban character of the island was striking:

> The narrow streets and high houses, the former not remarkable for cleanliness, and the latter partly of a dirty yellow colour, impaired by neglect and decay...The windows seemed barred with lattices as if the town abounded in thieves retained to obviate the heat by the free admission of air.

This from the pen of a British visitor, Captain James Prior, who came to Mozambique in 1812.[12] Mozambique in fact was probably at its

---

[12] Cited in Malyn Newitt, *A History of Mozambique* (Bloomington: Indiana University Press, 1995), 134.

peak as a town in the eighteenth century. In a greater state of decay yet was the original capital of the Cape Verde islands, Ribeira Grande, on the island of Santiago, also originally established with all the accoutrements of a Portuguese town and declared the seat of a bishop in 1533. It fell into decline when the slave trade with Brazil began to bypass the Cape Verdes and pirates menaced the small and isolated community. After a French pirate attack of particular destructiveness in 1712, it became a forlorn ruin; the Portuguese attempted nothing so impressive again on this arid archipelago.

By contrast, Luanda, the nucleus from which Angola would be created, retained many of the structures with which it was endowed after its foundation in 1575. In the Angolan and Mozambican interior, a number of urban settlements also were established, of which an outlier, which we have already glimpsed, was the long-dead town of Dambarare in what is now Zimbabwe. However, settlements on the Zambezi, Tete, Sena, and Zumbo – the latter at the confluence of the Luangwa – were also important in the gold, ivory, and slave trades. Their more tentative existences did not mean they lacked all of the appurtenances of Portuguese urbanism. Indeed, when the trade flourished they were fairly sizeable. Here traders and "landholding" possessors of *prazo* grants, who functioned as military leaders and chiefs, owned substantial town houses. Zumbo in the nineteenth century, by then long past its peak, was said to cover two miles of ruins. In its heyday its dominant figure was *frei* Pedro, a priest who fathered many African children, traded widely, and held the reins of power in what is today a massive borderland tract covering parts of Mozambique, Zambia, and Zimbabwe.

Mozambique City itself had an African as well as a European character. Captain Prior, whom we have quoted, was also able to note the existence of an African settlement of simple structures but full of healthy children alongside the Portuguese island city. All these towns were enlivened with a mixed and acculturated population rather than fed by a stream of European immigrants. Only at the end of the period covered in this chapter did southern Angola begin to receive Portuguese immigrants in significant numbers who founded towns with a new and more thoroughly European core character, such as the ports of Moçamedes and Porto Alexandre, towards the middle of the nineteenth century.

David Birmingham's short study of the Luanda carnival, an institution which existed at least as far back as 1620, provides insight on urban life in Portuguese Africa. Carnivals, contrary to currently fashionable interpretations, were not really institutions where townspeople could temporarily reverse the social and political order of urban life and create a new republic for a night. In fact, they tended, as with the St. Louisien *fanal* and the Coon Carnival that developed later in Cape Town, to avoid confrontation or reference to authority. The Luanda carnival was suitably loyalist; it promoted Portuguese pretensions. But it became invested with elements of representation that reflected pre-Catholic traditions, for instance in the propitiation of a sea god who could work miracles. Moreover, representation in carnival became a way that different sections of town could create a sense of identity and confront rival sections. Intimations of incest and witchcraft were part of the ritual. Carnival was one institution that reflected the antiquity of this African city whose wealth was so long based on the slave trade aimed especially at Brazil. This history created a continuity of Portuguese cultural influence that was separate from the actual role of immigrants from Portugal, a relative rarity in the city. The formal documentation on early Portuguese colonial towns in Africa invented on paper an artificial world modelled on a European grid, and it is easy to contrast this dramatically with actual narratives of decline and decay as well as with more modest but also more vital African realities on the ground, as seen by actual observers. However, this should not take away from the real prosperity that such towns enjoyed in phases, the influence of their institutions, and their success in establishing a presence on African soil over a very long time-span.

These are points that hardly need to be insisted on in the case of Cape Town and South African colonial towns. The reality of Portuguese control away from islands and certain strategic centres can be queried, but in the far south of Africa, from the establishment of Cape Town in 1652, a fully colonial world began to sprout. In the course of the following two hundred years, that world developed an important urban component. Cape Town was also a refreshment station; under the Dutch East India Company, it harboured a large garrison and catered to the needs of travellers between the Netherlands and the East Indies to which it was subordinated. The trade in livestock, which gradually was joined by systematic agricultural cultivation, was also geared to serving this world in transit. Cape Town, the "Tavern of the Seas," held a large percentage of the colonial population from the start, a percentage which in fact gradually diminished. From the beginning of the nineteenth century, population figures for the city are approximately fifteen thousand, a figure for African urban life which we have often encountered elsewhere. As a result of the gradual development of commercial life in the interior and the decline of urban slavery, that figure grew only very slowly for decades. It was approaching thirty thousand at the time of the great diamond discoveries in the vicinity of Kimberley in 1867, no bigger then than Lagos and smaller than Zanzibar.

The focal point for the early Cape was the massive castle, just as we have noted for other early European outposts. Perhaps the next most critical were the gardens laid out nearby. The gardener was the first individual permitted to live outside the castle perimeter. What was distinctive here was that, instead of the gradual development of a commercially orientated urban community by indigenous peoples, a process of privatisation took place that brought about an immigrant free burgher population, together with growing numbers of slaves and eventually freedmen of diverse origins. Only in the earliest years could a cattle kraal with local Khoi herding people be found anywhere near the castle.

Instead, it was decommissioned Dutch East India Company employees and other immigrants who came to provide the key services that the economy required. As land loans in the vicinity of the castle gave way to outright land purchase, such people provided food in the form of crops and meat as well as other necessities. It was often the women of the town who organised all-purpose shops, drinking establishments, and boarding houses, which were so characteristic of early Cape Town. The history of the town, despite the massive early presence of the garrison, is one of the gradual development of a more and more autonomous urban population with its own varied interests, a civil society.

Even before the British take over in 1795 (permanently from 1806), the free citizens organised a variety of cultural and social activities, had begun to build some fine houses after the prosperous commercial phase of the 1780s, and were catered for by an imitation of Dutch urban planning. In early days, the main streets lined canals, which became with time an inconvenient eyesore and were eliminated. The Burgher Senate provided the principle of political representation into the British period. It was abolished in 1827 but reconstituted in 1840. By this time what had been largely a Dutch-speaking town with a small British minority was rapidly becoming Anglicised through the arrival of new immigrants as well as administrative pressures.

The humbler and low-status services were provided by slaves and the descendants of slaves and convicts. The Company slave lodge, home to many women who bore children to both slave men and free, was the most intense focus of slave life in the town through the Dutch period; here all slaves belonging to the Company itself were supposed to spend the night. If conditions in the lodge were often very degrading, it was equally noticeable that Cape Town slaves varied in condition and status. As with Zanzibar, the highly commercial nature of urban slavery was such as to half-emancipate many individuals in time. Many slaves were effectively hired out but forced to give their masters and mistresses some of their earnings. Even in the eighteenth century, some services were associated with free people of colour, who for example were the majority of the town's fishermen. Slavery was finally abolished in 1833, although quasi-free arrangements such as apprenticeships remained for a while longer. These free and slave elements melded to form the basis of the popular class of the city. Often they turned to Islam, introduced by captives from South East Asia, as the foundation of an autonomous belief system; Christianisation also became widespread in the nineteenth century. If what we are terming the popular class was extremely heterogeneous in origins, it consisted mainly of people of colour. However, the indigenous element in it was certainly weak. From an early date, the Khoi herders of the Cape vicinity were driven out by force and disease.

Few ex-slaves at the Cape succeeded in going very far up the social ladder, although intermarriages across race lines remained far from rare. In effect, the mid-nineteenth century witnessed an increasingly residentially and occupationally distinct urban middle class, very largely white in origin and increasingly pressured to identify itself as British. By contrast what we might call the popular class (there was still too little wage labour to talk systematically of a proletariat), racially mixed but largely brown or black, clustered in crowded and poor dwellings near the waterfront. Slaves had sometimes been the source of considerable fears and rumours of rebellion; with the end of slavery, there was much less obvious social antagonism in Cape Town. The Cape carnival, which developed only in the nineteenth century, was notably lacking in any critique of the existing social order. At the same time, the mid-Victorian period witnessed the creation of various bourgeois-formulated institutions such as the South African Public Library (new premises opened by Prince Alfred in 1860), the Mechanics' Institute, various secondary schools, the Somerset Hospital, modelled on the ideas of Florence Nightingale, and the Roeland Street Gaol. Middle-class family life was beginning to remove itself to suburbia. The physical carapace of the Tavern of the Seas remained as it was in Dutch times, but a social order where industrialisation would be situated and growth would be more explosive was on the verge of creating a new dynamic.

By 1870, there were other colonial towns in South Africa, such as Cape Town's rival, Port Elizabeth, which expanded on the basis of the wool trade, Grahamstown in the Eastern Cape, and Pietermaritzburg in Natal, the latter two both able to exploit the trade of a vast interior market focussed in large part on livestock. Then there was the Natal port of Durban and the new centres generated by the expansion of Dutch settlers outside colonial frontiers into the interior of the southern African Highveld. All were however small and much less varied and remarkable than Cape Town at this stage. South African urbanism, rooted very largely in colonial forms and according to models created in Europe, was still quite unusual in Africa and far less significant than very much older and deeper patterns.

From the sixteenth century onwards, incorporation into an emerging world-economy increased African urbanisation on the whole and gave it a much more dominant commercial theme. This chapter has tried to capture some of this variety and the sense in which expanding commercial patterns were creating hybrid patterns, sometimes very ephemeral but often with lasting and original features that would themselves represent a historic layer of urban structure and urban culture which would survive into the imperial age to come. We have, for instance, seen the emergence of urban networks, the importance of slavery, and the beginnings of private property and urban household formation in various locations. The cities are the headquarters of those who live from the produce of cultivators in rural areas; they are exploitative. However, they begin to agglomerate craft production and tie together more commercial networks while creating more possibilities for human development through growing social complexity; as such they are a stimulus. The early urban patterns identified in Chapter One have become modified, while and the colonial age to come is in some places foreshadowed.

Selected Readings

Many of the books and articles cited for Chapter One continue to be relevant for this chapter and were used as sources, such as Raymond and Abu Lughod on Cairo. Other readings below seem more focussed on the material in this chapter.

For Portuguese trading towns see David Birmingham, "Carnival at Luanda," *Journal of African History*, XXIX, 1988, 93–103; Michel Cahen, ed., *'Vilas' et 'cidades': Bourgs et villes en Afrique lusophone* (Paris:l'Harmattan, 1989); James Duffy, *Portuguese Africa* (Cambridge, MA: Harvard University Press, 1959); Malyn Newitt, *A History of Mozambique* (Bloomington: Indiana University Press, 1995), and H. Ellert, *Rivers of Gold* (Gweru: Mambo Press, 1993). In the case of Cape Town, there now exists an excellent, superbly illustrated social history with comprehensive references: Nigel Worden, Elizabeth van Heyningen, and Vivian Bickford Smith, *Cape Town: The Making of a City* (Cape Town & Hilversum: David Philip & Verloren, 1998).

On urban life on the West African coast, a classic study of early developments is Ray Kea, *Settlements, Trade and Polities in the Seventeeth-Century Gold Coast* (Baltimore & London: Johns Hopkins University Press, 1982). For additional insights, an interesting range of reading would include Moustapha Dieng, "Naissance et evolution d'une fête: St-Louis du Sénégal et son fanal" in Odile Goerg, ed., *Fêtes urbaines en Afrique* (Paris: Karthala, 1999), 37–50; A. G. Hopkins, "Property Rights and Empire Building: Britain's Annexation of Lagos 1861," *Journal of Economic History*, XL, 1980, 777–98; Kristin Mann, *Marrying Well: Marriage, Status and Social Change among the Educated Elite in Colonial Lagos* (Cambridge: Cambridge University Press, 1985); John Parker, *Making the Town: Ga State and Society in Early Colonial Accra* (Oxford, Portsmouth, & Cape Town: David Philip, Heinemann & James Currey), 2000; and Alain Sinou, *Comptoirs et villes coloniales du Sénégal: Saint-Louis, Goree, Dakar* (Paris: Karthala/ORSTOM, 1993). Most recently, Robin Law has added a comprehensive monograph to this list: *Ouidah: The Social History of a West African Slaving 'Port' 1727–1892* (Oxford & Athens, OH: James Currey & Ohio University Press, 2004).

For architecture and lifestyle, Anthony D. King, *The Bungalow: The Production of a Global Culture* (New York & Oxford: Oxford University Press, 2nd edition, 1995) and Jacques Soulilou, ed., *Rives coloniales: architectures de Saint-Louis à Douala* (Marseille & Paris: Eds. Parenthèses, Eds. de l'ORSTOM, 1993) have a great deal to offer and provide wonderful illustrative matter.

On commercialisation of the early modern era and its impact on the interior of urban Africa, see for example J.-F. Boutillier, "La cité marchande de Bouna dans l'ensemble économique Ouest-Africain pré-coloniale" in Claude Meillassoux, ed., *Development of Indigenous*

Trade and Markets in West Africa (London: Oxford University Press, 1971), 240–52. For the central savanna, see the comments on nineteenth-century urbanisation in Michael Mason, *The Foundations of the Bida Kingdom* (Zaria: Ahmadu Bello University Press, 1981). This chapter uses quotes from Paul Staudinger, *In the Heart of the Hausa States* (Athens, OH: Ohio University Press Monographs in International Studies, Africa Series 56, 1990), and Louis Binger, *Du Niger au Golfe de Guinée par le pays de Kong et le Mosi*, I (Paris: Hachette, n. d.), on Kano and Kong respectively. However, for some more, see excerpts in Thomas Hodgkin, *Nigerian Perspectives: An Historical Anthology* (London: Oxford University Press, 2nd edition, 1975).

On the changing towns of the East African coast, especially Zanzibar, Abdul Sheriff, ed., *The History and Conservation of Zanzibar Stone Town* (Oxford, Portsmouth NH & Cape Town: James Currey, Heinemann & David Philip, 1995), and Abdul Sheriff, *Slaves, Spices and Ivory in Zanzibar*, (London: James Currey, 1987) are very useful. For a sense of how development took place in Ethiopia from the late nineteenth century, see W. A. Shack, "Urban Ethnicity and the Cultural Process of Urbanization in Ethiopia" in Aidan Southall, ed., *Urban Sociology* (London: Oxford University Press, 1973), 251–86.

For some of the cities that thrived in this period or parts of it in North Africa, see Gaston Deverdun, *Marrakech des origines à 1912* (Rabat: Editions Techniques Nord-africaines, 1959), Hamza Ben Driss Ottmani, *Une cité sous les alizés: Mogador des origines à 1939* (Essaouira: La Porte, 1997), and Paul Sebag, *Tunis au XVIIe siècle* (Paris: L'Harmattan, 1989). On Tunis more generally, see Paul Sebag, *Tunis: histoire d'une ville* (Paris: L'Harmattan, 1998) and J. S. Woodford, *The City of Tunis* (Wisbech: Middle East and North African Studies, 1990). On economic aspects of life in Cairo during the early modern period, Nelly Hanna, *Making Big Money in 1600: The Life and Times of Ismail Abu Taqiyya, Egyptian Merchant* (Syracuse: Syracuse University Press, 1998) is very enlightening.

CHAPTER 3

Colonialism and Urbanisation

In the previous chapter, we have noted that intensified participation in the Classical, Islamic, and then the expanding capitalist European world all led to urban growth in Africa, growth of a kind that was linked to a more general commercialisation of society. The towns that developed in consequence could be described as exploitative: they lived off trade and state formations that systematically extracted wealth from pastoralists and peasants, although they also engendered communities with distinctive skills, cultures, and ways of life. Urban growth continued under colonial occupation from the late nineteenth century but extended itself by leaps and bounds, particularly in the final generation of colonial rule beginning with World War II. According to one estimate the percentage of Africans living in cities rose to 4.8 percent in 1920 and 14.2 percent in 1960.[1] This meant impressive growth both in the size of cities (see Table 1) and in the extent of urbanisation taken as a whole; it also meant that the commercial vocation of cities in Africa became far more intense.

To this, we should probably introduce two important qualifications. On the one hand, not all urbanisation should be linked directly to commercial expansion. Some towns and cities developed as sites of capitalist production, particularly in the case of mining operations. As we shall see, the remarkable expansion of towns on the central African Copperbelt, in the colonies of Northern Rhodesia and the Belgian

[1] Farouk Benatia, *Alger: agrégat ou cité? l'intégration citadine de 1919 à 1979* (Reghaia: SNED, 1980).

TABLE 1. *Population of Some Significant African Cities in the Colonial Era (in thousands)*

Date	c. 1900	c. 1939	c. 1960
Cairo, Egypt	910 (1897)	1,312 ('37)	2,852 ('59)
Alexandria, Egypt		686 ('37)	1,335 ('59)
Johannesburg, So. Africa	102 (1896)	283 ('31)	1,097 ('60)
Casablanca, Morocco	20 (1897)	257 ('36)	961 ('60)
Algiers, Algeria		264 ('36)	834 ('60)
Ibadan, Nigeria	210 (1900)	387 ('31)	600 ('60)
Accra, Ghana	18 ('01)	61 ('31)	491 ('60)
Addis Ababa, Ethiopia	35 ('08)	300 ('38)	449 ('61)
Léopoldville, Belgian Congo	5 ('08)	27 ('35)	420 ('61)
Tunis, Tunisia	146 ('01)	220 ('36)	410 ('56)
Dakar, Senegal	18 ('04)	92 ('36)	383 ('60)
Lagos, Nigeria	74 ('10)	127 ('31)	364 ('60)
Three Towns (including Khartoum), Sudan	77 ('05)	176 ('38)	315 ('60)
Salisbury, S. Rhodesia		26 ('31)	300 ('61)
Nairobi, Kenya	12 ('06)	119 ('48)	267 ('62)
Tananarive, Madagascar	50 ('00)	142 ('45)	248 ('60)
Luanda, Angola	20 ('00)	51 ('30)	220 ('60)
Bulawayo, So. Rhodesia		53 ('46)	195 ('61)
Kumasi, Ghana	19 ('11)		190 ('60)
Elisabethville, Belgian Congo			190 ('60)
Mombasa, Kenya	30 ('06)	85 ('48)	190 ('60)
Lourenço Marques, Mozambique	10 ('04)	47 ('35)	184 ('61)
Abidjan, Ivory Coast	1 ('10)	17 ('36)	180 ('60)
Kano, Nigeria	30 ('03)	89 ('31)	176 ('60)
Douala, Cameroun		28 ('31)	150 ('61)
Dar es Salaam, Tanganyika	25 ('06)	69 ('48)	140 ('62)
Brazzaville, French Congo	5 ('00)	24 ('36)	129 ('61)
Freetown, Sierra Leone	34 ('11)	65 ('47)	125 ('60)
Bamako, French Soudan	7 ('10)	37 ('45)	120 ('60)
Conakry, Guinea	6 ('10)	26 ('45)	113 ('60)

Source: William Hance, *Geography of Modern Africa* (New York: Columbia University Press, 1964), 54–55. Additional figures from Brian Kennedy, *A Tale of Two Mining Cities: Johannesburg and Broken Hill 1885–1925* (Johannesburg: Ad Donker, 1984); Fouad and Barbara Ibrahim, *Egypt: An Economic Geography* (London: I. B. Taurus, 2003); T. N. Goddard, *Handbook of Sierra Leone* (London: Grant Richards, 1925); Phyllis Martin, *Leisure and Society in Colonial Brazzaville* (Cambridge: Cambridge University Press, 1995); Paul Sebag, *Tunis: histoire d'une ville* (Paris: L'Harmattan, 1998); Douglas Wheeler & René Pelissier, *Angola* (London: Pall Mall Press, 1971); Brigitte Lachartre, *Enjeux urbaines au Mozambique* (Paris: Karthala, 2000); André Adam, *Casablanca*, I (Paris: Editions du CNRS, 1968). Populations reckoned in thousands. The accompanying table and map indicate graphically and in numbers the size and growth of bigger urban settlements in colonial Africa.

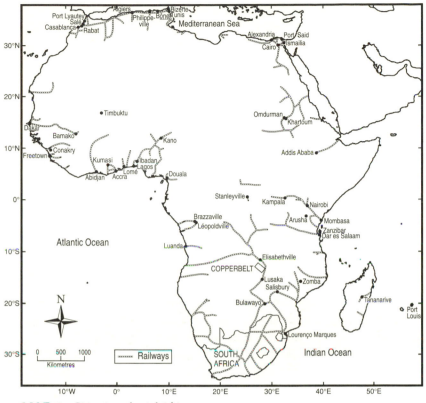

MAP 3. Cities in colonial Africa.

Congo, became a kind of benchmark for colonial African urbanisation more generally. This kind of production, however, was narrowly tied in to colonial Africa's vocation as a supplier of raw materials for the West. In addition, colonial administrative facilities attracted both rural migrants and outsiders to the continent towards capital cities, which contained the greatest variety of new services. "Primate" cities, those which dominate the urban process, were thus expanding far more rapidly than provincial towns, except where international commerce required a different focus of activity.

On the other hand, not all African towns and cities grew. Those which were associated with African states dissolved and crushed by colonialism often withered away; so did many others whose commercial life depended on caravan routes that were no longer operative, eliminated through the new colonial borders and through the establishment of roads and rail routes that no longer necessarily followed old patterns. Typically transport routes were now focussed on the evacuation of mineral and agricultural produce from the African interior to the port towns, many of which were also capitals, while Western imports were brought into Africa along these routes.

Urban sociology used to characterise some cities as parasitic rather than generative. This is a persuasive argument to the extent that the state is itself oppressive and manned by large numbers of officeholders who support many servitors but effectively live off an impoverished peasantry. The parasitic view of the city had an important element of truth in it before colonialism, but it subsequently became less true. Colonialism appears at times as a deliberately structured system for sucking up Africa's wealth. The primate city held the new forms of wealth in any territory to a disproportionate extent, but that wealth was based on forms of social control and exploitation that lay at the heart of colonialism. Wealth in Africa began to be commercialised on a larger scale, and it is through providing the sites for the processing, transport, and administration of that commerce that urban growth largely took place. This was simultaneously exploitative and stimulating. It was only in the towns that capitalism could be engendered, organised, and administered even in the raw state in which it was forming in Africa. Exploitative does not mean parasitic: the advance of capitalism in colonial Africa, albeit highly uneven, was dynamic and led to deeper and deeper changes in society. Previously, sophisticated and urbane communities could coexist for centuries with a minimally altering countryside, a peasantry constrained mainly by its relationship to the natural environment, and perhaps the tribute extracted from it by an elite. Now the town began to dissolve older relations of production in the countryside as the twentieth century proceeded. The relationship of town to countryside changed and, particularly as we move on into the independence era, transformation intensified. In the course of this chapter, this phase of urbanisation will be examined, but in addition considerable attention will be paid to academic and policy debates that took place around urbanisation at the time and afterwards.

Old African Cities; Degrees of Change

As many scholars have noted, a study of colonialism reveals a variety of types of African towns. For this chapter, it will be suggested that it may be useful to consider this variety in terms of a spectrum rather than a typology somewhat as follows: a) (superficially) unchanged towns; b) towns with a visibly hybrid character; and c) new cities. As one moves

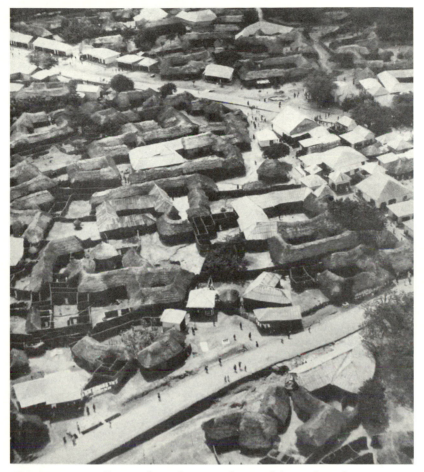

FIGURE 6. Hardly transformed: an aerial view of Ilorin, the only emirate adhering to the Sokoto caliphate in Yoruba-speaking southwestern Nigeria. *Source:* Buchanan and Pugh, *Land and People of Nigeria* (1955; reprinted 1971).

along this spectrum, the differing nature of large urban settlements becomes clearer.

We might start at one end of the spectrum, where we can find those towns which were essentially already established, not just spatially and demographically but also culturally, before colonial rule. Some examples on this end of the spectrum would be Zanzibar or Ibadan. In all these cases, a process of modernisation which seriously altered life in the towns and involved new physical infrastructure did take place. However, it might require a close look before a freshly arrived observer could pick up the changes that occurred. Continuity and accretion were more apparent than radical change.

In the Nigerian city of Ibadan, sprawling around neo-classical Mapo Hall on its hill, densely populated and difficult-to-negotiate passageways and alleys still separated compounds which remained the homes of extended families. A large portion of men continued to spend much of their week on adjacent farms beyond the outskirts throughout the six decades of British rule. Much of the craft and commercial life of this largest of Yoruba-speaking cities appeared to continue unchallenged. In particular, as A. L. Mabogunje, the outstanding Nigerian student of African urban life, long ago pointed out, the old markets, which so characterised urban solidarity in pre-colonial times, retained much of their vitality. Under Nigerian style indirect rule, whereby the British tried as much as possible to administer Africans through what were considered to be modified African institutions, Mabogunje's other pre-colonial Yoruba urban anchor, the palace, also retained relevance.[2] However, just as Mapo Hall was hardly representative of pre-colonial architecture, the chiefship and the disputes it invariably took on were hardly a continuation of the contradictions of some pre-colonial "constitution." The vitality of the internal commercial economy and the social relations that connected with it gave this huge conurbation an apparent sense of continuity that can, however, be exaggerated.

Colonial Ibadan, never conquered by the Islamic *jihad* states of the North in the turbulent nineteenth century, was rapidly becoming a majority community of Muslims. On the outskirts, a new commercial area arose, not incidentally focussed on Lebanon Street, where Middle Eastern immigrants dominated new forms of exchange. Indeed, here, on the periphery of Ibadan, large numbers of Nigerians, Yoruba-speaking and otherwise, agglomerated in response to economic opportunities and the territorial transport infrastructure that knit the colonial federation together. The important Hausa-speaking community, now linked to "Northern Nigeria," became detached from the authority of

[2] Ibadan, however, lacked a single palace representing city authority. Indeed, it was under colonialism that an attempt to create an *Olubadan*, or overarching ruler, of the city was first seriously made. The very high levels of violence and disorder which represented an inheritance from Ibadan's distinctive history were a problem the British had to deal with, as Ruth Watson has recently discussed in *'Civil Disorder is the Disease of Ibadan': Chieftaincy and Civic Culture in a Yoruba City* (Oxford & Athens, OH: James Currey & Ohio University Press, 2003).

the elders of Ibadan and more autonomous from the city in general. Muslim of course, its leaders followed the precepts of the Tijaniyya brotherhood, which distinguished them from Yoruba Muslims. In accordance with British ideas, ethnic cultural autonomy was thus given recognition; colonial states were about establishing pacified boundaries between those defined as culturally different from one another, not about nation-building. In addition, there was a spacious administrative quarter for whites as well as increasingly significant educational, health, and other new spaces in Ibadan. Colonialism enabled the *plural society* to form, where apparently separate and antagonistic culturally defined groupings met in the marketplace with peaceful dealings guaranteed by the colonial protector. Horace Miner, an American anthropologist, observed this clearly in Timbuktu, which had become an outlying provincial centre in the northern French Soudan, incorporated into French West Africa, on the eve of World War II. With the establishment of French suzerainty, this ancient town, in decline but not terminal decline, appeared sociologically to be a colonial plural ethnic space where different ethnic communities dominated different sections of town and sectors of the economy. Ritualised fights between community youths confirmed boundaries; there was a kind of assumption that the town had held together largely through the intervention of the colonial suzerain, lacking as it now did a common identity for all. This was a city without common citizenship.

The theme of continuity masking change can be pursued as well north of the Sahara. A careful study of early colonial Salé in Morocco shows that although the outward show of urban civility – in which respectability is related to the antiquity and piety of families, to the practice of particularly honoured craft activity, and to the combination of urban artisanal operations with farming in the vicinity – remained extremely visible, the reality was changing by the time of World War I. Commerce – as opposed to the honoured old naval craft of piracy at the expense of infidels – was of growing importance, and Jews, who focussed on commerce rather than industry, thrived; connections to the new colonial state were critical in accessing new forms of influence and power. Poor Berber speakers from the mountains arrived as migrants. Colonial Salé was not the dignified *chasse gardée* of a cooperative Muslim aristocracy, as the French hoped, but an encapsulated and in some respects ossified suburb of Rabat. Older elements in the town, in fact, felt threatened and disempowered through change and tended to withdraw from public life in bitterness. Both Salé and (relatively speaking) Ibadan were neglected by the colonial state. It was Lagos, the colonial capital of Africa's most populous territory, which experienced the most change while Casablanca, a place of previously minor significance, became the burgeoning economic centre of the new Morocco.

Omdurman on the Nile, the capital of the Khalifal state established in the 1880s on the ruins of the Egyptian Sudan, represented a somewhat similar kind of urban experience. After the conquest of 1898 and the proclamation of the Anglo-Egyptian Sudan, it lay cheek by jowl with the restored and replanned colonial capital of Khartoum. Khartoum North, a third attached urban community, tended to house the growing number of colonial employees, for instance on the railways. Omdurman became an inward-looking and relatively sleepy town. Its complex property and social relationships did not fit the theories with which the British sought to govern the colonies, and its importance dwindled dramatically. Yet it survived as a reminder of different times and was testimony to continuities in the economic activities of older urban compounds. In the Khartoum complex, the heart of the new working class, which was active in service, transport, and artisanal activity, probably consisted of emancipated slaves and their children. Omdurman itself lay near the starting end of our spectrum, but, if we consider the whole of the so-called Three Towns – the entire Khartoum-Khartoum North-Omdurman complex – one moves somewhat further away from the continuum end of the spectrum compared to cities that seemed the most "traditional," such as Ibadan towards the hybrid middle. The totality was a mixed urban community with very contrasting sections.

In other cases, ostentatious colonial suburbs eventually engulfed older communities, marginalizing them or rendering them less and less relevant to the broader patterns of social dynamism. For instance, Accra had its origins in three old Ga settlements which enjoyed a rich urban tradition. After British rule was established, these settlements gradually become overwhelmed by a colonial city in which the proportion of Ga people diminished while modern commercial and administrative sections were established. With time, the old Ga central neighbourhoods became less and less fundamental to the life of the city as a whole. They were not marginalized exactly, but they were not easily integrated into a new Accra. Less than a decade after independence, the American anthropologist Marion Kilson grasped the feel of the old Accra, which was her own subject of interest, but she realised as well its diminishing role:

> Central Accra is a densely populated, active, noisy centre of African urban life in the heart of the national capital of Ghana . . . A visitor walking through the byways of Central Accra senses that he might be in any comparable residential area of marginal elites and manual labourers in any West African capital. The smells, sights and sounds which he encounters are as characteristic of Treicheville [sic] in Abidjan or Ginger Hall in Freetown as they are of Central Accra: the deep, open, trash-filled gutters, the sizzling smell of frying plantain, the occasional whiff of urine, the small open shops of artisans, the barber cutting hair under a tree; children chasing home-made wheel toys; men playing checkers in the shade of a house; women carrying sleeping infants on their backs and possessions on their heads; the sharp clank of aluminium pails, the reprimanding shouts of mothers, the rhythm of highlife pulsating from an open window, the warm laughter of good fellowship. Nevertheless these superficial sensory similarities mask wide social and cultural variations in the lives of the inhabitants of such urban areas.[3]

Janet Abu-Lughod, in a paradigmatic study of the Moroccan city of Rabat, uses the South African term of "apartheid" to describe the process by which another old city with its rich and distinctive traditions becomes a kind of cultural museum, less and less relevant to much of the dynamic of colonial Morocco, while apparently surviving physically intact. The French assumption was that the Moroccan population of Rabat would remain unchanged as befitted the charming yet decadent world of Islam, pickled with medieval spices; there could be no expectations of dynamism, growth or in-migration.

Of course this was Morocco, not the Transvaal; no pass laws or racial codes permanently and consistently determined the movement and residence of Arab, Jew, or European. Repressive legislation played a much smaller role than the thrust of urban colonial planning in creating an urban bifurcation. For, outside old Rabat, as Gwendolyn Wright has explored more generally in Morocco, Islamic atavism was paired with the promotion of a relatively avant-garde modernism in architecture and city planning for the new colonial city, populated by thousands of "Europeans," that developed outside the perimeter of old

---

[3] Marion Kilson, *African Urban Kinsmen* (London: C. Hurst, 1974), 1–2.

Rabat. Such a modernism, promoted by French planners and archi-
tects, could embrace Moorish architectural motifs, providing a local
grace note. They thought these to be more tasteful than the awkward
and overly commercial addenda to older structures and facades that
were generated by the eclectic locals. From the 1930s, Wright argues
in fact that a yet more thorough and universalist modernism became
dominant, eliminating the local colour. Moroccan preservationism had
fitted very well the increasingly dominant theories of indirect rule by
which the "natives" were encouraged to rule themselves along "traditional" lines, making administration cheaper and easier (and obviating
claims towards membership in the emerging colonial society) while
dynamic colonial society expanded freely.

The largest Mediterranean port of Africa was Alexandria, whose
Stock Exchange dominated the Egyptian cotton trade. There was
little left of ancient Alexandria before the nineteenth century. The city
was virtually reborn under the deliberate patronage of Muhammad
Ali (who was himself actually a Muslim Albanian and not an Egyptian
by birth), the Turkish governor who became effectively an independent ruler of Egypt and his successors. This was a new Alexandria
which arose, deliberately intended to cater for commerce with Europe
and as a home for Europeans and migrants from all over the Mediterranean and Near Eastern world, of whom the most numerous were
Italian and Greek. In this context one can hardly talk about analogies with apartheid. Yet it is equally true that the huge population of
"outsiders" in Alexandria had relatively little to do with Egyptians on
a basis of social equality, were not administered under Egyptian law,
typically held strong anti-Egyptian prejudices, and certainly did not
think of themselves as Egyptian. Eventually, when the monarchy was
overthrown and the nationalist tide rose in the 1950s, almost all
departed. As in the Maghreb, this did not prevent a cosmopolitan population – perhaps a quarter of the total urban population – from creating its own cultural life. Alexandria rivalled Athens as a centre of Greek
literary culture until well into the twentieth century, for instance, and
was the beloved lifelong home of the great poet Constantine Cavafy.

The case of the Egyptian capital of Cairo is also perhaps salutary.
It was not really the plots of the British or their discourse about Ori-
entals but the press of the modern city, of capitalist thirst for change,
that led to a gradual transformation. The city expanded dramatically
to the west; the Nile was first bridged in 1872, and a massive drainage
programme of low-lying and previously neglected land instituted in

1907. Between 1882 and 1937, Cairo physically expanded sixteen-fold.[4] Modern highways and bridges were constructed, as well as light-ing and transport facilities. Even for Egyptians, the good life was sig-nalled in Baron Empain's suburb of Heliopolis, constructed in the desert on the road that led to the airport. Better-off Egyptians left the inconvenient quarters they had called home for life in a Europeanised and more convenient city. Old Cairo became a quaint part of a larger city, picturesque but known for crowding, overpopulation, poor ameni-ties, and poverty – this without direct colonial planning aimed at it. These North African cities – Cairo, Alexandria, Rabat – were hybrids, with the modern style particularly dominant in Alexandria. But hybrid cities were also found elsewhere.

For the British, Northern Nigeria under the administration of Frederick Lugard and his successors provided a model of indirect rule applied elsewhere. In its numerous towns, the pattern was one of "native administration" within the old-walled *birane* while direct administration covered the emerging administrative and commercial sections as well as the New Towns or *Sabon Garis* inhabited by a grow-ing "native foreigner" population. The authoritative late colonial geog-raphy text on Nigeria had this to say on the great savanna city of Kano.

> Note, as in the case of Ibadan; the composite character of the city; the old Hausa city, incompletely occupying the space within the twelve mile circuit of walls and centring upon the great market-place which has replaced the sacrificial grove of pre-Islamic days; the Strangers Settle-ment outside the walls occupied by immigrants from the south such as Yorubas and Ibos; the commercial-administrative zone in proxim-ity to the station; and the government residential area insulated by its building-free zone.[5]

This "composite character" clearly did not emerge from human nature unguided.

European authorities in general were reluctant to acknowledge and sustain the property rights of established African populations. Even in West Africa, plans for the destruction of existing African residential communities were often ruthlessly pursued before World War I. Strug-gles over such plans in the German-controlled port city of Duala in

---

[4] André Raymond, *Cairo: City of History* (Cambridge, MA & Cairo: Harvard University Press & American University of Cairo Press, 2001), 322.

[5] K. M. Buchanan & J. C. Pugh, *Land and People in Nigeria* (London: University of London Press, 1955), 72.

Cameroun reached a peak when the authorities hung Rudolf Manga Bell, who had led the struggle against redevelopment, for treason. There were plans in this period for the destruction of the old city of Mombasa on the coast of Kenya while the British also toyed in 1908 with the idea of destroying the old sections of Accra following a plague epidemic. The French authorities were keen to dismantle and entirely destroy the *medina*, or native quarter, that existed alongside the market of the increasingly grand capital of French West Africa, Dakar. The future of the *medina* hung in the balance after the plague epidemic of 1915, a typical episode in the colonial struggle to segregate African cities. It was perhaps characteristic of the milder French approach that although the *medina* was reconstructed on more salubrious lines, it was not actually removed. The French could put aside entirely neither the claims of the native Lebou population, some of whom lived in the *medina*, nor of the voters born in the *Quatre Communes* (often Lebou in fact) and thus qualified as French citizens in the Third Republic, who constituted a significant part of its population. Overcrowded, insalubrious, but economically vibrant and convenient for a variegated population, it has remained an important part of the modern city. Gervais-Lambony has shown the long (and benign) shadow cast on the once-German colonial capital of Lomé in Togo by the authorities' willingness to recognised urban property rights from before conquest. As a result, Lomé was a relatively integrated town by colonial standards.

Stubborn opposition to colonial racism and removal policies have continued to have a long shelf life. Where older urban property rights and customs were threatened, Africans proved very reluctant to endorse urban reform in later years, even if clearly justified in terms of traffic, hygienic, or planning needs. Thus the old Ga fighting companies, the *asafo*, were adapted into organisations that were very successful at resisting the creation of any form of modern tax system in Accra that might have paid for amenities. Indeed this kind of resistance significantly slowed up the engulfing of the older urban communities within the colonial city.

New Cities in Africa

With hindsight, continuities with the pre-colonial past are perhaps clearer now to writers on African cities. By contrast, a generation ago the focus was much more on discontinuities, based in particular on the "typical" new cities of the southern half of the continent. It has to be said that here urbanisation had previously been on a small scale or had hardly existed at all, although this point can be exaggerated, as previous chapters have stressed. For instance, the Ndebele capital of Bulawayo in Southern Rhodesia had been the important centre of a strong kingdom; it was also chosen as the focal point for the new colonial province of Matabeleland and as such became an important railway, commercial, and, to some extent, industrial town with close links to South Africa. Through much of the colonial period, it was larger than Salisbury, the capital. Yet the pre-colonial population had scattered, and traces of the past are impossible to find beyond perhaps the fact that Ndebele speakers were much quicker than Shona speakers to find domiciles in town. This sharp discontinuity is only somewhat less true for Kampala, where one can still see the royal huts of the Buganda *Basekabaka* (kings). The capital of the new colonial Uganda was located in the suburb of Entebbe alongside Lake Victoria Nyanza, but in Kampala itself a new commercial and administrative centre took pride of place in what became the reconfigured city centre. Yet these cities are close to, or at the far end of, our spectrum: they were virtually new colonial towns.

Other colonial cities were really entirely new, such as Nairobi, the capital of Kenya, Lusaka, the capital of Northern Rhodesia, Zomba, the tiny capital of Nyasaland, or Elisabethville, the provincial capital of the copper mining province of Katanga in the Belgian Congo (today Lubumbashi). Indeed, even in northern Africa, the desired forms of economic exploitation seemed to require new urban settlements, for instance Port Said and Ismailia on the Suez Canal, Bizerte, the naval base and port on the Tunisian coast, Philippeville (now Skikda) in Algeria, and Port Lyautey (now Kenitra) on the Atlantic shores of Morocco. The main African Red Sea port south of the Isthmus of Suez was Suakin, located for security on a small island; in consequence, the British constructed Port Sudan from scratch to replace it.

Sometimes such new settlements had at first a noticeable militarised element with a fortified core; they were islands of control dominating a potentially hostile countryside. Thomas Spear has created a dramatic image of early Arusha in northern German East Africa, rising like a ship from the great savannas of that part of the continent and only too obviously placed in order to dominate.[6] Here there were dramatic signs

---

[6] Thomas Spear, "'A Town of Strangers' or 'A Model Modern East African Town'" in Anderson & Rathbone, *Africa's Urban Past* (Oxford & Portsmouth, NH: James Currey & Heinemann, 2000), 199.

of an urban space sharply delineated from its surroundings. Especially noteworthy were the cases where European settlers were numerous enough to establish business and residential communities that broke radically with the world around.

Such communities were absolutely central to the colonial purpose. From the late nineteenth century, segregation was the colonial watchword throughout the continent. The colonial city emerged and differentiated itself, often very ruthlessly, from preexisting patterns. As has long been noted, the growth of urban segregation was typically linked not merely with the establishment of racial theories of superiority but with panics about epidemics and the need to keep the new ruling class of the colony healthy through isolation from contact with the bulk of natives. An early example goes back to the devastation of malaria on the sugar-growing island of Mauritius in 1866–68. In consequence, the state created the rail system that allowed the white population of Port Louis to leave the city every day for the apparently more salubrious and higher Plaines Wilhelms, admittedly not on a racially defined basis. The pestilence carried off one-seventh of the population, including a particularly high portion of the remaining ex-slave population and their children, who had lived in town after leaving the sugar plantations following emancipation.

The British Colonial Office medical advisory committee opined in 1911 that "it has been proved that the separation of the European from the natives is one of the most efficient means of protection against disease endemic amongst native races."[7] A 1914 report from Kenya on "sanitary matters" called for racial segregation as essential urban policy barring all but the "highest class Indians" from the white town and, as a matter of course, using these as a barrier between white settlers and migrant African unskilled workers.[8] Settlers dreamt of entirely reconstructing the landscape, recentred around their needs and desires and taking America or Australasia as idealised models. Racial segregation in its heyday was made also into a moral imperative: white peril episodes in the history of colonial Rhodesia expressed settler anxieties about contacts between white women and black men at the domestic level.

---

[7] Philip Curtin, "Medical Knowledge and Urban Planning in Tropical Africa," *American Historical Review*, XC, 1984, 606.

[8] From Luise White, *The Comforts of Home; Prostitution in Colonial Nairobi* (Chicago: University of Chicago Press, 1992), 48.

One of the most dramatic cases was that of Freetown, the West African capital of Sierra Leone, precisely because it was so unlikely. Freetown was established in 1788 as a centre for ex-slaves returned to Africa. In the nineteenth century, it became an important commercial town with a noticeable Anglicised professional class known as Creoles. In some respects, it already was a "modern" town, a classic nineteenth-century commercial entrepôt. White residents lived interspersed in a lively and diversified urban community. Health was the primary reason given for trying to transform this situation: above Freetown, Hill Station was planned as a healthy home for whites only, focussed around bungalows constructed for colonial officials. From 1902, British-made prefabricated dwellings were hauled up to this site while a special railway was constructed to serve its favoured inhabitants. Politically this marked sharply the decline of the Sierra Leone Creole elite in the colony in favour of imperial officials with their racist world-view.

However, Hill Station was not especially successful as a new suburb intended to mark a bold step forward in colonial development: "It was originally intended that no African should be allowed to sleep in the reservation, but it was found impossible for Europeans to live there without having at least one servant residing on the premises."[9] Whereas urban reconstruction may have sometimes led to substantial improvements in health as they allowed for higher standards of hygiene, the "sanitation syndrome"[10] was largely an excuse to justify intensified racial segregation. Malaria, the apparent cause for the creation of Hill Station, was just as prevalent there as near the waterfront. However, the concomitant creation of an all-white social club and an all-white tram service was bitterly resented by the Sierra Leone Creole elite.

Creating entirely new quarters for existing towns involved considerable town planning, in which the homes of those who laboured in the city were consigned to irrelevance. In the new Kenyan capital of Nairobi, founded on the line of rail in the centre of the new colony in 1899, massive suburban tracts were laid out with tree-lined boulevards and no expectation of public transport whatsoever. This was an English Garden City in the tropics – for the privileged. White (and to a lesser extent Indian) property speculators were able to make substantial profits from the sale of privatised land. The African quarters that emerged near the centre were an afterthought, wretched and

[9] Michael Banton, *West African City* (London: Oxford University Press, 1957), 17.
[10] A term used in a classic article on Cape Town, South Africa by M. W. Swanson.

FIGURE 7. Colonial makeover: Vila Algarve, Lourenço Marques, Mozambique. The former headquarters of PIDE, the Portuguese secret police. *Source:* Michel Loye; used by permission.

unplanned. This meant small purpose-built rooms, intended to serve single workers on the most Spartan of models. The real economic heart of the population of such towns was in fact excised and treated as an unwelcome appendage. African migrants to town were essential to their functioning but unwelcome to any claim of citizenship; their comings and goings deemed them to be forever "impermanent." In these precarious circumstances, poor African neighbourhoods got flattened and removed when they were seen as inconvenient. The early history of Nairobi is marked by such episodes. Areas initially demarcated for Africans in Nairobi, for example, although characterised mainly by neglect, were simply demolished as the city centre expanded and land was required for more "significant" purposes.

Nor were such ideas peculiarities of the British. Lourenço Marques, the new capital of Portuguese East Africa, was a raw, unserviced frontier settlement with an extraordinarily mixed population in the 1890s. By the time of the First World War, it had been transformed; its heart now consisted of a well laid-out town with wide boulevards and some impressive public buildings, what the locals called *Xilinguine*, the white man's place. Shacks, mud, and garbage were expelled to the city outskirts. When urban neighbourhoods, whether constructed or just laid out by the state, were authorised for Africans clearly essential to the labour force required in towns, they were constructed on Spartan lines and on marginal locations. However, as economies grew, these neighbourhoods were never sufficient. In such North African cities as Algiers and Casablanca, *bidonvilles*, shack settlements, began to spring up beyond the planned perimeters by the end of the 1920s.

This kind of urban process has been conceptualised *in extremis* at the other end of the continent for the eastern Algerian city of Bône, now known as Annaba. What was once a walled Turkish garrison town, focussed on its mosque and fortifications, was remodelled by the early twentieth century. The old town, most of whose Muslim population fled into the interior initially after the French conquest, was marginalized and swallowed up by a much larger city – two-thirds of its population at peak was European – whose economy was based on the evacuation of mineral products from the interior, with the port and line of rail critical factors. European trees lined graceful boulevards while public spaces were marked out with statuary commemorating French colonial figures. The great promenade, named in honour of French Bône's most remarkable politician, Jérome Bertagna, swept up from the harbour to culminate at the foot of a neo-Gothic cathedral. The town hall, with

187. — BONE.   Le cours Bertagna   ND Phot.

FIGURE 8. Colonial makeover: Cours Bertagna, Bône, Algeria, ca. 1900.
Source: Courtesy of the Bibliothèque Nationale de France, Depártement de la reproduction, Paris, France.

its mansard roof, took on the aura of a well-constructed metropolitan *hôtel de ville*. Commercial life was dominated by the typical French artisanal and mercantile activities, and there was hardly an Arab face to be seen in a promenade through the town core. Arab survivals were relegated to the picturesque – and to the slum.[11] Not merely was Bône drastically Europeanised; it evolved with other Algerian towns a *colon* culture that was distinctive and potentially autonomous in terms of dialect, folk heroes, political culture, cuisine, and so forth, not unlike the situation at the other end of the continent in South Africa. Indeed, if French, Maltese, Italian, and Spaniard tended to fuse into a single European "community," if that is the right word for it, this evolution also brought increasingly articulated internal class distinctions, albeit in a context where there was little secondary industry to discipline working class life.

Peasants or Workers? The New Urbanites

Nowhere in colonial Africa was urbanisation rawer and newer than on the Northern Rhodesian Copperbelt. Here towns grew with great speed from the time of mineral development in the middle 1920s to 1964 when Zambia became independent. There was no question about the demand for Africans to live in towns here on the part of the employer, although the white labour force on the copper mines was proportionately larger than in South Africa The administration of urban Africans and the whole question of *citizenship* which urbanisation brought in its wake represented a particular dilemma for the British rulers of the colony who conceptualised Africans as tribal residents living under the control of chiefs in a suitably pacific and modified manner, caring for their cows while their women harvested crops. The problem, however, lay in the need for labour in an era when so many Africans, while basing themselves on continued membership in rural societies, spent varying phases of their lives in towns and when the labour needs of capital were consequently enormous. It required the involvement of hundreds of thousands in order to attract tens of thousands of labourers to do the hard and poorly paid work of colonial capitalism at any one time. On the Copperbelt, a particular onus

---

[11] It should perhaps be noted that much of the "European" population was fairly poor. Some distance from the centre, a segregated working-class suburban environment for Europeans emerged from the late nineteenth century onwards. This was the birthplace of the French novelist Albert Camus.

was left with the mining companies which did amass large amounts of capital and had the direct interest in creating a stabilised, if not an urbanised, workforce and were prepared to research and experiment to find solutions to their problems. Until the eve of independence in 1964, the vast majority of Copperbelt Africans were resident on mines property, although some 20 percent were estimated to be living in informal housing on the edge of the mining cities.

This worry brought administrators to introduce into the colony a set of anthropologists to attack the problem of the "detribalised Bantu" that they felt they would be facing, more urgently given large-scale industrial action in 1935 and 1940. Those anthropologists associated with the Rhodes-Livingstone Institute were in fact pioneers in the intellectual construction of urban life in the southern half of Africa. As has been recently discussed by James Ferguson, they were in a sense the left wing of the settler world of southern Africa, a left wing that aspired to a breakdown of the bifurcated colonial society offering some kind of multiracial citizenship focussed on the opportunities that social transformation might bring. The pioneer urban anthropologists operated on an emerging agenda: Northern Rhodesia was experiencing a kind of Industrial Revolution of which they were observing the early stages.

In the heyday of colonial rule, this was not an easy task. Colonial administrators, by contrast with the anthropologists, took for granted that the African was a naturally rural inhabitant whose urban experience was a danger to the integrity of African society as well as to colonial authority. As Dame Margery Perham, an influential and in some respects liberal colonial ideologue wrote, "this situation subjects them [Africans] to an intense social strain."[12] The work of more critical intellectuals was tolerated in the hopes of relieving the strain.

Yet starting with Godfrey Wilson, the anthropologists wrote increasingly complex and sophisticated accounts of what was at first called *detribalisation*. Max Gluckman famously pointed out that "an African tribesman is a tribesman; a miner is a miner";[13] workers were above all workers and needed to be treated as such in the context of labour disputes and labour organisation. Gluckman, along with J. Clyde Mitchell and A. L. Epstein, tried to examine the new habits, tastes, and aspirations of black townsmen. They were all superb observers and recorders of new cultural phenomena. One of Epstein's most important books

---

[12] Cited in Jean Comhaire, *Urban Conditions in Africa; Select Reading List on Urban Problems in Africa* (London: Oxford University Press, 1952).

[13] In "Tribalism in British Central Africa," *Cahiers d'Etudes Africaines*, I, 1960, 57.

examined the growing importance of first, trade unionism and then, nationalist politics as an urban phenomenon. However, he still felt obliged to point out that "the urban African remains a tribesman and yet is not a tribesman."[14]

Even writers such as the Rhodes-Livingstone scholars lived in the shadow of assumptions about the dominance of tribes and custom. One of the enduring strengths of these scholars, notably Max Gluckman, however, was their understanding that many African residents of Copperbelt towns and cities aspired to the modern, the cosmopolitan; however, they defined it *in their own terms*. Indeed, as the years went by, and especially with the approach of independence, they increasingly tended to see themselves as sociologists and to drop the conceptual baggage of anthropology as it existed. The Rhodes-Livingstone scholars never really tried to conceptualise the urban community as a whole; they concentrated fairly strictly on the African migrant. Somewhat paradoxically, their subjects were in one sense unable to be normal townsmen in that they continued to reside on mine company property.

The British anthropological approach tended to explain African life in cities in large part through ethnic diversity. Ethnicity, important a subject as it was, could clearly be stretched by others virtually to dissolve any idea of the modern and transformational. In a classic study along these lines in a collection that tended in this direction, W. A. Shack wrote about the Gurage unskilled workers of Addis Ababa, Ethiopia, not of course a colonial city, very much as a coherent and intact "tribe" that came to the city to fulfil particular expectations without ceasing to be in any sense Gurage. If they encountered any new ideas in the city, these represented adherence to another tribal ethic – the Amhara prestige pecking order dominant in town. Ethnic identity overshadowed urban change. Indeed, in West Africa, emphasis for

---

[14] In a later evolution, Epstein moved to a position that saw urbanization as a profoundly important but not entirely predictable or straightforward process ("Urbanization and Social Change in Africa," *Current Anthropology*, VIII, 1967, 275–95). Mitchell for instance promoted the more "sociological" concept of social networking to understand Copperbelt transformation and described neo-tribal elements as historically transitional (Mitchell, ed., *Social Networks in an Urban Situation*, Manchester: Manchester University Press, 1969). Eventually he compared the Copperbelt town to the US city attracting immigrants and rejected anthropological concepts of "culture" as being irrelevant to the city (*Cities, Society and Social Perception*, Oxford: Clarendon Press, 1987). It can be argued, and has been most eloquently by James Ferguson in *Expectations of Modernity* recently, that in so doing, he moved to a point where he could no longer grasp the failed modernism of the economically decaying contemporary Copperbelt.

observers of the cities in the decade before independence lay on social fragmentation and new forms of ethnic identity. The discipline of social anthropology provided a wonderful stimulus to "fieldwork", original observation that allowed new paradigms to emerge and new phenomena to be highlighted. But the cultural biases of social anthropology as it was also made it hard for this school of writers to conceptualise very effectively a new urban lifestyle. At best, urbanisation needed to be comprehended as part of a "folk-urban continuum" (Southall, ed., 1973). And of course, tens of thousands of new townsmen and townswomen in Africa were what later social scientists call straddlers, people who passed their lives between town and countryside and used opportunities that opened for them where possible in either or both context. In the Great Depression, it was particularly notable that the extreme recession of the copper mining industry did not lead the whole black population to vacate the urban settlements to which they were still relative newcomers. On both sides of the Belgian-British frontier, many still found enough in town life to cling to the urban setting. When Belgian authorities attempted to deport unemployed Africans out of Elisabethville, they met with sturdy resistance. Yet the question posed for intellectuals focussed continually on how much of the older African culture was surviving in the harsh world of the towns.

Catherine Coquery-Vidrovitch has insisted with some justice that this has not really been a significant issue in French scholarship in Africa to the same extent. For one thing, French colonialism coincided in good part with those parts of Africa where clearly an earlier urban tradition existed and had to be acknowledged. However, the emphasis on reconstituting tribalism along lines that could safely be managed under colonial development was very much less consistent. If there is a Francophone figure comparable to the Rhodes-Livingstone school of anthropologists, it must be Georges Balandier, who published an influential study of the rapidly expanding equatorial city of Brazzaville in 1955. Balandier was a sociologist, not an anthropologist, and the weight in his work lay in identifying original cultural and social features of the African town – "une veritable culture négro-urbaine" – and as such he built his social model around the évolué – the educated man – not the rural tribesman come to town. He too generalised from the African community *within* the town rather than spend much time on considering Brazzaville, colonial capital and home of thousands of French merchants, officials and their families, as a totality. However, he laid the groundwork intellectually in which Africans could claim the city, and not just an apparently traditional walled town preserved by tasteful colonists, as their own. In contrast to the hesitant and careful views of British anthropologists, we can note the early celebration of the African city in the work of the British writer on African politics, Thomas Hodgkin, who even before independence suggested in English that the cities represented a "new indigenous civilisation" quite distinct from what rural Africa had ever brought forth.

The exploration of a new urbanity in Africa was handled with particular effectiveness by the radical French anthropologist Claude Meillassoux. Meillassoux, in a study of social groupings and associations in the Malian[15] capital, Bamako, showed a succession of institutions and cultural forms that were integrating established residents and immigrants of Bamako into a new, distinctive culture. Meillassoux recognised that ethnicity had a very ancient pedigree in the West African city, where it could be remoulded but also form part of a larger urban pattern without disintegrating. In Bamako, the Muslim religion and what Meillassoux calls the Banaba language [Bambara] as lingua franca became defining elements of urbanity that transcended ethnicity in important ways. In looking at urban associations, which partly reinforce but partly crosscut ethnicity, he identified the social glue which held neighbourhoods and urban life together. It is the *quartier,* or neighbourhood, which defines Bamako urban life rather than ethnicity while the family compound contains mostly that which is familiar to social structure and built environment in rural Mali as well. But this importance of neighbourhood was no doubt very great in many African cities.

It was not only the lack of access to cars and the absence of decent public transport systems but also the fragmentation of the colonial city and the exclusion of the masses from central facilities to which the authorities paid the most attention that led to what would be called in French *enclavement.* Most interesting are Meillassoux's discussions of organisations that perform and that dance. Such public spectacles involving voluntary participation are particularly significant in taking new cultural forms forward in Africa. At first dance forms tended to reproduce older cultural values and have a rural feel, but over time they change. Here, he argued, young people questioned or even ignored older forms of seniority and paternalist authority. "Beyond the apparent license and futility of the clubs, we can perceive a groping attempt

---

[15] The French Soudan before 1960.

to shape a new society, a new social order and new sex relationships."[16] This attempt was less developed before independence in 1960, when older forms of authority and ethnic adherence received far more obvious adherence in the structure of dances then still dominant. At about the same time in the Belgian Congo, Jean Lafontaine captured the significance of the *matonga*, the typical and large-scale urban funeral rite of Léopoldville where kinship groups and older spiritual forms played little part but ceremonial was dominated by the widow and friends of the deceased and was essentially secularised.

Scholars of West Africa such as Michael Banton and Kenneth Little had already laid much weight on the emergence of voluntary associations as new forms of social glue in African cities. Such associations are at once eminently practical in the creation of networks that sustain economic linkages and providers of prestige and status. Parker has shown for Accra that whereas such associations were not very significant to the native Ga, who had a plethora of older integrative cultural and social associations of their own, they were especially significant for the growing number of Gold Coasters of other origins who flocked to the colonial capital in the twentieth century.

In his landmark study of the working class of Mombasa, the historian Frederick Cooper has taken apart a variety of elements for examination that reveal some aspects of this variegated and fragile civilisation. Mombasa's working class did contain members who belonged entirely to the old world of this commercial coastal town. However, many of its workers in the colonial period were men who shifted usefully between town and countryside. Cooper drops the discomfort of the Rhodes-Livingstone anthropologists with this apparent contradiction. The availability of much casual work, notably on the docks, suited such straddlers' quest for more autonomy following the dissolution of slavery. They sought membership in the cultural world of Muslim Mombasa but not on the terms of slavery and disrespect that the poor had known in the past. Their relationship with landlords in Majengo (the neighbourhood where many lived) was usually exploitative if paternalistic but also contained elements of autonomy and mutual respect. Mombasa also attracted, however, up-country workers, notably Luo from the shores of Lake Victoria Nyanza at the other end of Kenya, who worked on the railways and were complete

[16] Claude Meillassoux, *Urbanization of an African Community* (Seattle: University of Washington Press, 1968), 141.

outsiders to the Islamic world of Mombasa. Thus there were different types of workers who made different types of claims on the city.

More recently Laura Fair has taken up a similar set of themes with regard to colonial Zanzibar. Fair considers, as has Ahmed Sikainga for the urban Sudan, how slave populations in Islamic societies coalesced after emancipation into a new working class distinct from the old master class but retaining relatively little from their often distant societies of origin.[17] Observers like Cooper and Fair who wish to consider the city as a new remarkable social formation are looking at features such as dance and music, clothing and costume, conviviality based on drinking spots, sport, and other forms of social communication. Cooper noted, as the Copperbelt anthropologists had long before, the remarkable importance of dance and dance societies in the nature of social cohesion in African cities. Fair has recently commented that men enjoyed participation in cross-dressing dance displays just as much as participation on football teams along the lines that British sponsors took to be conventionally masculine, much to the astonishment of white observers. Urban sport was also not always played according to white man's rules. Parry, Phimister, and van Onselen have recounted urban boxing contests in Bulawayo, the railway junction city in colonial Southern Rhodesia, which operated according to distinctive local rules and represented structured ethnic competition. They were contests replete with symbolic significance in which magic played as much a role as skill.[18]

With regard to clothing, it is remarkable that Godfrey Wilson, the first important Rhodes-Livingstone scholar, commented that no less than 60 percent of early copper miners' wages went on clothing. Wilson looked on this as an economic issue while realising that clothing bore a great importance as carrier of prestige; today's scholars are more apt to ask what type of clothing was bought and how clothing worked as cultural signifiers. The use of European clothing elements would seem to entangle African workers in the fine net of capitalist accumulation, but with time clothing display could also reflect new forms of

[17] This point has also been made by Cooper for Mombasa and by Post & Jenkins for Ibadan.
[18] Parry's piece is included in the Raftopoulos & Yoshikuni collection. For Phimister & van Onselen, see "The Political Economy of Tribal Animosity: A Case Study of the 1929 Bulawayo Location 'Faction Fight'", *Journal of Southern African Studies*, VI(1), 1979, 1–43.

respectability and identity that were independent of how Europeans actually clothed themselves in the colonial setting.

Long ago, the linguist Joseph Greenberg pointed out that African cities were often the site of dramatic linguistic invention in the colonial period as new lingua francas spread and became accepted as characteristic of particular towns. Thus Lingala, a language that spread to further trade relations on the lower Congo River, became such a lingua franca amongst Africans in Léopoldville, capital of the Belgian Congo. The cities also incurred the attention of indigenised religious movements, Muslim and Christian, even if white Christian missionaries generally preferred to target peasant communities for their outreach. Parker considers for Accra that, in the earlier colonial phase, "an ongoing, uneasy dialogue between Christianity and indigenous belief" was typical.[19] In many West African cities such as Ibadan and Lagos, the poor converted in very large numbers to Islam, which became associated with the indigenous and local popular culture. By contrast, in colonial East Africa, the early prominence of Islamic urbanism sometimes gave way to the dominance of Christianity as converted peasant migrants became more numerous and the earlier urban core population was marginalized.

Most of the new cities were very heterogeneous in ethnic terms. Their residents were associated with a very wide variety of "tribal" groupings as classified by colonial administrators. If in some cities there were massive continuities with the immediate countryside, for example in Yoruba-speaking south-western Nigeria, others were populated very largely by migrants coming from much greater distances with a sense of identity very distinct from that of the "indigenous" population. Arusha (in contemporary Tanzania), for instance, had very few residents from the Arusha-speaking population of the environs; for much of the colonial period, moreover, its population became more and more European and Asian in percentage terms. The greatest colonial conurbation of the East African interior, Nairobi, attracted many Kikuyu speakers from the densely peopled agricultural lands in its vicinity. Colonial Salisbury makes an interesting case. Initially its core urban inhabitants came largely from outside Southern Rhodesia, and short distance migrants, Shona speakers, tended to use the city, as with the Kikuyu in Nairobi, moving in and out in complex intersecting

---

[19] John Parker, *Making the Town: Ga State and Society in Early Colonial Accra* (Oxford & Portsmouth, NH: James Currey & Heinemann, 2000), 155.

migration patterns. Chi Nyanja was originally the dominant Bantu language of Salisbury as it still is in Lusaka. However, with time a Shona-speaking elite and a Shona proletariat fixed themselves in Salisbury and became dominant gradually after World War II.

The great majority of immigrants to the Copperbelt, both British and Belgian, were long-distance migrants, and workers were cut off to an extreme extent from the surrounding countryside. Here even the white population had a transient and raw feel to it, understandable from the mining context. It was Clyde Mitchell who used the *kalela* dance on the Northern Rhodesian mines as a kind of symbolic touchstone for grasping the new urban life in the territory in a classic essay published towards the end of the colonial era in 1956. During the dance, different "tribal" groups displayed typical characteristics and differentiated themselves from others in good-natured ways that aimed at creating a new sociability while advertising their participation in the economic life of the Copperbelt. The dance belonged to the copper workers; there was no representation in it of any element of the educated stratum of the population.

Ethnicity remained very important but took on a different cast in the city. Abner Cohen, writing on Nigeria, has proposed that "ethnic groups are in fact interest groupings whose members share some common economic and political interests and who, therefore, stand together in the continuous competition for power with other groups."[20] This is a strong definition of how ethnicity operates in those parts of Africa where it is most potent. Often particular ethnic discourses that come together define very dynamic elements in society that are able to create wealth and play a very powerful role in the urban environment.[21] New settlers especially needed relatives and friends from home to provide them with the housing and potential access to income that would make urban life feasible. This engendered ethnic associations.

Often ethnic distinctions that would be important at home were eviscerated in the urban situation where such a variety of people lived side by side. John Iliffe thus refers to the creation of "supertribal" identities in colonial Tanganyika. When Parry writes about boxing in colonial Zimbabwe, his use of "ethnic" also indicates supertribal

---

[20] Abner Cohen, *Custom and Politics in Urban Africa; A Study of Hausa Migrants in Yoruba Towns* (Berkeley: University of California Press, 1969), 192.

[21] For example, the Igbo in Port Harcourt as portrayed by Howard Wolpe, *Urban Politics in Nigeria; A Study of Port Harcourt* (Berkeley: University of California Press, 1974).

agglomerative identity that made sense only in the new urban context. The city also evoked a sense of wider identity yet. Perhaps we need to examine as well the emergence of territorial or national identities, something which has interested scholars less. It must often be in the city that men and women discovered that they were Kenyans or Togolese or Congolese. This is not to suggest that a new national identity was rapidly taking shape, although it is no doubt in the cities where it would become most relevant.

In fact, the new ethnicities often brought about intense rivalries marked by violence. This was notably true for instance in Balandier's paradigmatic city of Brazzaville in 1959 and after. Brazzaville, the capital of French Equatorial Africa, has been the pan in which new ethnic identities have been cooked. The two distinct African *quartiers* of the colonial city, Poto Poto and Bacongo, according to Florence Bernault, stimulated a division between north and south identities for the entire French Congo,with ominous long-term consequences for national peace in the future Republic of the Congo. Van Onselen and Phimister have shown how the structured and symbolic fight contests of early Rhodesia could degenerate in phases of economic downturn and intense competition into genuinely widespread and disruptive ethnic "faction fights." In Nairobi, during the 1950s, the Mau Mau insurgency had finally spurred the British to engage in massive expulsions of Kikuyu workers from the city, with their places often taken up by Africans from other ethnic groups uninvolved in Mau Mau. This is one of the circumstances that helped bring about the highly charged "tribal" politics of late colonial and independent Kenya.

The typical African city contained far more men than women, especially in eastern and southern Africa, and it is hard to escape the impression that short-term and youthful male migrants must have maintained a massive presence in the eyes of any beholder of colonial African urban life. However, those women that did come to live in the cities had an importance often considerably beyond their numbers. In West Africa, where urban compounds exhibited so much continuity with the past, women both rich and poor could occupy a variety of economic roles and held a time-honoured place in the market and in a range of craft activities. However, urban women also succeeded in making an early and important contribution in early colonial towns and cities of southern and eastern Africa where they had no traditional presence. Luise White has shown for early Nairobi that the women judged by authorities as prostitutes actually could be divided into various economic categories and were in part involved in providing a range of services beyond sexual favours for men. Such women were the bedrock of social stability in the new, precarious, and violent townships which housed African workmen. They had far more at stake in securing access to housing in their own names and gaining legal recognition as residents. Such women frequently became Muslim in East Africa because Islam was a legitimating factor in casting off any uncomfortable association with a tribe or ethnic group that could empower male elders.[22] Susan Geiger demonstrated that independent Muslim women were often very significant in the formation of early nationalist politics in late colonial Tanganyika, the territory to the south of Kenya.[23]

Throughout the southern half of Africa, women were pushed into exercising their rights on the fringes of legality – selling cooked foods and other goods on the streets, offering their sexual services along a variety of lines or "forms" as White calls them, taking in laundry and brewing beer with its strong associations of sociability and community formation. Such women were really the pioneer African urban entrepreneurs in many cases here. Rarely were they waged employees except as domestic workers, and often their existence in the city was threatened unless they formed marital (or less formal) alliances with men, men whose legitimate role in the urban economy was much more secure in the eyes of the authorities.

For African women, despite the precariousness of life in the city, there was the possibility of liberation from oppression to family obligations and situations of extreme dependence as well as misery that emerged in the rural context. The relationship of colonial authorities to such women was complex. Often they were seen as offensive to patriarchal ideals and highly expendable to the modernising city. They were part of an early urban fringe that lived on the edge of colonial law, with subcultures of "alcohol dealers, gamblers and prostitutes" prevailing.[24] However, as White and, in the case of Salisbury, Teresa Barnes, contributing to the same collection as Parry, indicate,

---

[22] Later in the colonial period, Nairobi attracted many women who worked as prostitutes and defined themselves as Bahaya. These women, from northern Tanganyika, did not become Muslim.

[23] Susan Geiger, *TANU Women: Gender and Culture in the Making of Tanganyikan Nationalism, 1955–1965* (Portmouth, NH, Oxford, Nairobi & Dar es Salaam: Heinemann, James Currey, EAEP & Mkuki nya Nyoka, 1997).

[24] Parry in Raftopoulos & Yoshikuni, 1999, 57.

there was also often a grudging tolerance based on the contribution of what stabilised women offered to a potentially difficult-to-discipline working class.

An Era of Resistance

> Don't think you've snuffed out the Casbah
> Don't believe you can build your new world on our ruins.[25]

In this final section, having looked at varieties of African urban communities and neighbourhoods, the emphasis lies in disaggregation and struggle. The attempt by colonial authorities to shore up some of these elements while disestablishing others, or to maintain some kind of stable balance, crumbled after World War II. One part of postwar urban history in Africa lay in a reactionary struggle, a struggle in the late colonial period on the part of the privileged against concessions and for the extension of the city white. In the Camerounian port city of Douala, the end of World War II initiated a wave of violence on the part of white settlers afraid of concessions that would decentre their ambitions after the Brazzaville address of General de Gaulle seemed to threaten a deracialisation of French colonial policies. Increasingly extreme incidents mark the later colonial history of Bône, where decolonisation in 1962 would mean the physical departure of almost all the "Europeans" who had formed the majority of the urban population and the deconstruction of the colonial town as it had been conceived by the French – starting with the physical demolition of the cathedral and the colonial statuary. In Nairobi, whites who dominated the City Council struggled constantly for enforcement of pass laws, repatriation of vagrants, removal of informal housing wherever it was deemed inconvenient, and the establishment of curfews and no-go areas for Africans. Lusaka, established as a new capital for Northern Rhodesia in 1930, was, so far as its white population were concerned, a "planned" city with huge residential lots and curving tree-lined streets in place of the conventional grid pattern. The copper boom allowed for the emergence of a private building sector that actually constructed the homes and offices whites used; even the apprenticeships in the industry were

---

[25] Quote from Kateb in M. L. Maougal, "Algérie capitale Alger" in the collection *La ville dans tout ses états* (Algiers: Casbah, 1998); my translation.

largely confined to whites until independence in 1964. Up to this time Lusaka developed mainly along lines focussed on its expanding white middle-class population, although purpose-built municipal housing for Africans did gradually get allocated and formal racial segregation began to dissolve. Carole Rakodi is right to characterise this kind of planning as "debased" even when it contained elements that were considered the last word in the twentieth-century city.[26] As we shall see in the next chapter, this thrust went together with the triumphal urban planning of apartheid in South Africa, but it was doomed even there and from a much earlier phase.

In some respects, the quintessential male urbanites of Africa had been the elites. As colonial states created social services and allowed for the emergence of a new African leadership, the sites where such elites could make a living were disproportionately urban. In the cities they set the stage for new social and cultural forms that were admired and later spread further down the socioeconomic ladder. They were proud of town ways and of their access to the world via the towns, even if colonial authorities exaggerated their isolation from rural forms of organisation and prestige. However, policies based on accommodating small elite numbers became less relevant over time.

Limited categories of Africans then had been afforded tentative urban space, albeit in a contradictory way. Even outside western and northern Africa, where indigenous urban life was so prevalent, colonial authorities had also usually recognised the existence of established urban communities where white settlers were not too exigent. Towards the end of the colonial period, the anthropologist Valdo Pons studied the city of Stanleyville in the Belgian Congo. Belgian authorities recognized that there was an old urban population that preceded colonial control and performed some useful economic function – the *arabisés*. To accommodate them, the *centre extra-coutumier* was created where Africans could build "traditional" homesteads and start businesses along controlled lines, although of course the state insisted on continuing to own the land. In Léopoldville, Africans, women included, were eventually given the right to own freehold land in such settlements, but most preferred the longer-established occupation rights to what were called in French *lotissements* as sufficient. Moreover, "in 1958 a study of housing estates by Albert Attunou showed clearly that the average

[26] Carole Rakodi, "Colonial Urban Policy and Planning in Northern Rhodesia and its Legacy," *Third World Planning Review*, VIII(3), 1986, 213.

Congolese would prefer to acquire his[sic] own *parcelle* and build a house to his own specifications, rather than live in a housing estate."[27] On such a *parcelle*, the landlord could become a sort of chief and he could acquire tenants as clients, especially if the spatial allotment was fairly large. This policy accompanied the rigid, legal racial segregation that had typified Belgian rule from the end of the nineteenth century. The historian John Iliffe has underlined the role of landlords, *fadhahausi*, in Dar es Salaam, Tanganyika, during the interwar years under British rule. In the centre of town, notably the district of Kariakoo, they represented bulwarks of stability and used compound rents to accumulate capital. "Kariakoo" referred to the World War I carrier corps, and the term elided into a sense of respectability and importance in the colonial order. The lively Kariakoo market was fundamental to the neighbourhood's economic existence.

However, the property rights of such individuals were usually hedged and everywhere the availability of plots was insufficient. And in cities where Africans did hold entrenched property rights, colonial authorities were ill at ease. The authorities waged a major struggle in Zanzibar to force what was termed *waqf* land – which engendered no rent and had been in the gift ultimately of the Sultans – into a more commercial system. The gift of such land enabled many poor Zanzibaris to live rent-free across the lagoon from the Stone Town. Such pressure led to a major rent strike in 1928, where solidarity held to the point that the authorities had to yield. As late as the 1940s, a district commissioner in the Sudan considered that "no where else in the world is there so large a community which is so unproductive" as in Omdurman.[28] In Omdurman, life operated still according to social norms over which the colonial economy held little purchase. Homeowners could live off rents while an internal economy of crafts and commerce remained vibrant.

A further element in many African towns were poor peripheral commuters who were not so much acknowledged as tolerated, the straddlers Cooper has introduced to us. Thus in Dar es Salaam, native Zaramo speakers from the vicinity were rarely found in the town centre but tended to construct homes on the urban periphery if they were able

---

[27] J. S. Lafontaine, *City Politics: A Study of Leopoldville 1962–63* (Cambridge: Cambridge University Press, 1970), 119.
[28] Ahmed Sikainga, *Slaves Into Workers: Emancipation and Labor in Colonial Sudan* (Austin: University of Texas Press, 1996), 176.

to access money from urban activities. In Nyasaland, a poor colony, the limited space made available for Africans in the vicinity of Blantyre and Limbe was so dreadful – "windowless hovels" – that far more people preferred to make their homes at some distance from town and commute. In early Rhodesia, the prevalence of "private locations" and tribal areas near towns made this kind of commuting a feature from an early period.

With regard to migrants, we are able today to recognise that for the workers themselves the question was not how urban they proposed to become but how to access the resources of town in a way that enabled their lives to be improved. Urbanisation as a process was something that came second to this and workers were inclined to struggle to maintain their situations at both ends rather than be defined by the state as either peasants or proletarians. Because poor urban migrants had themselves valued the importance of a transient and ambulant existence, there was some collusion between their self-defined needs and the systematic tendency of colonial rulers to minimise spending on urban planning and infrastructure. Nairobi's African population had its first purpose-built housing in the form of a squalid and unsanitary series of tiny rooms and, as we have seen, such housing was seen as highly expendable. Communal laundries and dormitories were initially typical features and stressed the extent to which migrants were conceived of simply as indistinguishable "labour" rather than human beings with a foothold in an expanding urban environment.

Using the South African model to which we shall be referring in the next chapter, we note that lasting improvements for long depended on revenues derived from municipal attempts to control beer drinking with municipal beer houses rather than any system of property rates that might be associated with tenure. In this setting, where a large settler population was resident, the state tried as well to control the physical movement of poor African individuals within urban space through pass laws, an endless source of harassment, and shakedown street politics. Indeed, in Nairobi, the entire town-planning model and most of the employed town planners came from South Africa, something that was largely the case in colonies further south as well. In general, the resources involved in trying to control African drinking habits were too limited for the so-called Durban system to really take effect, although it existed in some form throughout the British colonies in the southern half of Africa and even spread into Belgian colonial usage. Thus in Salisbury, the municipal brewery actually supplied malt to African brewers, as authorities were unable to wipe out African beer production. No wonder Africans preferred, and fought for, the preservation of neighbourhoods where they had rights and where economic activities were possible, even if such neighbourhoods were also relatively squalid.

With the rapid expansion of African urban populations from the late 1930s on, the plans of colonial administrators for cities based on segregation and on an urban ideal aimed at the affluent began to look less secure and less relevant. Swollen townships alive with underpaid workers and poor people trying to keep their heads above water became the source of resistance to authority. This sometimes provoked forceful strikes, notably of public sector workers, which in turn often played a critical role in creating a mass base for nationalist political leaders and parties but which were also typically concerned with urban conditions. The authorities saw in growing cities the potential source for social and even political disruption, a home for agitators and those who failed to "fit" into colonial paternalist expectations. The "struggle for the city" in Cooper's terms was partly about shaking authority so as to allow for conditions of extended reproduction where only temporary amenities designed for a small and ambulant population were provided for. Collusion between worker abstemiousness and state stinginess ceased to hold at critical junctures. In conceptualising key struggles, Cooper shed entirely worries about just how "urban" African urban dwellers were in the colonial period; instead he focussed on the consequences of rural Africans domiciling themselves in the city, their basic needs and aims, and how this clashed with the reluctant reception they received from authorities.[29] As they succeeded, they threatened to change the very nature of the colonial African city.

In some cases, the city became the site of resistance to colonial authority, resistance which blended with demands for improved economic conditions in the light of wartime and postwar conditions. If most historians have emphasized the positive aspects of urban leisure time in recent years, one notes that by the 1940s Fair notes also a violent and tense element in urban life. In contrast to more cheerful narratives about structured dance societies, a few writers have taken seriously claims about the extension of delinquency and the spread of crime, especially given the large population of male youths and the

---

[29] Frederick Cooper, *Struggles for the City; Migrant Labour, Capital and the State in Urban Africa* (Beverly Hills & London: Sage, 1983).

emergence of a quite uncontrolled, raw consumerist "cowboy" culture, in the words of Andrew Burton. Its proponents did not want
to be told what elements of capitalism and new forms of wealth to
accept and which to abstain from. African urban culture was beginning to acquire an insurgent character, especially in the new colonially
generated towns. And authority's not-entirely-unjustified fears about
disorder were also not-entirely-unjustified fears about politics. Thus
the "African crowd" of Nairobi represented a major source, in British
eyes, of recruitment for the Mau Mau rebellion of the early 1950s.[30]
Operation Anvil uprooted and expelled workers from the city on an
unprecedented scale. It was notable also that new workers from parts of
Kenya where Mau Mau was not significant were sometimes rewarded
with better-quality housing (creation of Makadara and the beginning
of family housing units for Africans in Nairobi) than had ever previously been made available.

Purpose-built state housing of a decent quality by the middle 1950s
was no longer entirely a novelty. In Dar es Salaam and elsewhere,
new and more enlightened colonial policies did begin to authorize
the construction of municipal housing for African clerical and worker
families. Magomeni in Dar es Salaam, where workers in government-
owned dwellings held down relatively secure jobs, was far more integrated into the colonial economy than was Kariakoo. In Khartoum
North, African workers in steady employment were permitted to erect
homes on government-assigned plots just as they were in sections of
Abidjan, the new capital of the Ivory Coast, near the port, after World
War II. Yet nowhere did colonial planning envision the emergence of
great cities marked by African proletariats or conceive systematically
of the need for cultural and economic continuities and infrastructure
aimed at the survival of poor people in large numbers. At best, later
planning efforts moved away from racial segregation (except of course
in South Africa and neighbouring territories) and began to try to apply
modernist ideas based on the social democratic and liberal ideals of
contemporary Europe, whether appropriate or not. Efforts at modernising and sanitising West African cities in response to mild dol-
lops of political democratisation met with stalemate; African electors
proved profoundly reluctant in coastal Nigeria and the Gold Coast
to pay systematic rates that would underscore modernisation. As we

---

[30] Just as did New Bell in postwar Duala. Cameroun witnessed a sustained and violent
anti-French insurrection just after the peak of Mau Mau.

have seen, the early history of slum clearance associated with segregation and hygiene cast a long shadow; urban residents fought shy of cooperation with the state.

Attempts to create suitable confined homes for a proletariat, often coupled with removal campaigns aimed at expunging the unwanted, did not begin to resolve the burgeoning advance of the shantytown, the *bidonville*. Cooper has shown both for Kenya and for Senegal that when the colonial state was unable to force Africans back into their older situation, they instituted reform plans which were not so much badly intended as contradictory and unworkable. African wages remained painfully low and formed the basis for savings or for petty accumulation only with difficulty. In particular, the capital costs of constructing working-class family-based neighbourhoods on the European model for the majority of town dwellers proved too high, and the attempt to deal with their inhabitants as though they were inscribed in European nuclear families proved too unrealistic. As late as the beginning of the 1950s, for instance, Herbert Werlin noted that Africans in Nairobi still lived largely in a context where paved roads, drainage, and electricity did not exist. These reform schemes continued, especially in the wealthier colonies, into the postindependence period, but it would then become clearer not only to conservatives but also to those who admired the rise of African nationalism that African cities could not keep pace with the demands for a basic improvement in living on the part of the masses. The potentially antisocial "urban crowd" presented an ever greater challenge to the philosophy of development tied in to a desire for order.

An underdeveloped area in the study of colonial towns lies, perhaps surprisingly, in politics. Particularly in the later colonial period, distinctive forms of urban politics did emerge. On the one hand, old centres such as Ibadan, Kano, or Accra held out scope for patronage to forces clustered around changing networks of African authority structures. In Lagos, Pauline Baker argues that the British, surprisingly given their ideological predilections, sidestepped the chiefly "house of Docemo" but in so doing unintentionally accorded it resistance significance and status as a political player. She thus shows that it was the survival of older forms, as well as the charisma of specific individuals such as Lagos' Herbert Macauley, that brought urban politics to life. Sometimes urban politics took the form of bitter contests, notably in West Africa, when impinged on by colonial attempts to squeeze taxes out of residents for modernization plans. Even when shorn of

any racist element, they could evoke intense hostility. The relationship
of indigenes to newcomers often bedeviled political development as
the newcomers, often ahead in terms of wealth and education, refused
to accept the authority of the long-established. Struggles could be
dissipated through political concessions, reforms, and divide-and-rule
tactics that rigidified ethnic, regional, or religious divisions.

Even in settler colonies such as Southern Rhodesia and Kenya,
advisory councils were created so that trusted Africans could assist
with the practical side of urban administration, but they invariably
had little power, even of a patrimonial sort, and were not viable sites
for vibrant political activity. Colonial rulers tended to create modern
political representative structures as cities grew in size and importance. These were most effective and important when dominated by
white settlers. In British colonies, the vote was based on the payment
of property rates, and municipal structures were formed to serve the
ratepayers. Thus in Northern Rhodesia the Townships Ordinance gave
some kind of self-government of this sort to a number of municipalities. Settler rule was often more parsimonious with expenditure and
gave even more short shrift to African services and needs than officials from Europe. Only on the eve of Zambian independence was
the municipal franchise extended substantially to Africans, and still
they constituted only a minority. In East Africa, Indians were usually
included in urban government structures but invariably on a less than
equal basis; Nairobi's white mayor was complemented by a brown-
skinned vice-mayor, although the Indian population was perhaps twice
as large as the white population.

By contrast, the advisory councils and elected councils of West
Africa had too little in the way of resources and autonomy to attract
or engender a new African politics. However, there were colonial
towns where postwar trade unionism gave urban politics a strong
working-class cast; but more typically, the most educated and well-
to-do Africans were often able not merely to organize their own class
around grievances but to emerge successfully as champions of the
masses. As some writers have shown for Nigeria, the urban arena
became very attractive by the 1950s to African politicians eager to
build up a following and able through provincial and territorial self-
government to command resources with which to create the beginnings
of urban machine politics and offer symbols of "progress" to con-
stituents. A classic study of a typical late colonial politician in Nigeria,
Adegoke Adelabu, makes clear the central role of the Ibadan town
council in his rise to power and notoriety. Such politicians did not

really try to engage with the contradictory and challenging problems involved in planning modern cities and accommodating the mass of new urbanites in late colonial Africa. One should not underestimate as well the difficulties involved in organizing the very disparate urban populations of colonial Africa. This was not merely, as we have seen, the question of the racial minorities (or "Europeans" in the case of North Africa) but also of differences between indigenes and migrants, homeowners and tenants, traditional chiefs and educated elites. The struggle for the city had more than one angle.

This chapter has tried to indicate the substantial scale of growth in colonial cities, especially primate cities, to give a sense of the diversity of economic activities that made urban life possible and to consider the social forms that Africans themselves created in this environment. In some cases, the cities sprang up from nothing at all, although continuities and links to rural life remained very important; in others, pre-colonial cities changed perhaps only marginally and subtly but often through marginalization in new colonial structures. This did provoke important differences. Colonial rule, characterized by economic functionalist policy and racist segregation ideas, often tried to impose idealized norms from the metropole, but African realities continued to creep in repeatedly. Though colonial cities experienced stabler phases, they were often the source of social and political crises that revealed the contradictions in colonial ideas about development.

Selected Readings

By contrast with the specific subject matter of the previous chapters, colonial cities in Africa have interested many modern scholars, and there is much to be read on them. Thus the following reading list is far from comprehensive. Again, many of the titles already given for previous chapters – such as Parker, Miner, Peel, and Lloyd et al. – are very relevant to this one as well. A typology of colonial cities that is widely influential is a feature of Anthony O'Connor, *The African City* (London: Hutchinson, 1983). Some thoughtful essays widely cited by students of colonial urban Africa are J. R. Rayfield, "Theories of Urbanization and the Colonial City in West Africa," *Africa*, LXIV, 1974, 163–85; J. D. Y. Peel, "Urbanization and Urban History in West Africa," *Journal of African History*, XXI, 1980, 269–78; and Catherine Coquery-Vidrovitch, "The Process of Urbanization in Africa," *African Studies Review*, XXIV(1), 1991, 1–98. See also David Simon,

Cities, Capital and Development (London: Belhaven, 1992). Gwendolyn Wright, *The Politics of Design in French Colonial Urbanism* (Chicago: University of Chicago Press, 1991) is a distinctive contribution.

Retracing urban debates among scholars takes us back at least to the 1950s if not earlier. A strong classic "anti-urban" statement might be Bert Hoselitz, "Generative and Parasitic Cities," *Economic Development and Cultural Change*, III, 1955, 278–94. Those interested in how cities were being studied in the late colonial period itself can make use of J. Comhaire, *Urban Conditions in Africa: Select Reading List on Urban Problems in Africa* (London: Oxford University Press, 1952). For the major writings of the Rhodes-Livingstone Institute school, eager to make a space for the urban African, see Godfrey Wilson, *An Essay on the Economics of Detribalization in Northern Rhodesia, Rhodes-Livingstone Papers 6* (Manchester: Manchester University Press, 1942); Max Gluckman, "Tribalism in Modern British Central Africa," *Cahiers d'Etudes Africaines*, I, (1960), 55–70; A. L. Epstein, *Politics in an Urban African Community* (Manchester: Manchester University Press, 1958), "Urbanization and Social Change in Africa," *Current Anthropology*, VIII,(1967), 275–95, and *Urbanization and Kinship* (London: Academic Press, 1981); J. Clyde Mitchell, *Cities, Society and Social Perception* (Oxford: Clarendon Press, 1987), *The Kalela Dance, Rhodes-Livingstone Papers* 27 (Manchester: Manchester University Press, 1956), and the volume edited by him, *Social Networks in Urban Situations* (Manchester: Manchester University Press, 1969). There is an interesting critique in James Ferguson, *Expectations of Modernity: Myths and Meanings of Urban Life on the Zambian Copperbelt* (Berkeley: University of California Press, 1999).

The more comfortably urban tradition in French scholarship is represented by Georges Balandier, *Sociologie des Brazzavilles noires* (Paris: Presses de la fondation nationale des sciences politiques, réed, 1985) and Claude Meillassoux, *Urbanization of an African Community* (Seattle: University of Washington Press, 1968). It was echoed long ago by Thomas Hodgkin in his classic *Nationalism in Colonial Africa* (New York: New York University Press, 1956). Another entirely positive urbanist was the American anthropologist Hortense Powdermaker, who also wrote about the Zambian Copperbelt: *Copper Town: Changing Africa* (New York: Harper & Row, 1962). Also see H. J. Simons, "Zambia's Urban Situation" in Ben Turok, ed., *Development in Zambia* (London: Zed Press, 1979).

Later social scientists often focussed on ethnicity, voluntary organisation, and community construction within the African city: Michael Banton, *West African City* (London: Oxford University Press, 1957); Abner Cohen, *Customs and Politics in Urban Africa: A Study of Hausa Migrants in Yoruba Towns* (Berkeley: University of California Press, 1969); Merran Fraenkel, *Tribe and Class in Monrovia* (London: Oxford University Press, 1964); Marion Kilson, *African Urban Kinsmen* (London: C. Hurst, 1974); Kenneth Little, *West African Urbanization: A Study of Voluntary Association in Social Change* (Cambridge: Cambridge University Press, 1970). D. J. Parkin, "Urban Voluntary Associations as Institutions of Adaptation," *Man*, N.S. I, 1967, 90–95; Valdo Pons, *Stanleyville* (London: Oxford University Press, 1969); and Elliott P. Skinner, *African Urban Life: The Transformation of Ouagadougou* (Princeton: Princeton University Press, 1974) are some of the important studies of the 1960s and 1970s. Such studies, typically by anthropologists and usually researched before independence or not long afterwards, repay rereading. Aidan Southall, ed., *Urban Anthropology: Cross-Cultural Studies of Urbanization* (New York: Oxford University Press, 1973) collected much of this material. On one under-researched issue, note Joseph Greenberg, "Urbanization, Migration and Language" in Hilda Kuper, ed., *Urbanization and Migration in West Africa* (Berkeley: University of California Press, 1965), 50–59, and Johannes Fabian, *Language and Colonial Power: The Appropriation of Swahili in the Former Belgian Congo 1880–1938* (Cambridge & Berkeley: Cambridge University Press and University of California Press, 1986).

Segregation and racism with their links to urban reconstruction/renewal have intrigued scholars for some time. See for instance on this theme Leo Spitzer, "The Mosquito and Segregation in Sierra Leone," *Canadian Journal of African Studies*, II, 1968, 49–61 and Philip Curtin, "Medical Knowledge and Urban Planning in Tropical Africa," *American Historical Review*, XC, 1985, 594–613. Related to this is R. F. Betts, "The Problem of the Medina in the Urban Planning of Dakar," *African Urban Notes*, IV, 3, 1969, 5–15. On southern Africa see Jeanne Penvenne, *African Workers and Colonial Racism: Mozambican Strategies and Struggles in Lourenço Marques 1877–1962* (Oxford & Portsmouth, NH: James Currey & Heinemann, 1995); Richard Gray, *The Two Nations* (London: Oxford University Press, 1960); Carole Rakodi, *Harare: Inheriting a Settler Colonial City* (London: Wiley, 1995) and, on Northern Rhodesia, "Colonial Urban Policy and Planning in Northern Rhodesia and its Legacy," *Third World Planning Review*, VIII(3), 1986, 193–216; and Philippe Gervais-Lambony, *De Lomé à Harare; images et pratiques des villes africaines* (Nairobi & Paris: IFAS & Karthala, 1994). Valuable comparisons can be drawn elsewhere with Janet Abu Lughod, *Rabat, Urban Apartheid in Morocco* (Princeton: Princeton University Press, 1980); Zeynep Çelik, *Urban Forms and Colonial Confrontations: Algiers under French Rule* (Berkeley: University of California Press, 1997); Bruce Fetter, *The Creation of Elisabethville* (Stanford: Hoover Institution University Press, 1976); and David Prochaska, *Making Algeria French: Colonialism in Bône 1870–1920*, (Cambridge: Cambridge University Press, 1990). Moving towards more general themes, a very substantial study written not long after independence is André Adam, *Casablanca*, 2 volumes, (Paris: Editions du CNRS, 1968). As an example of a smaller city, the Moroccan border town of Oujda, Yvette Katan, *Oujda: une ville frontière du Maroc (1907–56)* (Paris: L'Harmattan, 1990) is interesting. Moroccan urban development under the French experience was distinctive and far more nuanced than generally was the case in colonial Africa and is in its complexity not done justice in this chapter. For a thoughtful study see Abderrahmane Rachik, *Ville et pouvoirs au Maroc* (Casablanca: Afrique-Orient, 1994). Kenneth Perkins, *Port Sudan: Evolution of a Colonial City* (Boulder: Westview Press, 1993) traces the development and contradictions of an entirely new colonial city with only a commercial expatriate element. For fine, largely literary evocations of Mediterranean African cities, see Michael Haag, *Alexandria: City of Memory* (New Haven: Yale University Press, 2004) and Iain Finlayson, *Tangier: City of the Dream* (London: Harper Collins, 1992).

An early collection of articles showing a sense of tension and crisis in African colonial cities was published in 1969 in the special issue (III[2]) of the *Canadian Journal of African Studies*, which notably included Peter Gutkind, "Tradition, Migration, Urbanization, Modernity and Unemployment in Africa: The Roots of Instability." Urban studies in Africa were transformed by a collection edited by Frederick Cooper with an important introduction: *Struggle for the City: Migrant Labor, Capital and the State in Urban Africa* (Beverly Hills & London: Sage, 1983). This paved the way for new social historical studies of cities which emphasized first class and then culture and gave some definition to certain previous studies. A few titles along these lines would include Florence Bernault, "The Political Shaping of Sacred

Locality in Brazzaville 1959–97" in Anderson & Rathbone, cited in Chapter One; Laura Fair, *Pastimes and Politics: Culture, Community and Identity in Post-Abolition Urban Zanzibar 1890–1945* (Oxford & Athens, OH: James Currey & Ohio University Press, 2001); Phyllis Martin, "Contesting Clothes in Colonial Brazzaville," *Journal of African History,* XXXV(3) 1994, 401–26 and *Leisure and Society in Colonial Brazzaville* (Cambridge: Cambridge University Press, 1996); Frederick Cooper, *On the African Waterfront: Urban Disorder and the Transformation of Work* (New Haven: Yale University Press, 1987); Jane Parpart, *Labor and Capital on the African Copperbelt* (Philadelphia: Temple University Press, 1983); Ahmed Sikainga, *Slaves into Workers: Emancipation and Labor in Colonial Sudan* (Austin: University of Texas Press, 1996); Richard Parry, "The 'Durban' System and the Limits of Colonial Power in Salisbury 1890–1935" and Charles Ambler, "Alcohol and the Control of Liquor on the Copperbelt", both in Jonathan Crush & Charles Ambler, eds. *Liquor and Labor in Southern Africa* (Athens, OH: Ohio University Press, 1992); and Andrew Burton, "Urchins, Loafers and the Cult of the Cowboy: Urbanization and Delinquency in Dar es Salaam 1919–61," *Journal of African History* XLII, 2001, 199–216. Obviously emphases vary fairly widely.

A gendered reading of the colonial city owes much to the pioneering work of Luise White, *The Comforts of Home: Prostitution in Colonial Nairobi* (Chicago: University of Chicago Press, 1992). See also Diana Jeater, *Marriage, Perversion and Power: The Construction of Moral Discourse in Southern Rhodesia 1894–1930* (Oxford: Clarendon Press, 1993). For an earlier interpretation, see Kenneth Little, *African Women in Towns* (Cambridge: Cambridge University Press, 1973).

A range of readings on aspects of urban politics in colonial Africa might include Pauline Baker, *Urbanization and Political Change: The Politics of Lagos 1917–67* (Berkeley: University of California Press, 1974); Richard Joseph, "Settlers, strikers and sans-travail; The Douala Riots of September 1945," *JAH*, XV, 1974, 669–87; Dominic Fortescue, "The Accra Crowd, the *Asafo* and the Opposition," *Canadian Journal of African Studies*, XXIV(3), 1990, 348–75; Frank Furedi, "The African Crowd in Nairobi," *Journal of African History*, XIV, 1973, 275–90, Roger Gocking, *Facing Two Ways: Ghana's Coastal Communities Under Colonial Rule* (Lanham, MD: University Press of America, 1999); John McCracken, "Blantyre Transformed: Class, Conflict and Nationalism in Urban Malawi," *Journal of African History*,

XXXIX (2), 1998, 247–69; Kenneth Post & George Jenkins, *The Price of Liberty: Personality and Politics in Colonial Nigeria* (Cambridge: Cambridge University Press, 1973), a study of the political boss of late colonial Ibadan; Herbert Werlin, *Governing an African City: A Study of Nairobi* (New York: Africana, 1974); and Howard Wolpe, *Urban Politics in Nigeria: A Study of Port Harcourt* (Berkeley: University of California Press, 1974).

Finally, a few other works to add to the brew. For a monograph of a Moroccan town pushed aside by colonial development, I found valuable Kenneth L. Brown, *People of Salé: Tradition and Change in a Moroccan City 1830–1930* (Cambridge: Harvard University Press, 1976). Not specifically on a single city but still a classic is A. L. Mabogunje, *Urbanisation in Nigeria* (London: University of London Press, 1968). With important things to say about colonial African cities, although also on many other things, are John Iliffe, *A Modern History of Tanganyika* (Cambridge: Cambridge University Press, 1979) and Ian Phimister, *An Economic and Social History of Zimbabwe 1890–1948* (London: Longman, 1988). Andrew Hake's *African Metropolis: Africa's Self-Help City* (London: Chatto & Windus, 1977) contained a very good account of African housing and life in colonial Nairobi, although its focus was post-colonial. Jean Lafontaine provided a perceptive survey of African life at the end of the colonial era in the capital of the Belgian Congo: *City Politics: A Study of Léopoldville 1962–63* (Cambridge: Cambridge University Press, 1970). An excellent recent collection on urban colonial history in one country is Brian Raftopoulos & Tsuneo Yoshikuni, eds., *Sites of Struggle: Essays in Zimbabwe's Urban History* (Harare: Weaver Press, 1999).

CHAPTER 4

Cities in Revolt: The Long-Term Crisis of South African Urbanism

In many respects, the history of the South African city resembles that of cities elsewhere in Africa. In particular, the urban policies of the colonial era, for which South Africa was often a model, show continuities and similarities to a large extent. This is true particularly with regard to cities such as Lusaka, Harare, Nairobi, and the string of Copperbelt towns which were created out of nothing (or on the completely effaced sites of earlier settlements). To an extent, of course, the scale and antiquity of immigrant establishment on South African soil is such that the cities which European settlers founded are larger and, in particular, more institutionally and spatially complex than what one might find elsewhere. The "white" town with its recreational and cultural amenities, its official structures and its historic peculiarities, typically covered most urban space and seemed to define urban life. Moreover, the distinctive presence of a Coloured (most easily defined as mixed race) population, culturally moulded in the colonial era, and a large population descended from Indian immigrants, is also on a very significant scale. If the whole urban space is now entirely integrated, the presence of more than nine million "non-blacks" of various shades at the start of the twenty-first century remains important and even, in many respects, a still-dominant feature of civil society.

While the "white" city will remain relevant to this chapter, it will not receive so much direct attention. Instead, much of our focus will be on the emergence of a genuinely urban culture which might be said to form the basis of a common South African culture (to the extent

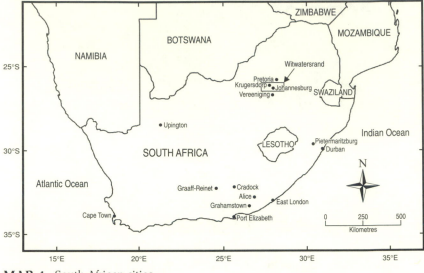

MAP 4. South African cities.

that one exists). This is obvious enough in terms of elite culture, but it can also be made with regard to popular culture as well. Underlying this is a history of the struggle on the part of a great variety of men and women to remain in the city and to explore the autonomous life possible in the modern city, despite its many snags. This will be taken up in conjunction with the contradictory nature of the state and its attempts to force distinct social and political forms on the city, leading up to some investigation of the urban factor in the last generation of intensified struggle against the *apartheid* system in the 1980s.

However, relatively little space will be taken up in exploring the administrative history of South African cities, both because much of the story is not so different than that covered previously and also because there are a slew of excellent South African urban studies. By contrast with most African countries, a large portion of the academic literature available on society and history is urban in nature and widely available. Every major city in South Africa has its own impressive historiography. For instance, the history of South Africa's fifth largest city, Port Elizabeth, has benefited from the attentions of three significant active academic writers – Gary Baines, Joyce Kirk, and Jennifer Robinson – and some of the work of A. J. Christopher, doyen of South African historic geography. Durban, Cape Town, Johannesburg (although not Pretoria) are all even better studied.

The Rise of Segregation

In essence, one can very briefly sum up the conundrum that afflicted South African urban planners for a century. The cities that they had in mind were designed to be "white," blank slates in terms of any earlier social formation and entirely modern in character. In the classic phrase of Maynard Swanson, "the underlying question was one of overall social control: how to organize society to provide for the mutual access of black labourers and white employers in the coming industrial age without having to pay the heavy social costs of urbanization or losing the dominance of white over black."[1] However, the reality was that the labour market called to life by the urban economy was very mixed in character and included ever larger numbers of native Africans, despite the white mind-set which assumed that African culture was inherently tribal and rural.

As early as the 1840s, "frontier" towns in the eastern Cape Province and newly annexed Natal confronted this problem. Xhosa-speaking Africans in the Cape, whether residents of territory recently conquered by the British or from beyond the frontier, came to these early towns to seek access to cash, which they were beginning to find useful, and, in time, necessary. A study of early Pietermaritzburg in the colony of Natal from mid-century by Keletso Atkins tries to recreate how African men assimilated the colonial capital into their own social and eco-nomic ideas. The laundry washermen were organised into something like a guild which organised parallel specialised forms of work that could be found in rural Zulu society. Early African urban settlements were found also in Grahamstown, Alice, Cradock, and Graaff Reinet towards the eastern end of the Cape Colony. In consequence, author-ities began to lay out distinct African townships, generically known as *locations,* to fill a need for what was taken to be transient basic hous-ing. Thus segregation went back into the early days of urban life in South Africa.

In early Port Elizabeth, it was Xhosa men who brought passen-gers and cargo from ships to shore, and colonial logic was to create a "Kafir village" nearby for them to lodge on the edge of the urban settlement. In 1855 a "Native Strangers' Location" [*sic*] was set up to

---

[1] Maynard W. Swanson, "The Urban Origins of Separate Development," *Race*, X, 1968, 31.

accommodate others. Even in this era, perhaps the heyday of Cape liberalism, the idea of planning for an integrated urban environment in which Africans could be assimilated as citizens was completely unthinkable, although debates on how to extract some revenue from them began very early. Black people were associated with all the vices of slum life, with poor sanitation and hygiene, and their homes were seen as the source of epidemics of plague, cholera, and malaria. Clean-ups after such epidemics were often the excuse for shutting down spaces where Africans congregated.

However, in reality the separation of the white town and the encampment for Africans was breached in numerous ways. The locations designed by authorities were problematic for many of their putative inhabitants. It was possible in many instances for individuals to live better in settlements that were less controlled by the state. Before the Union of South Africa was formed in 1910, the majority of African people in most South African towns were found outside the location. In Port Elizabeth, for instance, private individuals began to set up small private locations on the town periphery for profit. This was a pattern which cast a long shadow.

In the early twentieth century, such private housing emerged in and around the city of gold – Johannesburg – where it remained very important. A generation later, when the city was beginning systematically to destroy such property and remove the inhabitants, an early social science study, *Rooiyard* by Ellen Hellmann, gives a remarkable written snapshot of how "yards" in the neighbourhood of Doornfontein, a neighbourhood where housing was giving way to purely commercial property, looked in 1933/34. Rooiyard was the (profitable) property of a white landlord and consisted of dozens of small rooms inhabited by largely employed black men and largely unemployed black women (apart from some domestic workers), most of whom brewed beer illegally. There were also Indian and Coloured residents. Here was a population living in squalid conditions with partly communal facilities. It was constantly at odds with the authorities, with the police, in fear of imminent removals – for which no replacement housing was provided. The Doornfontein yards were in the process of disappearance. However, the two big concentrations of private housing in Johannesburg available to Africans – Sophiatown and Alexandra – continued to grow in the 1930s. Not coincidentally, both were initially close to noisome garbage dumps and unable to attract white residents. Gradually, they became important centres of black life for lack of any alternative. The former was destroyed, a cause célèbre of the 1950s, while the latter survives to the present, an enclave within the city's northern suburbs, although much of its housing was replaced with hostels.

Other black people simply took themselves to poor areas in towns. As such areas became poorer, the skins of their inhabitants tended to become darker, a pervasive phenomenon in the historical development of South African society. Cape Town's racial settlement pattern harked back to the conditions briefly described in Chapter Two. There was no systematic housing segregation by race, and Coloured people of heterogeneous origins rather than African migrants from coherent precapitalist social formations were overwhelmingly the majority of those not adjudged to be white. However, in the twentieth century, some Africans, mainly from the eastern Cape, found their way to the crowded tenements and one-storey houses that lay just beyond the city centre of Cape Town – District Six. Initially District Six held a very mixed population; in the early years of the century, it attracted thousands of poor Jewish immigrants from eastern Europe. However, with time, white residents found their way out of the neighbourhood and the population became overwhelmingly Coloured. Indeed, after World War II, better-off Coloured people also began to move on. Nonetheless, often the white landlords and businesspeople remained, as in Sophiatown, a remnant of earlier times.

Cape Town also is the best example in South Africa of another, older phenomenon whereby, in this commercial town, even the best neighbourhoods led on or down to a cluster of poorer dwellings where the service people and domestic workers could be found. There were poor people of colour found in cottages in virtually every urban neighbourhood in the Cape Peninsula and, to a lesser extent, in the smaller communities of the Western Cape by the early twentieth century. Whites may have dominated commerce overall, but the ordinary shops where working people bought their necessities were often owned by Indian or Coloured proprietors, typically Muslims. Finally, the borderline between African and Coloured, between Indian and Coloured, between white and Coloured, was often very hazy, reflecting a long history of intermarriage and coupling in a creole population. Racial statistics may not have been very accurate in this kind of society, but they certainly reveal a distinct pattern of racial mixing compared to other parts of the country.

Durban, the commercial city that came to serve as South Africa's main port once the cut to the Bay of Natal offered large-scale safe harbourage in the years after the Anglo-Boer War, became the home in time of two-thirds of South Africa's population of Indian descent. If Indians came to the colony of Natal as indentured workers intended for the sugar plantations, once indenture ended, more and more made their way to the towns, especially to Durban, where they would out-number whites, or to the immediate periphery of Durban. Indians at first stayed on the land in significant numbers so long as cheap prop-erties could be found. But as this possibility closed down, they eagerly acquired urban skills, tried to enter urban trades while their com-mercial and later professional men sought to create permanent fam-ily homes in desirable urban neighbourhoods. On the edge of town, a predominantly Hindu population provided laundry services, veg-etable and fruit gardens, and fish as they gradually established per-manent communities. Beside the centre city emerged a densely peo-pled, largely Muslim, commercial community that could hardly have been more urban. Segregation was imposed more ruthlessly than at the Cape and was more pervasive, but nonetheless the nature of the Indian claim on the city was such that it could not be dismissed in terms of assumptions about the immanent whiteness of the South African urban settlement.

Returning to the world of the location, it must be emphasised that from an early date, Africans resented efforts to tax them and to limit their freedom. The failure of the South African economy to offer wage work to black women other than as domestic help meant that women were desperate for independent access to earnings. As elsewhere in Africa, African women were attracted to town life when their oppor-tunities in rural communities were closed down due to widowhood, witchcraft accusations, unsuccessful marriages, desertions, family dis-asters, or other reasons. Here however it was often necessary for them to find a means of latching on to a man who could earn a regular wage. Alternatively, they could provide other services, notably the brewing of beer, which signified sociability and nourishment to those men. Another possibility, if one could get access to some kind of housing, was renting out property. Lodgers' permits in the hands of some black residents, which legally allowed residents to take in lodgers, became a source of government income in some towns.

These imperatives led to intense conflicts over the right of women to brew grain beer and over the right of Africans, men and women, to own property in town. Property ownership from the nineteenth century signified a form of citizenship, a testament of rights, which could potentially be extended into other fields such as health and education. Africans found themselves under the constant pressure of obeying laws which were not laws that made sense in terms of their own cultural code and which invited criminal breaches and constant possibilities of corruption of law enforcers.

White opinion on these issues was for long not very clear. On the one side of the spectrum, more paternalist white decision makers were eager to acknowledge and encourage the rights of black property owners as anchors of stability and respectability; this of course by implication went together with accepting the notion that black people were permanently a part of the town. On the other end of the spectrum was the view that recognising permanent property rights across the colour line did not fit the evolving ideology of white South Africa. In early Port Elizabeth, and elsewhere, the first locations, initially in easy walking distance of workplaces, were eventually threatened with removal and torn down as the city grew. This was the fate of Ndabeni location in Cape Town, a miserable locale whose construction was associated with a plague scare in 1903 but whose site was required for industrial expansion in the 1920s. If the location was to acquire a permanent place in South African life, it must be humbly situated beyond the gaze of white citizens in their normal course of activity on a peripheral site that minimised its use of space.

From the time of Union in 1910, the state continually tried to regulate matters, to establish a firmly based urban policy, and to iron out contradictions. Although these policies certainly made a difference in people's lives, it cannot be said that a completely consistent and effective regulatory environment ever was successfully established from the point of view of the authorities. One commonly observed threshold was crossed legislatively with the passage of the Natives (Urban Areas) Act of 1923. It contained elements of the more segregationist Stallard Commission proposals, which crudely promoted white supremacy, and the older Godley Commission perspective that retained more of the older paternalist thrust. On the one hand, the urban administrations already had the right to surveillance of the black population in towns through a pass law system which allowed for expulsions of the unwanted. Moreover, middle-class white suburbia was arming itself with covenants that restricted home purchase to whites in particular defined areas. On the other hand, while prescribing segregation, the

Act did not provide resources that would actually remove the black population physically. Pass law legislation, however demeaning and however much providing petty authority figures with day-to-day power to be used or abused, could not be effective in phases where the economy was growing and labour required. Some urban areas were "proclaimed" for one race only, but it was difficult to make this system stick. Poor people were apt under duress simply to move from one humble abode to another, yet unnoticed, one. The energies of small capitalists were often in fact inclined to undermine racial legislation that could interfere with profits.

One financial device that was typical of "native administration" in South Africa but imitated further north was to force Africans to drink "native beer" only at specific municipal beer halls set up by municipalities as sources of revenue to pay for services. This was often known as the "Durban system" from the city which adopted and popularised it even before Union. However, in Durban massive resistance from women brewers led to the system collapsing at the end of the 1920s. By contrast, it was really introduced into Johannesburg only in 1937. In some places, the granting of lodgers' permits was another way for the municipality to extract money from black residents. A common principle, however, was that whites must not have to pay for even the most minimal services of the remainder of the population. There was simply no official concept of a common urban citizenry to which at some level everyone belonged.

Later legislation pointed to harsher management. The Slums Act of 1934 did point the way to destruction of housing inhabited by people of colour while only constructing new public housing for whites. The 1937 Natives Laws Amendment Act paved the way to the creation of higher and wider barriers that would fence off locations and isolate them from normal city life while reinforcing segregatory powers. Yet in reality this legislation was promulgated just as South Africa was entering into a long boom period where black labour was increasingly required in the urban setting, a period which peaked during World War II when the pass laws were actually suspended for a couple of years as virtually superfluous.

The 1940s are the decade associated with a sharp increase in the proportion of black women in South African towns, with black family life emerging there on a large scale and with substantial migration of farm workers to the city. According to official figures, the percentage of Africans living in urban areas rose from 17 percent to nearly 24 percent between 1936 and 1946.[2] In those areas where African communal land tenure and the chiefly administrative system remained in force, large numbers of men went to the mines as migrant workers. Now many migrant workers shifted from mines to factories and began to explore the city for new opportunities.

This was undoubtedly the period when the "urban question" most exercised the minds of the authorities. The Smuts government put into place the Fagan Commission of 1946. This commission reported on the need to acknowledge permanent black residence in towns, but it was not prepared to create political structures that crossed racial lines or ponder the planning of towns on a basis other than race. It reflected the views of a government that fully embraced South Africa's rapid industrialisation but was unwilling to make the political concessions that went with this transformation. The good intentions of industrial paternalism were also undercut by the very low prevalent wages and huge backlog of poverty amidst which black urban dwellers lived. By contrast, the opposition National Party put into gear the Sauer Commission, which emphasized the need to keep cities white. It was equally contradictory, however, in its message; it recognised the need to work with economic realities and provide for those black people who were required for urban employment. This commission report would be the guiding light of the *apartheid* years but it is difficult to see that the "liberal" alternative contained clear answers. Both tendencies look with hindsight simply shot through with contradictions.

On the ground, how did the world look to urban dwellers? The early and middle 1940s were marked by some intense conflicts caused by the pressures to be associated with urbanisation. One was the series of bus boycotts that marked the rise in transport fares covering the community of Alexandra in Johannesburg. These boycotts, the most notable of which occurred in 1944, were marked by very public pedestrian marches right through the heart of the northern suburbs of the city. The fare hikes affected not only workers, they affected those employed less regularly, such as women taking in laundry, and they attracted the attention of angry black bus owners who had been driven out of business by the municipal monopoly. Intelligent publicity gave the boycotters the sympathy of large numbers of whites, who were forced to

---

[2] From David Welsh, "The Growth of Towns" in Monica Wilson & Leonard Thompson, *Oxford History of South Africa*, II (London & New York: Oxford University Press, 1971), 173.

acknowledge their dependence on black urbanites for satisfaction of their own daily needs. This was not in the end a truly explosive movement, however; it was resolved through reversal of the price increases. Not unrelated was the rapid increase in trade unions aimed at organising black urban workers. They achieved much success under the banner of the Council of Non-European Trade Unions, especially on the Reef with regard to light industry orientated to mass consumer market. In inflationary wartime conditions, the state was again willing to compromise on informal recognition and some pay raises.

More problematic for the state was the large-scale squatter movement situated on spare ground southwest of the city. This movement involved entrepreneurs who promised their followers cheap rents and promised that they would die resisting the government if it tried to move them. James Mpanza, leader of the Sofasonke movement – "we will all die" – and an ex-convict, was the most engaging and notorious of the squatter leaders. The shacks took in for affordable rents those who could no longer squeeze into location shanties and yard rooms. Moreover, they offered real potential for petty accumulation by shack-lord leaders and others – and they were very difficult for police to patrol. By this time, a substantial amount of new housing for Africans had been constructed in Johannesburg, but it was very insufficient to the new needs, let alone to any ambitious plans for removing poor people who had acquired a toehold in the city. During the 1940s all the major centres began to be the focus for squatters. Cato Manor Farm became the home of tens of thousands of African shack dwellers east of the Durban city centre, while Windermere and other localities housed poor Coloured and Africans near Cape Town. Clearly the urban context as laid out in pages of legislation was not the same one that people experienced.

At the same time, despite the state and despite the harsh conditions that material life offered, there is abundant testimony of the emergence of a distinctively South African life style that was urban. It is audible in the sing-song accent of Cape Town where English was mixed with Afrikaans and in the slang used in the ghetto where Indians lived on the verge of downtown Durban, as well as the *tsotsi taal* of the Reef which started to mingle Zulu with other African languages as well as Afrikaans. It was also audible in music: the arrival of jazz from America came into a context where even the poor often had access to phonograph records. In the towns, it was adapted to African ears and then passed into the countryside by migrants. According to Eddie Koch, the *marabi* styles of the interwar years were particularly suited to the newly urbanised because they were inexpensive to acquire and possible to perform on the cheapest of instruments – a world of "pennywhistle virtuosos"[3] and barroom ("shebeen") chanteuses formed. Anthropologist David Coplan emphasises that this music was completely divorced from tribal association and something new and heterogeneous.[4] One source of the new music was the cinema. The perceptive American social worker, Ray Phillips, wrote up an astonishing array of films from the 1930s that were banned from the gaze of black viewers in one of his books on urban black life in South Africa; nonetheless, this very list suggests that there was much to be gleaned from what was still available.

From music and film, one can turn to literature. The 1940s was the era of *Drum* magazine, a kind of South African imitation of the new photo-journalism popular in Western countries. Liberation was tied to consumerism and a bold effort to portray black South Africans as sophisticated modern people – separate, that is to say, from "traditional" models that could be associated with racism – in the style of American movies. The magazine also employed a string of reporters who wrote lively accounts of crime, sex, amusing incidents, and conflicts with authority. The city, with all its harshness, was still the source of the new civilisation for which attentive audiences were supposed to hunger. The countryside, if it figured at all, was at best a residual source of the picturesque. Some of the *Drum* writers achieved a level of artistry in their short stories and poems that marked them out as a new literary school, in fact the first one conventionally recognised amongst black intellectuals in South Africa. Coloured writers of fiction in Cape Town such as James Matthews, Richard Rive, and Alex la Guma were at the same time creating a parallel imaginative world that was equally rooted in a popular urban culture.

And people read and found other amusements that were characteristically urban. Some of these have been captured by South Africa's first important black artist who painted in a Western idiom, Gerard Sekoto.

---

[3] The term in David Coplan's "The African Performer and the Johannesburg Entertainment Industry: The Struggle for African Culture on the Witwatersrand" in Belinda Bozzoli, ed., *Labour, Township and Protest* (Johannesburg: Ravan Press, 1979), 202.

[4] Of course, this is not to say that the cities were often the site of cultural performance intended to sustain and reinforce ethnic and rural loyalties, as for instance Deborah James' studies of women's music and dance in more recent Johannesburg locales indicates.

FIGURE 9. Johannesburg. Gerard Sekoto: "In the Orlando
train," ca. 1940/41. *Source:* The Gerard Sekoto Foundation;
used by permission.

Sekoto's finest work captures the rhythms, the dignity, the accents, and
the pathos of his urban surroundings. He spent important phases of
his life in Sophiatown and in District Six. The passengers in the train
bent over a newspaper depicted in *In the Orlando Train* (ca. 1940/41)
captures the intensity with which black men were held by the pictures
and words that came together in print media. This intensity gives the
picture its emotional impetus. Sekoto's *Game of Draughts in a Crowd*
portrays, also in the washed-out colours of South African urban reality, another form of entertainment which took on urban characteristics.
Sport was also a largely urban world of activities, which contributed
richly to the argot of South Africa. Boxing, football, bicycle racing,
and, perhaps above all, horse racing, had their followings. If organised
sport was increasingly segregated, it certainly provided a common discourse for male communication that crossed colour lines. Gambling –
partially associated with Chinese entrepreneurs – acquired a familiar
structure in the cities.

Such interaction was happening in the shadow of South Africa's
first skyscrapers and the attractive Art Deco style that characterised
the boom years from the middle 1930s in the white core of the bigger
cities. All this happened despite the intensification of segregation and
because of the pervasive and increasingly industrialised character of

FIGURE 10. Johannesburg. Gerard Sekoto: "Game of
draughts in a crowd," ca. 1940/41. *Source:* The Gerard Sekoto
Foundation; used by permission.

urbanisation. While high-minded social workers and university lectur-
ers worried intensely about how to define "urbanised" and "proletar-
ianised" in the South African situation, or whether the natives were
becoming "detribalised" and exactly to what extent, a situation was
increasingly developing where the borders between urban/rural and
proletarian/self-sufficient were beginning to be blurred and the beginnings of a common South African culture could be found. Africans
themselves had names and nicknames for those who were a mix of
town and country.[5]

Yet into the middle of the twentieth century, much of the urban
African population did consist of rural migrants who self-consciously
rejected the influence of the town. They hoped to save their money
and return to the pastoral household where social lives were moral and
comprehensible. In a famous anthropological study, Philip and Iona
Mayer captured this for a small city, East London, in portraying "Red"
men who made use of the town but were not of it. Their "School" culture counterparts, already committed to church and school as morally

---

[5] According to Eddie Koch's "'Without Visible Means of Subsistence': Slumyard Cul-
ture in Johannesburg" (in Belinda Bozzoli, ed., *Town and Countryside in the Transvaal*
[Johannesburg: Ravan Press, 1983], 151–75), *amaphakati* – those in between – was a
Zulu word used in Johannesburg in this context.

determinant institutions, were far more amenable to assimilating the ways of the town. Yet in the big city, this kind of distinction was no longer entirely operational even by the 1940s. Who could be more rural than the blanketed BaSotho miners identified in the 1940s as MaRashea – the Russians? They were men with "a deep suspicion of urban life and particularly of urban women."[6] But the MaRashea, if they were seemingly constantly at war with the wide boys of the town, the *tsotsis*, who threatened to take their hard-earned money and disputed territory with them, were not interested in confining themselves to mine compounds or indeed to legal gainful employment. As Phil Bonner reports, they invested the town looking for women, fights, and consumer goods and willy-nilly became part of the urban environment. Indeed gang life and the tendency of the ambitious but desperate to find ways of shaking down marginal businesses and living off the poor was spreading, not just in black Johannesburg but also among Coloured and Indian urban dwellers elsewhere at the same time.

David Hemson has recreated the career of the Durban dockworker, Zulu Phungula. Phungula was the working-class hero of black men in Durban in the 1940s par excellence. In one sense, Phungula was a classic Zulu migrant worker for whom the rural homestead was critical and who stood entirely outside the organisational history of South Africa's future main black resistance bloc – the African National Congress and South African Communist Party. Yet he is identified as the leader of intense worker resistance at the docks based on the need for higher wages befitting the urban environment. His was the militancy of migrant workers who demanded something from the city without entirely wanting to be part of it.[7]

At the same time, the racial structuration of the city powerfully shaped people's minds. It is sobering to recall the hostility of white South Africans to the surviving integrated elements within the city, even while it held cultural fascination for them and drew them too into some aspects of a wider culture. From early on in urban South Africa, the single male "digger" migrating from some part of the Empire was a key figure, and his chance at status and a settled life depended, if he did not strike it rich, on establishing a racial order on which he could come

---

[6] Bonner, 172, in Philip Bonner, Peter Delius & Deborah Posel, eds., *Apartheid's Genesis 1935–62* (Johannesburg: Ravan Press, 1993).

[7] For the parallel context in other parts of Africa, see the work of Frederick Cooper, and especially his *Decolonization and African Society* (Cambridge: Cambridge University Press, 1996).

tops. This was a seductive philosophy as well for Afrikaner entrants from the countryside who had few resources or suitable skills and had now lost their property. One reason for the destruction of Sophiatown from 1955 was the violence towards blacks from whites in surrounding neighbourhoods as blacks passed through on their way home. This kind of violence can be attested at the same period for young white men in Durban who saw those who transgressed the racial code as threatening to the social order. Much as we may blame the state for its institution of a racially differentiated system, it was based in good part on the fears and hostilities of a white population which urbanised rapidly in the first half of the twentieth century and was unable to pick itself up out of the urban maelstrom without the force of a racist state.[8]

South African Townships

> The inhabitants of the location live like a captured people. They are bound and tethered by laws that have no application to the residents of the white town. There is a mass of prohibitions-and what is not prohibited has to be specially permitted. Wherever a man [*sic*] goes, whatever he does, he runs the risk of breaking a law. There is a multitude of papers – green papers, pink papers, buff papers – for everything must be written and authorised. Life in the location is stifled by the dense web of bureaucracy. A man in the location goes about with the superintendent's signature all over his person. He becomes a piece of paper, his family becomes a cluster of papers, his house a number in a register, his job a yellow form; and his life and security exactly as valuable and durable as the scraps of paper that fill his pockets. The work of the police is all too easy, for every man is a likely wrongdoer.[9]

Yet the location itself was beginning to outgrow the imaginative grasp of parochial city fathers. Initially it was possible to identify a paternalist regime where the managers of locations knew the local populations and dispensed favours and minor justice based on face-to-face arrangements. The Native Affairs Department had nurtured this kind of system which operated relatively autonomously from the social norms that prevailed outside, a little tribal territory to administer apart from the white city in the surrounds. However, in general, it was not

---

[8] The percentage of whites living in urban areas increased from 51.6 percent in 1911 to 78.4 percent in 1951 (Welsh, 1971, 173).

[9] Harry Bloom, *Transvaal Episode* (Berlin: Seven Seas Books, 1959), 14–15.

difficult for the inhabitant to step out of the location into the surrounding town – walls and limited entry access had not yet been established.
In Sophiatown, all a resident needed to do to leave was to cross the
road; there were no fences or walls surrounding it. In Port Elizabeth,
a "model" white administration actually resided within the location in
a special compound. However, the location was equally lacking in the
normal urban amenities – entertainment, schools, health facilities –
and paternalism could often fade into harsh and punitive administration from which it was difficult to establish much autonomy. "The
locations are gloomy places after work hours."[10] The location hardly
recognised social distinctions; its design made virtually no concession
towards the emergence of a middle class. Under the surface the common fate of the inhabitants was a constant social confrontation with
the authorities – the superintendent, "the location landlord", the management, and above all the police – "regarded as enemies."[11]

In general, some kind of health committee or location advisory
board was in place and did include local notables. In some cases,
these were the product of regular elections and were in fact able to
bring real grievances to the table. However, they had no executive
or administrative power and were completely divorced from the system of council management, imitated from Britain, which ran the
white towns. They had little or no economic power. If anything, it
was black workers who subsidised the white city, not vice versa. What
was lacking in this age was a political outlet actually based on the new
foundations of South African life. At first sight, looking northwards,
somewhat parallel urban contexts in Nairobi and Salisbury as well as
Algiers were finding a sharper and more effective political voice. The
urban and labour contexts were absolutely critical to the era of early
decolonisation and African nationalism. In all these cases, however, the
struggle against colonialism shifted sooner or later to the countryside.
Whether the state had short-term success as in Kenya in buttressing
a more conservative urban solution, or was able to retake the Casbah
by force as in Algiers, or could profit from violent divisions among the
political militants as in Salisbury, the city was temporarily constrained
even there.

As in Kenya and Southern Rhodesia, the authorities in South Africa
worried about and were concerned to establish some kind of long-term
control in the urban context. When the National Party came to power

[10] Ray Phillips, *The Bantu in the City* (Alice: Lovedale Press, 1935), 292.
[11] Ibid., 331, 198.

in 1948, they theoretically put into practice the ideas expressed in the Sauer Commission. In fact, *apartheid* brought two new aspects into play, or rather developed them intensively from limited earlier practice. Deborah Posel has called this "urban labour preference policy."

The first aspect was destruction. On a massive scale, and armed by the Group Areas legislation of 1950 which went further than the voluntary "proclamation" system established a generation earlier, the state systematically proclaimed every urban area in the country in terms of a specific "race group" and went about destroying housing that did not fit the pattern. It was particularly thorough about ruthlessly destroying areas which were in any sense ambiguous in their racial character, areas which inconveniently had the reputation of being too autonomous from state control, too far from the Foucauldian surveillance model so starkly captured above by the novelist Harry Bloom in *Transvaal Episode*. In general, such urban areas were doomed to destruction, although dilapidated slums had provided poor people with convenient access to sources of income, legal, semi-legal and illegal. They were difficult to control and patrol, especially given the presence of growing numbers of women in predominantly African areas such as Cato Manor who were not yet legally obliged to carry passes like men.

Poor but racially mixed and relatively central neighbourhoods were especially targeted. Thus Sophiatown was destroyed, Korsten in Port Elizabeth was destroyed, Cato Manor in Durban was destroyed, and eventually, in the 1960s, District Six in Cape Town was destroyed. These were really the arteries through which the lifeblood of the older urban popular culture had been developing. Much of the destruction was justified in terms of international models of modernising cities, of slum clearance and up-to-date kinds of urban planning, but of course with the South African twist of racial exclusiveness thrown in.

A large proportion of the destruction affected Indian and Coloured city-dwellers rather than Africans. In Durban, Indians, although much poorer than whites on average, were proportionately more likely to be home-owners. In Cape Town, there were Coloureds in "inappropriate" housing intermingled in every neighbourhood. Now this housing could be upgraded, made available for gentrification by a more and more prosperous white population. This often had the effect therefore of embittering and politicising populations that had not really presented any serious problem of control for white South Africa previously.

The 1950s were marked by important episodes of violent conflict which did have an impact (Vereeniging, 1937; Port Elizabeth, 1952;

East London, 1952; Durban, 1949, 1959, 1960, for examples of "race riots" and attacks on white passers-by and police). One marker was the shooting of several dozen people in a poor African township called Sharpeville outside the industrial city of Vereeniging near Johannesburg in 1959. The anger of Sharpeville residents, congregated to object to pass laws under the auspices of the principal African political organisation, the African National Congress' breakaway Africanist rival, the newly formed Pan African Congress, was perhaps the greater because of growing poverty and unemployment and because of a sudden and dramatic rent hike intended to resolve the problems of administering the township. The Sharpeville massacre was one of the incidents which led to proclamation of a State of Emergency, the banning of African political organisations and the end to the last real elements of the older authoritarian but paternalist system of colonial-style government of blacks in South Africa.

Destruction was not all that happened. The second thrust by the state was the willingness to engage in large-scale construction of new residential housing. By contrast with previous, relatively lacklustre attempts to segregate the city, the *apartheid* authorities were willing to try and resolve the urban question in South Africa by building large and racially defined townships beyond the edge of the white city. Black and white were often further segregated through the establishment of systematic intermediate layers of Indian and Coloured housing, all intended to allay conflict in official ideology. Soweto, the South Western Township complex serving Johannesburg, was the best-known such terrain; established in the 1950s, it became within a couple of decades the home of hundreds of thousands of inhabitants. It absorbed the much smaller Orlando Township, product of municipal housing efforts from the prewar decade.

Soweto was the living embodiment of the contradictory values of the South African establishment. On the one hand, it represented a major concession to the practical necessity of permanently situating very large numbers of black male workers in the urban setting as the only means of promoting the economic development of an industrialising South Africa. On the other, in many respects it lacked the human characteristics of a vital urban environment, reflecting the political imperative for the authorities to deprive or drastically truncate any impulse to common urban citizenship. That citizenship was available on a measly second-class basis for Coloured and Indians – not subject to a pass system and legally eligible to buy and sell urban property – but only within the rules that defined and protected white dominance. The element of surveillance established earlier developed further. Townships, which almost always otherwise lacked electric power, were marked by high lighting fixtures and wide roads to make control of people very easy. Often walled off from the white public, townships were in general only accessed by a limited number of roads, and whites were required to have a permit to enter them.

Pass laws and other documentation punctuated township life. From 217,000 convictions in 1951, they rose to 694,000 in 1968, the peak year.[12] From the middle of the 1950s, they covered women as well as men, despite a major women's protest movement march of 20,000 women to Pretoria in 1956. Gradually South African economic hunger for more and more low-skill African labour relaxed and the townships became characterised by unemployment and a pressing need for jobs. Pass laws in this context became more and more a means of trying to root out the unwanted and "differentiate" the labour force. In practical terms, this meant that surveillance took the form of continual police raids and daily confrontations that had at their heart a questioning about the right of African people to stay in the city at all. For virtually every township dweller, the police became a hostile occupying force, but simultaneously the potential for corruption and illegality was bottomless. At the same time, and as Bloom portrays at an early phase, surveillance took on grander and more impersonal aspects.

One of the dramatic features of township life was the growing presence of black subaltern authority, in effect the forerunners of the class that would profit considerably from the overthrow of *apartheid* after 1990. The white-run bureaucracy became more distant and more technocratic, governed by a "discourse centred on technical information, centralization, [and] bureaucratic hierarchy."[13] It was black police, black social workers, black clerks, and black nurses and teachers who began to define day-to-day authority in the township, as opposed to the paternalist world where white authority, for better and worse, "knew" their "people." Unlike the earlier location, and particularly in the largest cities, a notable feature of the township was the distinct evolution within of differentiated middle-class suburbia. A Dutch

---

[12] Doug Hindson, *Pass Controls and the Urban African Proletariat* (Johannesburg, Ravan Press, 1987), 68, 81.

[13] Ivan Evans, *Bureaucracy and Race: Native Administration in South Africa* (Berkeley: University of California Press, 1997), 51.

anthropologist reporting on this world at the start of the 1970s noted the presence in Soweto of this kind of subaltern hierarchy, more comfortable given the declining immediate presence of white authority and propped up by professional paper qualifications on which their status depended. There was nothing very specifically urbane about them: they organised their lives on a suburban and privatised model and their educational formation often took place outside the city. Yet, throughout South Africa, one aspect of removals and the creation of new townships was to bring this emergent class into existence. The position of Coloured and Indians in this regard, able to count themselves as home-owners, was stronger and securer, and their middle classes proportionately larger. Moreover, whereas the commercial world of District Six or Sophiatown had largely been in the hands of Jewish, Indian, or Chinese businessmen, in the new townships, the local "race group", Africans included, were given the local monopoly. However, licit commercial activity was also far thinner on the ground.

A second characteristic of this unfolding world was its pseudo-suburbanisation generally. Intentionally made somewhat difficult of access to white residential areas, the new townships were often far from the city centre. If affluent suburbanisation in the West has depended on the mass availability of the motor car, in South African townships private vehicles were a rarity and, until the advent of the black taxi at the end of the 1970s, the township space was very cut off from central urban circulation. By contrast to the international modernist model, whereby the urban working class typically has been housed in large apartment complexes that fit the technical and economic needs of the age, the South African township was less practically constructed around the ideal of tiny detached or semi-detached houses with small surrounding yards in characterless neighbourhoods. They also contained another important element typical of the South African situation, the large hostel complexes intended for (almost entirely) male populations with fixed jobs but rural homes and an assumption of circulating employment. The costs involved in sustaining township life were greater than those in the previous nondescript settlements where black people had been living. In conditions of widespread poverty, the environment was alienating, anonymous, and harsh, conducive to casual and violent interchanges and the very opposite of what *apartheid* ideologues had imagined might develop into peaceful family-based "native villages" so unlike the threatening, unplanned urban settlements they sought systematically to destroy.

A third major feature, however, was the continuing impact of the basic policy contradictions besetting South African urbanism. The constraints placed on urban development in new townships were crippling. Housing was often "sub-economic" and to some extent paid for through levies on employers. Basically, however, there was very little money to go around in the population for creating a more liveable and desirable environment. Whenever "reformers" tried to institute electrification, to take the most obvious example, rates and charges would go up to levels that people often found unbearable. Especially as long as the state served by and large as landlord, it was bound to take the pain of people's wrath and hostility at any aspect of township conditions that were oppressive.

But the greatest problems came more from the fact that people were settling down in the townships than from their resentment that they were driven to making their homes in them, although that was a source of grievance too. It came from the insistence of the state that in the long term, blacks had no rights in the city, in the short to medium term, the unwanted (by capital) should be "endorsed out," that the very instincts of people to root themselves in a new environment, however inclement, were unacknowledged. For better-off Coloured and Indian people, this was less true and their more prosperous neighbourhoods did gradually take on more human dimensions, but they were all the more inclined to resent what kept them from being full participants in the total life of the city.

The State vs. the People

> Were it possible to say.
> Mother, I have seen more beautiful mothers
> A most loving mother
> And tell her there I will go
> Alexandra, I would have long gone from you
>
> But we have only one mother, none can replace
> Just as we have no choice to be born
> We can't choose mothers;
> We fall out of them like we fall out of life to death . . .
>
> You frighten me, Mama
> You wear expressions like you would be nasty to me,
> You frighten me, Mama

> When I lie on your breast to rest, something tells me
> You are bloody cruel
> Alexandra, hell
> What have you done to me? . . .

The author of this poem, Mongane Wally Serote, was born in Sophiatown and wrote these verses about overcrowded, violent, beleaguered
Alexandra in a collection called *Tsetlo* in 1974.[14] Some of Serote's best-
known verses are tributes to Alexandra and Johannesburg. Paradoxically it is African writers who have celebrated their unlovely cities more
than white writers, who have far more memorably recounted their feel-
ings for meadows, ocean, desert, and mountainside. As one moves
into the 1950s and beyond, a larger and larger number of Africans
were born in, and came to know, only the urban environment. Paradoxically, the state regulations intended to limit African purchase on
towns had the effect of stiffening and strengthening the urban commitment of those who had the right to stay in towns – "Section 10 rights" –
amongst others and created a totally urban commitment far more strik-
ingly cut off from rural roots and older cultural patterns than in much
of Africa, just as equivalent legal barriers surviving from colonialism
were dissolving or being set aside through the continent. In South
Africa the argument about "detribalisation" was settled definitively in
the cities.

If the state was in some ways prepared to acknowledge the need
for an urban black elite, this elite continued to be hemmed in. The
ghetto-like character of the township tended to flatten out class distinctions compared to what an intelligentsia, a middle class based on
educational criteria, might have desired: it could hardly satisfy ambitious black would-be citizens. For the mass of working-class people,
although health and educational facilities were increasingly available
in town from the 1970s, unemployment began to be far more common. Secondary education of a poor quality spread rapidly but led
nowhere in the case of most graduates. The factories and mines continued to employ migrants, willing due to circumstance to settle for
far less and still critical for the running of the economy. The appeal
of urban nuclear family life under these circumstances was not great;

[14] From *Selected Poems* (Johannesburg: Ad Donker, 1982), 24. Used by permission of
M. W. Serote.

children were increasingly being born and brought up in (at best) one income woman-headed households.

The state gradually lost interest in providing the possibility of growth of a built environment for black urbanites as workforces ceased to expand. Instead, building programmes were frozen. The one main exception lay in cities which fringed onto the areas which had remained administered by African tribal authorities and were now restructured into apparently autonomous so-called Bantustans. Here new housing could be extended while local black authority could say who had the right to reside locally. Thus the old and miserable townships of the small city of East London were to be replaced from the end of the 1960s with a large area of new housing called Mdantsane, a virtual new city, within the Ciskei homeland. In Mdantsane, the population included a far more mixed community of Red and School people including, for the first time in a city, many Red women. Indeed the cultural distinctions between Red and School and particularly between rural and urban began to blur. Durban, the East Coast port city, also abutted on the Kwa Zulu homeland, and there was the intention of incorporating all remaining black housing in Durban into this separate nation-in-the-making. On the fringe of the national capital, Pretoria, conflict arose when a homeland authority, Kwa Ndebele, was created. Its officials flexed their tiny muscles and the non-Ndebele, the majority of inhabitants in large and spreading squatter communities, were treated in a discriminatory way by this subaltern elite. The state tried to slow urbanisation by enticing new industries to relocate first alongside and then within the Bantustans, a policy crowned with only modest success.

But there also was simply not enough housing as the black urban population continued to grow. Cape Town, for instance, was scheduled to rely on a Coloured working class now removed onto large tracts of the Cape Flats inland from the Cape peninsula. This was called "Coloured labour preference." In reality, the African population continued to grow through natural increase, but also the stream was equally fed by the migration of impoverished and jobless people from the countryside. In fact, employers in some contexts much preferred workers fresh from the country and in a vulnerable situation, thus continuing to offer a pull factor despite the intensified unemployment.

People began to erect shacks further out on the Cape Flats, setting the stage for intensified conflict over the future of the black population of the Peninsula. In one large settlement, Crossroads, determined individuals, particularly women – "the struggle to remain in the Western Cape was essentially a women's struggle"[15] – under a desperate leadership politically willing to turn any which way, resistance from 1978 was such that state attempts at removal became impossible. Finally the state relented and astonishingly agreed to allow the Crossroads people to stay on their site near the airport. In reality, the decision was not sincere; the covert intention was to create a relatively remote and secure (for white people) township called Khayelitsha yet further out and move all the Africans in Cape Town, including those in townships established well in the past, to this distant site. Recognise African rights of residence? OK – but only at the very fringe of the city. And at the same time, do everything to get rid of those who lacked proper documents and the "right" to stay in an urban area.

These were perhaps the most memorable ingredients of the black township explosions of 1976–77 which were first associated with Soweto but spread through the country. Central to the waves of demonstrations and resistance was the role of black schoolboys and girls protesting against the archaic forms of discipline and dearth of facilities in their schools but, more profoundly, against the bleak and confined future that seemed to await them. It was the introduction of Afrikaans as a medium of instruction which served as the spark of revolt and which symbolised precisely this confinement to a distinctively South African cage. The revolts, which led to the deaths of hundreds, were in turn dampened in good part because of the rage of the migrant workers from the compounds, resentful of the apparent privileges of the youths in schools, angry at the destruction of shebeens at the hands of the self-righteous, where they enjoyed drinking away their sorrows. In Soweto, an interesting development was the organisation of the notables, the Council of Ten, which did make coherent demands for improved living conditions that reflected some of the urban agenda and pioneered a conception of holistic urban development.

Soweto violence sparked a complex history of reform and resistance, an interwoven narrative punctuated with far more violence, far more intense politicisation and which for a long time placed the urban question on the political centre stage. Reform *apartheid* was significantly different than the pre-revolt situation. The state now moved dramatically to try to enrich and empower a stable black middle class. To a

---

[15] Josette Cole, *Crossroads: The Politics of Reform and Repression 1976–86* (Johannesburg: Ravan Press, 1987), 62.

large extent, it abandoned the effort to house the urban black population as landlord; indeed it tried to sell off rental housing increasingly as much as possible. It recreated so-called self-governing institutions and it allowed home purchase on long lease and then freehold basis. The late *apartheid* state favoured the institution of improved transport, electrification and a good water supply in the townships, certainly far more so than it would ever admit to its white electorate openly. Creating some kind of good order in the cities was a fundamental requirement to restoring profitability and attracting investment to South African capitalism. Shebeens? Those blacks with capital were more than welcome to get licenses and all were allowed to drink their fill to the extent that they could pay.

But who would pay for this better life that could ward off serious political change? As the state raised rates, slapped on electricity charges, tried to back up the powers of elected black officials whose elections had largely been boycotted or ignored, this covert question had to lie behind the questions asked openly. The new black municipal politicians, backed by only very small voting numbers, were not strong enough to move forward. And it was not possible that whites would freely pay for these improvements and changes. The township administrations created by the state quickly accrued enormous debts and suffered from systematic non-payments, non-collections. When charges were effectively shifted to an impoverished black population, the situation in fact became more explosive. Organisations based on residence started to form in townships all over. Thus, one of the most historically important, PEBCO, the Port Elizabeth Black Community Organisation, was established in 1979 to protest "water levies and rent increases."[16] The major explosion on the Rand would start with resistance to rent increases in Vereeniging and surrounding Vaal Triangle townships in 1984. Such increases were dramatic and followed an equally dramatic downturn in economic conditions after locally very prosperous times in the 1970s. They inevitably accompanied a collapse in the construction of black local housing by the state.

Nationwide resistance in black communities, now rural as well as urban and in some respects just as much affecting Coloured and Indian populations as African, became especially dramatic in 1984–86. Again

[16] Ineke van Kessel, "'Beyond Our Wildest Dreams': The United Democratic Front and the Transformation of South Africa," dissertation, University of Leiden, 1995, 265.

school issues, now affecting the majority of urban youth and children, were important. This involved, say with regard to a major militant hive in Alexandra, Minerva High School, protest "against the sexual harassment of female students by staff, locking of school gates, poor teaching aids, calls for an end to school fees and the wearing of uniforms, and the replacement of a prefect system with a Student Representative Council."[17] In time, the whole Department of Education and Training system for black youths fell into a state of collapse with destruction of school property and non-attendance. The powerful influence of the rapidly growing trade union movement in which black workers were learning to organise and take decisions themselves, winning important battles against businesses and breaking down long-established forms of workplace control, also was a factor. In some centres, union leaders played an important role in political events, notably in national stay-aways that eventually were able to affect millions of workers.

In addition to struggles in education and the workplace, there was also direct conflict over urban living conditions. The early 1980s were marked by accelerated struggles over bus fares, rentals, and service charges. In many areas a cycle of violence emerged, punctuated by shows of force, violent repression leading to severe injuries and deaths, use of funerals as a means of creating political solidarity, and the development of techniques such as consumer boycotts and people's courts which tried to wrest local power into the hands of self-appointed committees, sometimes with young people forming a violent and terrifying element. The black local authorities were often unwilling to enforce state decrees, yet this did not save their situations. Life for police and administrative officials resident in the townships was made impossible; some were murdered with the infamous "necklace" – rubber tyres around their bodies set alight.

We have a useful description of this kind of cycle in the raisin-producing desert town of Upington on the Orange River in the Cape Province (now the Northern Cape), by the lawyer who defended those brought to trial over this incident. Here the break-up of a demonstration, the closing down of civic protest space that had in an historic

---

[17] Charles Carter, "'We Are the Progressives'; Alexandra Youth Congress Activists and the Freedom Charter 1983–85," *Journal of Southern African Studies*, VII (2), 1991, 213ff .

moment been opened up in a very conservative part of the country, led to an aggrieved mob suddenly pushed back into the location precincts. Finding the home of a local policeman associated with repression in the township, they frightened him into fleeing his house, drove him into a corner and murdered him. The killers included many otherwise thoughtful and respectable men and women. Killing or hounding out of townships those designated as "sell-outs" was a constant feature of the years of revolt. Small cities and towns such as Upington, although neglected in the political headlines, were often particularly significant locales for resistance and in some cases were better rather than worse organised. Urban communities in the eastern Cape such as Cradock were the most remarkable and successful centres of insurrection with the greatest capacity for self-rule and organisation.

There was in all this an element of what Lenin famously called "dual power" in the context of the Russian Revolution. But in reality it was only possible in brief episodes for the township populations to expel the authorities. A reasoned assessment by Ineke van Kessel concludes that "few civics [as the impromptu urban organisations were characteristically known] were able to provide rudimentary services, apart from a form of popular justice, a clean-up campaign, illicit extensions of the electricity wiring and some protection against evictions."[18] She also points out that power tended to be largely male; women were often virtually written out of the insurgency even though their problems in the urban environment, given the frequency of women-headed households and the particular difficulty for women in finding jobs, were the greatest. Van Kessel herself provided us with an informative study of a community, Kagiso (near the small city of Krugersdorp on the West Rand), where resistance did remain largely in the hands of an older, often church-linked and responsible body of people. Such people were very uncomfortable with such new customs as people's courts sentencing antisocial or unpatriotic behaviour with "modelling" (walking naked through the streets) or much worse.

The state's capacity to manage the township population had declined remarkably. We have already noted the rapidly growing and almost uncontrollable squatter population on the outskirts of Cape Town. The expansion of Crossroads was eventually halted in 1986

---

[18] Van Kessel, 122.

when the state was able to make use of the men with white kerchiefs –
witdoeke – who rounded on new squatters and destroyed any potential
for unity in return for power and favours. Many indeed were sent to
Khayelitsha, but the possibility of really expelling the whole African
population of Cape Town to Khayelitsha was a chimera. And this
squatter explosion, which could possibly be channelled or manipulated
but hardly stopped, was occurring nationwide. For instance, Jeremy
Seekings reports that in an important East Rand township, Katlehong,
the number of shacks, estimated at about three thousand in 1979, had
exploded to forty-four thousand in 1983.[19]

The old story of removals went on well into the 1980s, but removals
became increasingly hard to put into practice as much elsewhere as in
Cape Town. Van Kessel points to the continuing saga of Oukasie, an
old location in the vicinity and abutting the centre of the town of Brits,
with its radicalising effect on the West Rand generally. Munsieville,
Krugersdorp's township, as a result of suburban development found
itself immediately across the road from a white neighbourhood. And
here there was still the imperative from white voters to remove the
unwanted; cries for its relocation were vocal but in the event could
not be met. Eventually this imperative failed. Munsieville was "saved"
with more substantial barriers being raised to isolate it from white
sights – a so-called Berlin Wall solution. In East London, the state
continued to try to destroy what remained of Duncan Village, the
central century-old location where people lived, unable or unwilling
to move to pleasanter Mdantsane. The realities of poverty obviated
upgrading plans that were bruited about. Eventually in 1985 this once
rather depoliticised community, dominated by migrants but become
intensely militant, was also "saved" for lack of alternative.

There were many new migrants to the cities, often coming from
smaller towns. In the countryside, white capitalist farmers had been
shedding large numbers of permanent workers. The semi-independent
or nominally independent homelands, after experiencing intensive
forms of resettlement intended to rationalise agricultural production,
were also changing as settlements that were very difficult to classify as
really urban or rural became the norm and people moved to near the

---

[19] Jeremy Seekings, "The Origins of Political Mobilisation in the Pretoria-
Witwatersrand-Vaal Triangle Townships 1980–84" in William Cobbett & Robin
Cohen, ed., *Popular Struggles in South Africa* (London: Review of African Political
Economy & Zed Press, 1988), 65.

South African "borders." The massive scale of what has been termed "displaced urbanisation" is very difficult to measure statistically.

Attempts to insert the power of particular Bantustans, such as the Kwa Zulu administration in Natal or the Kwa Ndebele one north of Pretoria, into the urban periphery, also met with violent resistance.

Hostels ceased to be designated domiciles for workers tied to jobs and became sources of cheap beds for the poor, inhabited by growing numbers of women and children as well as men. In the cities, tens of thousands of inhabitants of overcrowded small houses established themselves in shacks in backyards or elsewhere. And people were no longer paying any rent. Non-payment of rent was a particularly convenient and difficult-to-punish form of protest, ruinous from the perspective of the state's fiscal plans for urban development. In 1985, the state abandoned pass legislation, its most basic means of controlling the urban population with a history of more than a century and a half. It also finally authorised unqualified freehold tenure as legal for people of all colours.

Having said this, the state had one critical ace up its sleeve in fact. The physical layout of the townships, their isolation, the ease with which they could be shut off from the rest of the city, their lack of resources on which a poor community could survive, was not an accident. They had been planned and replanned for security. Eventually for this reason it was possible to restore order. The anger and turbulence and revolutionary energy of the township was almost entirely confined to township space. Ultimately the fire burnt itself out.

After the midpoint of the 1980s, moreover, the nature of protest had begun to change. The local issues and the urban context became less important. There was a dramatic revival in the fortunes of the exiled African National Congress, and politics started to focus on freeing leaders, returning exiles, and finding a political solution as defined in ANC terms. The United Democratic Front, an umbrella organisation for all the varied and variable civic organisations and in any event no longer able to function legally, tended to accept its role as a front for the ANC. The UDF, so impressive in its totality at first sight, was always limited by the area definition of most of its base components. Its concerns may often have seemed urban, but in the end, it was deeply fragmented and had no real capacity to make effective demands on a national basis. Its constituent bodies were very largely organised racially and failed to transcend the powerful divides created by the *apartheid* state beyond the call for a return of the ANC. Once that actually happened, the "civics" went into precipitous decline, and many of their most energetic leaders shifted into positions within a government in waiting.

From about 1990, local "stakeholder" bodies such as the Metropolitan Chamber in Johannesburg and Operation Jumpstart in Durban, meeting outside the normal administrative and political structures, began to map out the new urban landscape. Many surviving councillors, black and other, signed up for the now legal ANC. The new South Africa, which would undermine the legal basis for *apartheid* and start to reconstruct South Africa from 1990, would do so under the aegis of deals and compromises between new and old elites; its ability to reconstruct South African cities, though not negligible, would be constrained. In the words of the most eminent South African urban planner, David Dewar, at the dawn of the new era, "There are currently no cohesive ideas about the form of city South Africa should be moving towards. The urban problem is interpreted almost entirely as provision of shelter; as a consequence, kilometres of housing area are emerging but [with] few qualities or advantage of [a] 'city.' The emerging urban structure and form is exploitative."[20]

The challenge of reconstituting these cities continues and will be considered in Chapter Six. To conclude on an ominous note, one plant which the *apartheid* gardener certainly did nurture was crime. If we look at the history of District Six, once densely settled, it was a hive of casual labour and commercial activity that experienced relatively low levels of crime. As the neighbourhood altered, it witnessed the general emergence of Cape Town gangs who engage in protection rackets of various kinds with relatively little menace to the ordinary, impoverished working-class people of the neighbourhood. But the existence of this kind of criminal activity, growing alongside petty business enterprises and in some senses being simply the illegal end of a modest project of accumulation by a petty bourgeoisie of the wrong colour, gradually exploded into something far more menacing in the anomic, huge world of the Cape Flats townships. Families were moved out individually to buildings where they knew nobody. As elsewhere, jobs for those unfit for white-collar work and without the money or human capital to set up businesses were becoming progressively scarcer. Punished with prison sentences, Coloured youths found a perfect recruitment

---

[20] In David M. Smith, ed., *The Apartheid City and Beyond: Urbanization and Social Change in South Africa* (London: Routledge, 1992), 253.

ground for gangs in gaols. Membership became, beyond some access to the consumer society, a means of exerting manhood and identity and eventually a necessary means of survival. The new housing on the Flats was intended to solidify conventional family life and stabilise the life of the city poor; instead, the wrecking of older neighbourhoods and construction of a new environment from top down had the opposite effect exactly. This outlook shaped the purpose-built locations for Africans as well. The ordered structure of African family life was visibly marked out in the rural homestead; it was not reproducible in cramped urban quarters where it broke down dramatically and rapidly. Removals to townships were intended to recreate family life on a more modern basis but this they failed to do in most cases apart from the more affluent.

The figures show an explosive increase over time in the rate of violent deaths, figures which become even higher in African than in Coloured townships. In 1946 Cape Town registered five murders per one hundred thousand inhabitants, a figure not much worse than at the start of the century. This figure shot up to fifty-two in 1978 and seventy in 1995.[21] Police patrolling gave way in bureaucratic times to flying squads and spectacular occasional "swoops" that could be evaded. Gangs became eventually more and more antisocial and violent, and by the late 1990s, few months passed on the Flats without a child being killed in crossfire in gang warfare. By this time, the gangs led by far more sophisticated leadership were moving into anything outside the law – prostitution, gambling, forged documents, illegal exports (of, for instance, abalone for the Asian market) and, above all, drugs. And *apartheid* had come home to roost. Having taken over what they wanted on the flats, the gangs were now removing many of their activities to what was once respectable, even wealthy parts of the old lily white Cape Town, where they have so far proved impossible to push out.

Selected Readings

From the 1960s, the urban nature of political struggle in South Africa struck many committed writers and came to the fore in their strongly

---

[21] Vivian Bickford Smith, Elizabeth van Heyningen & Nigel Worden, *Cape Town in the Twentieth Century* (Cape Town: David Philip, 1999), 139.

motivated interpretations of South African society and history. Some
harked back to the struggles of the previous generation: Philip Bonner, Peter Delius & Deborah Posel, eds., *Apartheid's Genesis 1935–62*
(Johannesburg: Ravan, 1993); Philip Bonner, "African Urbanisation
on the Rand Between the 1930s and 1960s: Its Social Character and
Political Consequences," 115–31, *Journal of Southern African Studies*,
XXI, 1995, 115–31; Luli Callinicos, *A Place in the City: The Rand on
the Eve of Apartheid* (Johannesburg: Ravan/Longman/Maskew Miller,
1993); John Nauright, "'I Am With You as Never Before': Women in
Urban Protest Movements, Alexandra Township, South Africa, 1912–
45" in Kathleen Sheldon, ed., *Courtyards, Markets, City Streets: Urban
Women in Africa* (Boulder: Westview, 1996), 259–84; Baruch Hirson,
Yours for the Union (London & Johannesburg: Zed Press and University of Witwatersrand Press, 1989); Tom Lodge, "The Destruction of
Sophiatown" in Belinda Bozzoli, ed., *Town and Countryside* (Johannesburg; Ravan Press, 1983), 337–64; Sue Parnell, "Public Housing
as a Device for White Residential Segregation in Johannesburg 1934–
53," *Urban Geography*, IX (6), 1988, 584–602 and "Racial Discrimi-
nation in Johannesburg: The Slums Act 1934–39," *South African Geographical Journal*, LXX, 1988, 112–26; Andre Proctor, "Class Struggle, Segregation and the City: A History of Sophiatown," 49–89 and
A.W. Stadler, "Birds in the Cornfield," 19–48 both in B. Bozzoli, ed.,
*Labour, Townships and Protest; Studies in the Social History of the Wit-
watersrand* (Johannesburg: Ravan Press, 1979, 19–48). Even this long
list is far from exhaustive.

For a general appreciation, see Paul Maylam, "Explaining the
Apartheid City: Twenty Years of South African Urban Historiogra-
phy," 10–38, and Sue Parnell & Alan Mabin, "Rethinking Urban
South Africa," 39–62, both in *Journal of Southern African Studies*,
XXI (1), 1995; David M. Smith, ed., *The Apartheid City and Beyond:
Urbanization and Social Change in South Africa* (London: Routledge,
1992) and Mark Swilling, Richard Humphries & Kehla Shubane, ed.,
Apartheid City in Transition (Cape Town: Oxford University Press,
1991). A recent attempt to integrate material on one city for the twen-
tieth century can be located in Vivian Bickford Smith, Elizabeth van
Heyningen & Nigel Worden, *Cape Town in the Twentieth Century* (Cape
Town: David Philip, 1999).

For earlier periods, see Keletso Atkins, *The Moon Is Dead! Give Us
Our Money* (Oxford & Portsmouth, NH: James Currey & Heinemann,
1995); Joyce Kirk, *Making a Voice: African Resistance to Segregation*

in South Africa (Boulder: Westview, 2000); T. R. H. Davenport, "The Triumph of Colonel Stallard," *South African Historical Journal*, II, 1970; Gary Baines, "The Origins of Urban Segregation 1835–65," *South African Historical Journal*, XXII, 1990, 61–81; Philip Bonner, "The Transvaal Native Congress 1917–20: The Radicalisation of the African Petty Bourgeoisie on the Rand" in Shula Marks & Richard Rathbone, eds., *Industrialisation and Social Change in South Africa* (Harlow: Longmans, 1982); Maynard Swanson, "The Urban Origins of Separate Development," *Race*, X, 31–40, 1968; and A. J. Christopher, "Roots of Urban Geography; South Africa at Union," *Journal of Historical Geography*, XIV, 1988, 151–69. Maynard W. Swanson, "The Sanitation Syndrome; Bubonic Plague and Native Urban Policy in the Cape Colony 1900–09" in William Beinart & Saul Dubow, eds., *Segregation and Apartheid in Twentieth-Century South Africa* (London: Routledge, 1995; reprint), 25–43, has become a classic study. An extraordinary collection of studies on chapters mostly focussed around or after turn-of-the-century Johannesburg can be found in Charles van Onselen, *Studies in the Social and Economic History of the Witwatersrand, New Babylon, New Nineveh* (Harlow: Longmans, 1982).

There is a large literature on how urban life was constructed and reconstructed in various phases and sites of white authority. On this and other themes, the contribution of geographers, political scientists, and sociologists has been as important as that of historians. Notable are Doug Hindson, *Pass Controls and the Urban African Proletariat* (Johannesburg: Ravan Press, 1987); Ivan Evans, *Bureaucracy and Race: Native Administration in South Africa* (Berkeley: University of California Press, 1997); Deborah Posel, *The Making of Apartheid 1948–61: Conflict and Compromise* (Oxford: Clarendon Press, 1991); John Western, *Outcast Cape Town* (Minneapolis: University of Minnesota Press, 1981) and Jennifer Robinson, *The Power of Apartheid: State, Power and Space in South African Cities* (Oxford: Butterworth Heinemann, 1996).

However, readers can learn much also from classic older studies from the apartheid era and before: Mia Brandel-Syrier, *Reeftown Elite: A Study of Social Mobility in a Modern African Community on the Reef* (London: Routledge Kegan Paul, 1971); Ray Phillips, *The Bantu in the City* (Alice: Lovedale Press, 1935); Philip Mayer & Iona Mayer, *Townsman or Tribesman: Conservatism and the Process of Urbanisation in a South African City* (Cape Town: Oxford University Press, 1971, 2nd edition); Monica Wilson & Archie Mafeje, *Langa: A Study of Social Groups in an African Township* (Cape Town: Oxford University Press,

1963); Ellen Hellmann, *Rooiyard: A Sociological Survey of an Urban Native Slum Yard, Rhodes Livingstone Papers 13* (London: Oxford University Press, 1948) have all been very useful in writing this chapter. David Welsh, "The Growth of Towns" in Monica Wilson & Leonard Thompson, *Oxford History of South Africa*, II (London & New York: Oxford University Press, 1971) marked the transition to a newer and more historically shaped literature.

On urban struggle in the 1980s: Belinda Bozzoli, *Theatres of Struggle and the End of Apartheid* (Johannesburg: Witwatersrand University Press, 2004), which focusses on a single important township, Alexandra; William Cobbett & Robin Cohen, eds., *Popular Struggles in South Africa* (London: ROAPE & James Currey, 1988); Josette Cole, *Crossroads: The Politics of Reform and Repression 1976–86* (Johannesburg: Ravan, 1987); Andrea Durbach, *Upington: A Story of Trials and Reconciliation* (Cape Town: David Philip, 1999); Matthew Chaskalson et al., "Rent Boycotts, the State and the Transformation of the Urban Political Economy in South Africa," *Review of African Political Economy*, 40, 1988, 47–64; Ineke van Kessel, "'Beyond Our Wildest Dreams': The United Democratic Front and the Transformation of South Africa," dissertation, University of Leiden, 1995; Alan Morris, "The South African State and the Oukasie Removal," *Transformation 8*, 1989, 47–63. Mark Swilling, "Urban Social Movements Under Apartheid," *Cahiers d'etudes africaines*, IC, 1985, 363–79 and Jeremy Seekings, *The UDF: A History of the United Democratic Front in South Africa 1983–91* (Cape Town, Oxford and Athens, OH: David Philip/James Currey/ Ohio University Press, 2000) form a list of varied sources.

This chapter has made use also of a number of cultural manifestations of African urban life: Harry Bloom, *Transvaal Episode* (Berlin: Seven Seas Books, 1959); Mongane Wally Serote, *Selected Poems* (Johannesburg: Ad. Donker, 1982); Eddie Koch, "'Without Visible Means of Subsistence'; Slumyard Culture in Johannesburg" in Belinda Bozzoli, ed., *Town and Countryside in the Transvaal, op. cit.*, 151–75; David Coplan, "The African Performer and the Johannesburg Entertainment Industry; The Struggle for African Culture on the Witwatersrand" in Bozzoli, ed., *Labour, Township and Protest, op. cit.*, 183–218; and Lesley Spiro, *Gerard Sekoto: Unsevered Ties* (Johannesburg: Johannesburg Art Galley for the exhibition, 1990). For a visual study of urban South African history, try Peter Kallaway & Patrick Pearson, *Johannesburg: Images and Continuities; A History of Working Class Life through Pictures 1885–1935* (Johannesburg: Ravan, 1986).

A bit of light on more contemporary social conditions is shed by Colin Murray, "Displaced Urbanization: Africa's Rural Slums" in Beinart & Dubow, *op. cit.*, 231–55. Mamphela Ramphele, *A Bed Called Home: Life in the Migrant Labour Hostels of Cape Town* (Cape Town: David Philip, 1993); Alan Morris, *Bleakness and Light; Inner-City Transformation in Hillbrow, Johannesburg* (Johannesburg: Witwatersrand University Press, 1999); Douglas Hindson & Jeffery McCarthy, *Here to Stay; Informal Settlements in Kwa Zulu-Natal* (Durban: Indicator Press, 1994). On crime and its antecedents: Gary Kynoch, *We Are Fighting the World* (Charlottesville & Pietermaritzburg: University Press of Virigina & University of KwaZulu-Natal Press, 2005); on the history of the MaRashea: Wilfred Schärf & Clare Vale, "The Firm: Organised Crime Comes of Age during the Transition to Democracy," *Social Dynamics*, XXII, 1996, 30–35; Don Pinnock, *The Brotherhoods: Street Gangs and State Control in Cape Town* (Cape Town: David Philip, 1984); and Jonny Steinberg, *The Number* (Johannesburg & Cape Town: Jonathan Ball, 2005).

CHAPTER 5

The Post-Colonial African City

In this chapter, we shall consider how African cities seem to be shaping up as colonial rule passes out of memory. Urban growth now has proceeded at such a pace that a large percentage of all Africans today are town dwellers. This places them in a pattern which is discernable on every continent. However, major issues unfold in examining the post-colonial city in Africa which are not exactly universal. If African society is shaped by rural survival strategies and rural identities, what impact does life in big cities especially have? How can cities in Africa cope with their burgeoning populations when rapid industrialisation and economic development have failed to take place? Current world economic trends, bunched together in many accounts as "globalisation," marginalise Africa and with it, make the management of cities that work effectively for their inhabitants in Africa impossible to support financially in particularly bleak scenarios. There is no lack of literature that sees African cities as essentially dysfunctional and dangerous places. Contemporary Africa certainly has examples of city life that are nightmarish. However, there is also a counter-trend which highlights the economic rationality of much activity in African cities and sees them as well as the fount of cultural creativity as older rural-based ways of life fade or contain radically new elements. In this sense, the seed of a new Africa that can overcome present dilemmas lies there.

The dream of the successful city which certainly accompanied independence for African nationalists can be characterised as a modernist dream. The term "cosmopolitan" is used here also, as well as "modern." It is a dream which has faded painfully. Much of the literature

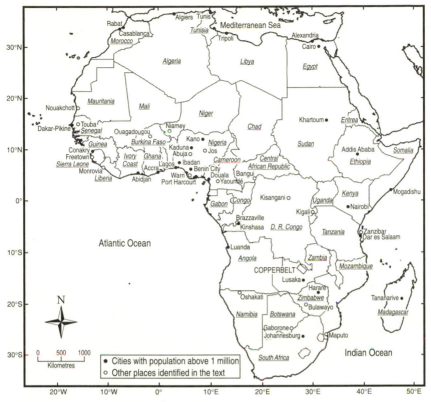

MAP 5. Contemporary African cities.

which honours new African urban social forms can be defined as post-modern by contrast. This chapter tries to avoid taking sides in the clash between modernist and postmodern visions while trying to make discernable what is attractive and contradictory in both. Let us begin by laying out the factual basis for looking at contemporary African cities.

The very rapid growth of postwar African cities continued and even increased with the coming of independence. Population growth of five to 10 percent per annum became typical for larger African cities in the 1960s and 1970s, much faster yet than the general population increase. By the end of the millennium, the urban population constituted a majority in South Africa and in the five Mediterranean African countries. In a number of other countries, notably Zambia, Angola, the Congo, the Ivory Coast, and Senegal, the percentage had reached 40 percent according to all estimates and 50 percent according to some. Large African cities embraced one million and more people.

The accompanying Table 2 indicates those cities according to relatively recent figures. Nonetheless, some differentiating patterns still
can be identified. To begin with, the independence era passed through
a phase of a more than a quarter-century. Independence year in Africa
is often taken as 1960; this is when Nigeria, the Belgian Congo, and
sub-Saharan French colonial Africa attained independence. They were
preceded by the Gold Coast (now Ghana) and Sudan, as well as North
Africa with the exception of Algeria. Within the next few years, Algeria
and the remaining British colonies of East and West Africa followed
this path. After 1965 there remained Southern Rhodesia, where the
local settlers had become independent, the Portuguese colonies, and
some remaining enclaves and islands. Apart from the special case of
South Africa, the last decolonisation took place in South-West Africa,
the present-day Namibia, in 1990. Thus the "independence era" does
straddle a period of global change that had its impact on the character
of urbanisation.

In certain cases, independence marked the break-up of larger colonial units with some effect on urban growth. The importance of Dakar
and Brazzaville, capitals of French West and Equatorial Africa, diminished. In some cases, the "need" for a national capital led to virtually
new towns called into being such as Gaborone in Botswana, Kigali
in Rwanda, and Nouakchott in Mauritania. In others, a new national
vision created new capitals in centrally located cities such as Abuja in
Nigeria, Dodoma in Tanzania, and Lilongwe in Malawi.

The question of capital cities is of real importance. It is not only
that the primacy of the primate cities became even more marked.
A noticeable feature of post-colonial Africa has been the particularly steep growth of administrative centres. Thus Lagos, for long the
Nigerian capital, surpassed Ibadan to become the largest Nigerian city
and indeed, the largest by far in Africa south of the Sahara. A remarkable feature has been one of reversal in the relatively few cases where
colonial economic structures had made a commercial transport focal
point larger than the capital before independence. Bulawayo, the main
industrial centre of colonial Southern Rhodesia, has been overtaken
by Salisbury, capital of the Federation of Rhodesia and Nyasaland in
the 1950s and early 1960s and then of Rhodesia, and subsequently
renamed Harare after black majority rule was established in 1980 –
in likewise-renamed Zimbabwe. Recently Yaoundé, the Camerounian
capital, has almost caught up with the port city of Douala in size,

TABLE 2. *African Cities with Populations in Excess of One Million*

City	Population	Date and Source
Cairo, Egypt	12 million (est.)	1994 (Yousay/Atta)
Lagos, Nigeria	10.5 million (est.)	2002 (Ahonsi)
Kinshasa, DR Congo	5–7 million (est.)	2002 (Nlandu)
Casablanca, Morocco	3.535 million	2000 estimate
Kano, Nigeria	3.329 million	2003 World Gazeteer
Alexandria, Egypt	3.328 million	1996
Johannesburg, S. Africa	3.226 million (2001)[a]	S A Cities Network, State of Cities Report 2004
Ibadan, Nigeria	3.140 million	2003 World Gazeteer
Ethekwini (Durban) S. Africa	3.090 million (2001)	State of Cities Report 2004
Luanda, Angola	3 million	2003 (Steinberg/Bowen)
Cape Town, S. Africa	2.893 million (2001)	State of Cities Report 2004
Abidjan, Ivory Coast	2.878 million	1997
Khartoum, Sudan	2.7 million[b]	
Algiers, Algeria	2.562 million	1998 Hadjedj
Ekurhuleni (East Rand), South Africa	2.480 million	
Addis Ababa, Ethiopia	2.3 million	1994 census
Pretoria (Tshwane) S. Africa	1.986 million	State of Cities Report 2004
Accra, Ghana	1.781 million[c]	1990
Conakry, Guinea	1.767 million	2003 World Gazeteer
Dakar, Senegal	1.659 million	1996 census
Kaduna, Nigeria	1.510 million	2003 World Gazeteer
Nairobi, Kenya	1.5 million	1994
Douala, Cameroun	1.448 million	1999
Harare, Zimbabwe	1.42 million	1992
Dar es Salaam, Tanzania	1.4 million	1996 Tripp
Rabat, Morocco	1.386 million	1994
Tananarive, Malagasy Republic	1.359 million	2001
Lusaka, Zambia	1.327 million	1995
Tunis, Tunisia	1.2 million	Stambouli
Port Harcourt, Nigeria	1.093 million	World Gazeteer 2003
Tripoli, Libya	1.083 million	
Benin, Nigeria	1.082 million	World Gazeteer 2003
Port Elizabeth (Nelson Mandela Metro)	1.006 million	State of Cities Report 2004
Mogadishu, Somalia	1 million	2000 estimate

[a] This and other South African figures refer to the large new metropolitan local government regions, some of which also have new names.
[b] Estimates for Greater Khartoum range up to 4.8 million.
[c] Greater Accra.

one of the last cases in Africa where a capital is not the primate city demographically. In the Congo, Kinshasa, the former Léopoldville, has become enormous, a city teeming with five million or more people. It was from early days the largest urban settlement in the Belgian Congo, but before independence, there was an important string of administrative, port, and mining towns in the provinces. After independence, many of the once-thriving provincial centres of Belgian times have stagnated or declined as the localised colonial economy of commerce and extraction has decayed or vanished.

This obviously reflects the enormous importance of government as a source of income and opportunity far beyond colonial times. It is in the cities that a new kind of modernity – typified by the presence of institutions of higher education, of significant health facilities, of development agency headquarters, and of such prestige structures as sports stadia and international grade hotels – has sprung up on an unprecedented scale. After independence, the Ivory Coast, with an economy based on cocoa and coffee, became the site of Abidjan *des tours*, as relatively high-rise structures arose above the Ebrié Lagoon. Prestige office towers marked the burgeoning centres of Nairobi and Harare as well as the oceanside Marina in Lagos. These structures were imitated on a more modest scale in provincial towns and poorer and smaller countries. Not only did government employment expand dramatically after independence, the government workers attracted services and commercial activity and acted as role models for friends and relatives in rural areas to come to the cities. The state itself formed the largest single element in the formal labour market in virtually every territory. Urban life became the stage for a desired and increasingly Africanised modernity – not of course necessarily defined as Westerners might define it – the place where Africans could become "cosmopolitan," as Jim Ferguson has poignantly captured for the Copperbelt cities of Zambia. For the good life was now theoretically open to all – the racial restrictions of colonial planning were everywhere eliminated. And the patron was in general central government; municipal or local authorities were usually usurped by appointees from headquarters. In Francophone countries, national ministries typically controlled the cities. On their largesse depended the smooth administration of towns.

Beyond deracialisation – and that was not everywhere necessarily of great importance – independence was not in fact a remarkable break in African cities. Generally speaking in the first years, the character of planning and the structures of the late colonial economy remained in place even if white managers became transients rather than settlers and modernism was harnessed to suit the self-image of a new elite. Indeed in many places the old elite did not disappear at first; thus in Abidjan the size of the white population rose quite rapidly after independence. Most bureaucracies leaned towards continuity in practice.

There were some striking exceptions, however, which pointed the way to the future. In Algiers, independence in 1962 was followed by the rapid, virtually immediate departure of half the population of the largest city west of Alexandria in North Africa. The new Algerian government had few bourgeois elements and a strong radical orientation. At the same time, the oil wealth of the Sahara gave it a reasonable resource base. The old European neighbourhoods quickly filled up with Arabic-speaking Algerians, sometimes from the old Casbah, while the Casbah itself attracted new and impoverished rural migrants, often Berber-speaking peasants from Kabylia. Much of older Algiers deteriorated physically. At the same time, emphasis lay in the creation of new industrial zones, certain prestige projects that celebrated the emergence of an Arab nation and in the construction of large housing projects intended for an urban working class. This was already foreseen in the last French reform Plan of Constantine of 1958 but greatly extended after independence. In Algeria, the arrival of poor country people who established squatter settlements on the periphery in defiance of modernist planning was met with hostility. Forced removals took place in the first years of independence. Turning to Egypt, the foreign character of Alexandria and Cairo was beginning to fade when the spectacular Black Saturday riots in Cairo marked a dramatic shift in 1952 that ended the monarchy. In these riots, perhaps one hundred people were killed, some of them lynched, and the very symbols of the typical urbanism of the prewar decades in Cairo, the Turf Club and Shepheard's Hotel, were destroyed. In fact perhaps seven thousand buildings were levelled. The radical government in Egypt under Gamal Abdel Nasser thereafter assaulted or eliminated the comfortable world of a cosmopolitan bourgeoisie while trying to plan the future of a modern city for a working class.

There are also a few sub-Saharan African cities, such as Zanzibar, where this kind of radical urban approach, concerned with social levelling and deeply influenced by the emergence of nationalism, was taken. Once independent, the former Portuguese colonial towns such as Lourenço Marques (now Maputo) and Luanda, after 1975 the respective national capitals of Mozambique and Angola, also experienced dramatic depopulation by colonists and settlers and a corresponding degradation of the dense urban built environment which they had designed for themselves modelled on Europe.

A more extreme case yet was the Congo. Independence in the former Belgian Congo was followed by waves of political instability, rebellion, and conflict. Belgian intentions to promote a fairly nominal independence, where little would alter, collapsed; after some years a new model began to emerge under Mobutu sese Seko's regime. If the new "authentic" Congo would live off what remained of mineral wealth still being harvested, most of this wealth that remained in Africa at all would rest in the capital. As the infrastructure decayed and with it many features of the Belgian colonial economy, the city of Kinshasa grew to massive proportions, becoming by far the biggest between Lagos and Johannesburg. In general, the draw of an older Africa was loosening; Africans in the countryside often wished to escape patriarchy and aspects of custom that oppressed them; they defined their goals in terms of cash more accessible in the urban environment. But in the Congo – renamed Zaïre under Mobutu – the countryside also became deeply disrupted by warfare and the breakdown of conventional economic networks in the early 1960s; urbanisation under conditions of fear of violence and rural catastrophe, which we have since seen repeated so dramatically in Khartoum, Luanda, Freetown, Monrovia, and elsewhere, already ensued in the early 1960s.

A disturbing feature of rapid urbanisation in Africa has certainly been the failure of the urban economy to offer jobs to the flood of new urbanites. It would be difficult to say, outside the far north and south of Africa, that industrialisation itself attracted people to real and existing employment on any scale. The urban populations of Africa expanded by the beginning of the 1970s to levels that the local business worlds could not absorb, and commentators began to refer to "overurbanisation." The colonial call of panic at the presence of impoverished, semi-educated concentrated masses of people was taken up in new forms. Such people were seen as social parasites, absenting themselves from the export-producing agrarian and mineral zones of rural Africa to settle in seething slum quarters where access to incendiary literature and ideas was easy. In the 1960s and 1970s, most African countries, wherever they belonged on the political spectrum, took up systematic round-ups and expulsions of urban dwellers living in self-constructed shacks. This was even the case in a city such as Abidjan where a rapidly growing economy was making use of this labour but was unable to catch up with the demand that existed for urban housing. One of the last such round-ups has been detailed by Aili Mari Tripp with reference to the *Nguvu Kazi* campaign in Dar es Salaam, Tanzania as late as 1983. The state attempted to define large numbers of urban dwellers as "unproductive," including twenty-two shiners of shoes and, more significantly, women who could not be categorised as officially married. This perspective was not really accepted by the population as legitimate and merely tended to drive more economic activity into the realm of illegality until, as was typical, the authorities tired and abandoned the campaign.[1]

But did all this make urban Africa genuinely urban? Didn't urban Africans continue to organise around ethnic associations? Didn't they continue to hold with belief systems created in rural areas? Didn't they react with indifference or hostility to key urban institutions? Did they not continue to retire to the countryside or allow their children to be brought up there?

In a sense, the numbers talk. They reveal a growing proportion of the population living at any point in cities, whatever the perambulations of individual trajectories. As we have already observed for colonial cities, a new culture was emerging characterised by festivities, music, cinema (now giving way to video programming), availability of print culture, associational activity, sport, and other activities that emanated from and took place largely on the urban terrain. "It was during [the late 1990s] where we have the development of 'reality' rap or 'Bongo' rap. 'Bongo' (Swahili for smart or clever) was the slang name for Dar es Salaam – the implication being that individuals have to be smart to survive in the city."[2]

Dorier-Aprill et al., looking at Brazzaville, point to these kinds of indicators – the importance of a Brazzaville Christmas and a Brazzaville New Year's Eve – and also emphasise that, while Brazzaville people may continue to believe in the supernatural and witchcraft, they live a life in which the ancestors who dominate rural ideology and legitimate rural life have faded in importance. In Brazzaville rather, it is a vast array of urban churches which provide forms of networking, sociability, and

---

[1] Tripp, *Changing the Rules: The Politics of Liberalization and the Urban Informal Economy in Tanzania* (Berkeley: University of California Press, 1997), 140ff.

[2] Sid Lemelle, "'Ni Wapi Tunakwenda?' Hip Hop Culture and the Children of Arusha" in Lemelle & Dipa Basu, eds., *The Vinyl Ain't Final: Hip Hop and the Globalization of Black Culture* (London: Pluto Press, forthcoming).

succour in times of need. The cities were filled with their own distinctive languages and idioms (in Brazzaville, Lingala, KiKongo/Lari, and the local inflections of French) and from them emanated a new sort of life. Particularly for the second and third generation, urban identification becomes of primary significance. It was true for Brazzaville even in the 1990s that a disproportionately small percentage of the population was elderly, but surely that too is apt to change with time. Even where ethnicity remained important, it often was defined in new ways that reflected urban competition and urban space. Thus those from the northern and western parts of the Congo became Niboleks, an amalgam that had no historic reality whatsoever.

In the middle to late 1970s, modernist Africa, where it had at first thrived after independence, for the most part became mired in crisis. The economic possibility of continuing to build up a prestige economy in the cities, to sustain import-substitution industries that brought in no profit, to build public housing that largely served the interest of relatively affluent civil servants – or alternatively was of a very low standard – declined as the value of African export goods diminished and debts to Western banks and governments accrued rapidly. The cosmopolitan dream that one could eliminate the unseemly and unsightly through government action turned into a nightmare. Big cities – with Lagos and Kinshasa in the lead – were vectors that triangulated the combined effect of several disastrous circumstances. They began to be seen as the problematic representatives of a new and troubled urbanism. They were great cities with little public transport, chaotic land tenure policies, poor access to remunerative structured employment, lacking in the public spaces that give the citizens of a city – at least in conventional modernist parlance – a sense of belonging and pride. As uncontrolled settlements spread on a far bigger scale, they threatened to overwhelm the functional urbanism inherited from colonial times when shack building was largely held in check.

Even in North Africa, where economic circumstances remained relatively more favourable, the decline, albeit not collapse, of the modern was notable. In Algiers, intensive state investment lost its grip and squatter settlements blossomed. Algiers and the far larger North African metropolis, Cairo, aspire to expand rationally through the creation of large satellite cities (15 May; 6 October) with at least some measure of planning, but certainly the Cairene experience has been viewed skeptically by experts who have instead seen city growth taking place in this incredibly densely peopled conurbation – 100,000 people

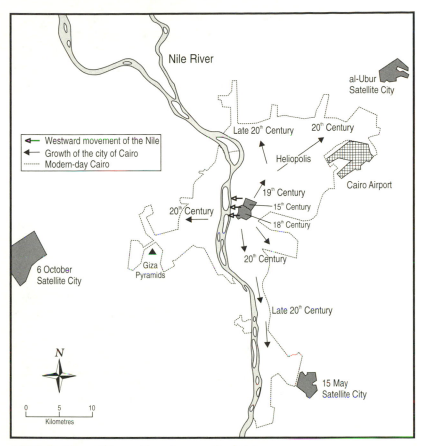

MAP 6. Great African cities: the growth of Cairo.

per square kilometre with figures of as much as four times that for some congested central areas – through the use of the historic city of the dead, through moving housing upwards to taller buildings, through crowding of the existing built environment and, on the periphery, through peasants selling precious green land suitable for cultivation in exchange for the purchase of better-situated bits of urban property nearer the centre. In one account, the average land available to citizens in the forms of parks is no more than five square inches.[3] In old cities, picturesque centres decayed as the affluent moved to suburbia, leaving slum conditions in the Algiers Casbah, the Tunis *Medina* and elsewhere. In stark contrast, "for dozens of kilometres the Nile now

[3] Max Rodenbeck, *Cairo: The City Victorious* (London: Picador, 1998), 20.

flows between a double wall of high-rise buildings, giving an indication of the changes Egypt has undergone in the last forty years."[4]

Casablanca also makes an interesting study. The 1952 nationalist riots led to a significant effort to replan the city, taken up again after 1980. There has been a willingness to create urban infrastructure away from the historic centre and to create viable public housing, although it is still difficult to argue that a new civic culture, equivalent to that in the pre-colonial Moroccan cities, is being successfully fostered and including poor migrants from the countryside.

James Ferguson in *Expectations of Modernity* has recently provided us with a disturbing and dysfunctional sense of this process where it has hurt almost the most, in the Copperbelt of Zambia, which was once infused with a sense of optimism and movement towards participation in a changing world. Since the 1970s, copper has suffered from declining world prices; the mines have not been very successful in creating a labour structure that makes them efficient and competitive. The once-extensive range of service and commercial activities in the bigger towns has shrunk enormously with the disappearance of most of the formerly large white minority, many of whom were entrepreneurs or skilled workers. And the informal sector provides very little secure income; it is underdeveloped compared to West Africa. Most African copper miners spend their working lives dwelling in company property; they have little to resort to when they become too old for work. The answer would seem to lie in a return to the countryside but the patrimonial ties that once bound lives together don't work easily for them and the return often becomes a disastrous end to life. Many have wives from other "tribes" unacceptable in rural areas. If making ends meet while working has become hard, surviving afterwards has become even more difficult. There is more despair than skilful opportunism in straddling between town and countryside today. Unsurprisingly this may be one urban zone where the population is stagnant, if not actually declining, according to geographer Deborah Potts.

Anne Schlyter, in her studies covering almost the whole period of independence of Zambia in the capital of Lusaka, does not provide a very different picture. The area she has chosen, George, was a squatter settlement once, saved from destruction by changing policies in the 1970s when the emphasis shifted to upgrading. But Lusaka has also, almost equally, suffered from economic degradation alongside the

---

[4] Raymond, 368.

Copperbelt towns. Far fewer households in George now are headed by
men in wage employment. Consequently the informal sector, which
mainly consists of petty commerce, has had to expand substantially.
Where once an optimism about the future flowed out of assumptions
about overcoming colonialism and racism and attaining an attractive
modern identity, now there is growing social dislocation while younger
people are terrified by the spectre of the AIDS virus. The small minority of families with successful accumulation strategies are apt to isolate
themselves more from the whole, and of course few can hope to repeat
the opportunities that were involved when the housing in George first
opened up; indeed rent from tenants are now a major source of income
for those who do own houses. The disappearance of UNIP, the single
party, as an effective patrimonial source of potential jobs and income,
is another negative which has not been countered.

At least the cities of Zambia have never suffered from serious political violence and collapse. A recent (ca. 2004) portrait of Kisangani,
once Stanleyville, the third largest town in the Belgian Congo on
the great bend of the Congo River, reveals a city where virtually no
"modern" activity functions anymore. Local "warlords" have controlled the town whose industry has been reduced to a limited amount
of beer brewing. There is little vehicular traffic, electricity, or even
pavement left of its once relatively developed urban infrastructure.
The only material reason for its inhabitants to remain in this city really
is security. Kinshasa, the huge Congolese capital city, retains a typical
city centre but its inhabitants very largely live in *les annexes*, the outskirts, that have been created through negotiations with local chiefs
and contain a life of their own that connects very little with that centre
and have few of the amenities one associates with urbanity. It is in
the *annexes*, however, that the music and art for which the *Kinois* are
famous gets produced. An even more extreme case is Freetown, the
capital of Sierra Leone, described by Sierra Leonean historian Ibrahim
Abdullah as a place "where every space in the city is under siege from
subalterns."[5] War-wrought devastation here follows on a gradual process of decay in a city which in essence was probably most dynamic in
the late nineteenth century.

No doubt many rural refugees in Freetown will return to their
homes when they feel that safer conditions prevail. However, in general, for all the important linkages many urban Africans keep with

---

[5] In *Under Siege: Four African Cities; Freetown, Johannesburg, Kinshasa, Lagos*, Documenta 11, Platform 4, Kassel Art Festival, (Ostfildern-Ruit: Hatje Kantz, 2002), 208.

FIGURE 11. Lagos 1960. Street scene on Lagos Island scheduled for demolition. *Source:* Peter Marris; used by permission.

the countryside, returning there is not an attractive option in phases of economic decline. In broad terms, what has happened has been a gradually declining *rate* in the growth of most African cities. Nowadays population increases consist far more of natural growth within the city than new migration from the countryside. There is a somewhat less straightforward tendency for smaller cities to experience a larger percentage of the growth rate. Such cities are sometimes centres of new commercial activities, including those that transcend boundaries more or less illegally. A good example of the latter would be the northern border town of Oshakati in Namibia, predicted to be the second city of the country in coming years. Trade with Angola passes through Oshakati which, due to the South African military activities of the 1980s, has excellent road links further south. In the next chapter we shall explore the Senegalese provincial city of Touba, growing very rapidly indeed, in part because of engagement in trade outside the control of the state.

This catastrophist view, however, is not shared by all specialists on urban development in Africa. At a remarkably early juncture on the eve of independence, Peter Marris produced a very critical and insightful study of urban removal in Lagos; he defended the way of life of the Lagosian slum-dwellers whose intricately linked if poorly serviced built environment served their needs, emotionally and sociologically, as well as economically. Only a relatively small percentage of the well-off would benefit from the proposed removal to distant purpose-built state housing far from Lagos Island.

This kind of voice gradually began to be heard more. With the crisis blocking modernist development, development experts, so often the main critical observers of African cities, began to propose a whole new take on African cities. The parasites, the shack-dwellers, the unemployed women instead of being seen as dragging down healthy forms of development in the city, began to be looked at as the authentic builders of African cities, as part of a process of development from below. Andrew Hake's classic study of Nairobi – the "self-help" city – as he called it, published in 1974, still makes an impressive case for this process. Far from being parasites, such poor dwellers in the city are there for a reason, to make themselves and their families a better life; they perform important services, create their own employment and make useful contributions to the economy. Such people, far from dragging down the economy, are actually engaged in building it up. The

FIGURE 12. Lagos 1960. Modernist reconstruction. New state-built housing on the mainland as part of urban renewal. *Source:* Peter Marris; used by permission.

large extensions of old townships, notably the Mathare Valley, have been pioneered here by landlords who provide limited rental space to tenants and permit Nairobi to extend itself further.

From this perspective, the city merely illustrated the general proposition rapidly gaining ground amongst aid donors and Western observers of Africa that the African state had turned swollen and corrupt and was more of a nuisance and a bully than a genuine contributor to development of any sort. The state provided planning ordinances and decrees that showed little real variation from colonial patterns except that the capacity to carry out such plans was no longer there. These plans were in some respects nefarious in the way they privileged some social groups and in other ways irrelevant to the real social processes at work in the city.

This sounds rather like the kind of excuse for colonial conquest a century earlier. But the appetite for colonialism has died in the West. Instead, the question was how to increase the burden of development for those who would be its beneficiaries. Thus the crisis in urban planning regimes was not entirely seen as a catastrophe – the poor "were doing it for themselves." Who needed the state? If they chose to live in urban areas, it must be because that was where market forces decreed them to go. Moreover, the impact of the World Bank–influenced policies of the 1980s and 1990s aimed at reducing what became known as urban bias through cutting out anything that smacked of state subsidisation, effectively making life in town more difficult than in the countryside according to many criteria.

According to this new received wisdom, development experts were urged to reject actual urban removals. By the late 1970s, such removals fell out of favour entirely unless they were grossly in the way of expanding elite needs. Instead, on the edge of cities, preparing site-and-service schemes was seen as the inexpensive and appropriate way to allow for urban growth. These schemes laid out greenfield sites and planned the "serviced" ground infrastructure with a minimum of services while assuming new residents would build the housing they wanted as and when they could. It fitted a self-help ideology well. This in turn gave way, as it proved too expensive and as the required infrastructure did not materialise or was very poorly maintained, to complete laissez-faire urban policy. After all, in the perfect market, prices would clear matters and naturalise suitable urban growth. Yet Deborah Potts, a sceptic about the merely market advantage of urban life, has written that "the savagery of the anti-urban politics of the Structural Adjustment Programmes has largely been misplaced,"[6] directed at people already impoverished and under siege. Whether urban bias had ever existed is questionable. Nonetheless Africans stay in cities. In practice, African cities continue to grow spatially through complex forms of negotiation that mix up the administratively regulatory with the realities of local legitimacy and power.

Following through from the eloquent work of Hake, there are two major propositions that can be taken up along the lines of "development from below." The first is essentially practical: how to make cities of the poor more liveable on the cheap. One element here is governmental reform, with the invention of the concept of *good governance* transcending conventional state forms and heavily promoted by international agencies. The state itself is meant to generate autonomous agencies closer to the ground and more sensitive to the people. A classic manoeuvre here was the imitation from France in Francophone countries of a local government system that broke up large municipalities into more people-friendly smaller units, sometimes directly elected by the populace. In other cases, cities experiment with distinct development agencies intended for particular purposes to uplift areas and find particular activities on which to concentrate. Local Economic Development, focussing integrated development on targeted localities, is a development buzzword for the first years of the twenty-first century.

Yet despite the insults flung at it over decades from the West, the role of the central government remains very prominent. The tendency to pull the patrimonial purse strings is great; the capacity of local authority to raise its own funds very poor. This creates space for fundraising Non-Governmental Organisations. Charity *cum* developmental organisations generate, and come to liaise here with, locally created outfits run by consultants and politicians, in part to net income and support. Such NGOs are able to do impressive work on an experimental basis through example and to alert outsiders to major problems; they are not very suitable for creating long-term systems run by local people that provide basic services, however.

[6] Deborah Potts, "Urban Strategies: Adopting New Strategies and Adapting Rural Links" in Carole Rakodi, ed., *The Urban Challenge in Africa; Growth and Management of Its Large Cities* (London/Tokyo/New York: United Nations University Press, 1997), 452.

Here it is possible to look as well at the CBOs, the community-based organisations that can potentially mobilise the masses effectively to pull the African city up by its bootstraps. As we have seen, cities with pre-colonial roots contain such organisations with old histories and symbolic meanings. However, they are joined today by innumerable new kinds of structure. Africans not only bring association into the city from the countryside, they create many novel forms of organisation, ethnic, religious, and based on other common interests. Networks are vital and they are created out of old and new material. Women in particular, freed from tradition-laden prohibitions on autonomous activity, are sometimes able to create very effective structures in African cities of a kind completely different than the patriarchal forms of rural societies.[7]

It has been argued that such associations can form the basis for forging a more civilised and acceptable urban life in Africa. The decline of industrial development from the 1970s has meant that classic working-class neighbourhoods are very atypical of African cities and with them, classic forms of proletarian organisation. But other forms of organisation more suitable to the diverse ways neighbourhood people make a living serve for some as a substitute. Urban politics responds in complex ways in Africa to more liberal policy shifts so long as they free people from unwanted restrictions and open up economic spaces. As private individual property ownership gets more deeply entrenched, most African cities are the sites of more and more accumulation projects based on house ownership. Landlordism can create apparent religious and ethnic loyalties and fissions and, where democratic contestation is significant, often determines how people will vote.

An impressive study of neighbourhood-based association has recently been recorded by Babatunde Ahonsi with regard to Nigeria's megalopolis, Lagos. Ahonsi believes that many sections of mainland Lagos have evolved from desolate stands of housing into liveable neighbourhoods characterised by varied forms of micro-enterprise and gradually acquiring basic amenities thanks to the collective capacities of Nigerians to organise and regulate their lives "from below." Community Development Associations, as they are known, "successfully paved streets, constructed security gates, routinely cleared and cleaned their surroundings (including dealing with the aftermath of flooding),

---

[7] Of course, in West Africa particularly, strong autonomous women's organisations have deep roots in many societies.

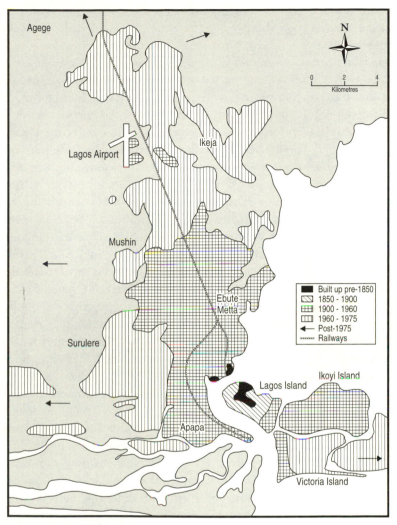

MAP 7. Great African cities: the growth of Lagos.

maintained public water pipes and taps and devised vigilante security arrangements for dealing with the problem of armed robbery,"[8] fending off the depredations of the notorious "area boys" who prey on the less organised. By contrast to J. Y. Peel's classic study of Ilesha, where urban organisation seems to revolve mostly around successful professionals sending support money to provide prestigious amenities

[8] In *Under Siege, op. cit.*, 283.

in their home towns while being oblivious to the urban environment around themselves, Ahonsi suggests a new civic identification and pride amongst very diverse Nigerians in the areas he considers.

In many African countries such organisations seem to point the way to the provision of basic services, such as the clearing of waste, where the state has entirely broken down. Gabriel Tati has explored for example the self-regulation of markets in the Congo, the construction of a bridge, also in the Congo, and the means by which waste is collected in one neighbourhood in Yaoundé in Cameroun.

For some observers, an answer lies also in promoting economic activities normally associated with village life in the urban setting. Undoubtedly, especially in small cities and indeed wherever there is substantial spare land, it makes sense for families to feed themselves to some extent through cultivation, not, as we have seen, anything new or unusual in African urban living patterns. There may also be some justification in setting aside appropriate, well-watered areas for market gardening activities that can improve the food intake of the city. Many African cities were planned in the colonial area with truly vast empty spaces that fitted the aesthetics of the would-be settler gentry – massive gardens that could hardly be sustained without plentiful inexpensive gardening help – and the desire for racial segregation. This emptiness really does fit very little beyond recreational needs today. Certainly it makes no sense for urban administrations to use their remaining capacity to destroy food plantations ruthlessly – as periodically happens in Harare or Nairobi on what are termed to be "raids" – in order to sustain questionable urban ordinances belonging to the colonial period. This argument can hold even if one realises that many of the denser African cities genuinely have little scope for urban agriculture and the more utopian green prospects urban agriculture has held out for a few are probably pipe dreams.

Lying behind such studies hovers the idea that this perhaps is how to construct real democracy in Africa. In Cairo, the traditional waste collectors have been Coptic Christians, poor and downtrodden and shunned by polite society (much of their work involved keeping pigs) but bound into a distinct community with links back to farming villages. Through the intervention of the church and of NGOs, the *zabaleen* have acquired elements of a much more advanced recycling operation where clean rags are woven into rugs and soil compost is manufactured in land-hungry Egypt. For Susanna Myllylä, the promise lies in the stimulation to self-help, although Cairo municipality continues to have its collective mind set rather on the creation of a "modern" state-run and capital-intensive waste disposal system that correlates with its world vision and with systematic bureaucratic processes.[9] In an influential recent monograph, Diane Sugarman has painted the portrait of a typical Cairene neighbourhood in which informal networks, patronage relationships, and political ties are critical in residents functioning effectively, by contrast to this official picture.

In contrast to the gloomy perspective on Zambia held by Schlyter or Ferguson, Aili Tripp, writing on Dar es Salaam in the new spirit, has tended to celebrate the decline of the state and the triumph of the market, releasing the people's energies in Tanzania, as socialist policies began to be abandoned. Tripp's studies of Dar es Salaam and Kampala suggest a lugubrious, incompetent, and still oppressive central state being effectively challenged by residents anxious to get on with their lives. In particular, she emphasises the capacity of women to organise themselves effectively. With the dramatic decline in the formal economy and the ability of the state to offer men decent employment, women's need to expand their range of activities and struggle for suitable conditions to facilitate these activities has grown dramatically.

Sylvy Jaglin has followed in depth the attempts by the radical Sankora regime in Burkina Faso from 1984 to restructure state-society relations in the urban context. In part, this was to break through the patrimonial web, which connected local initiative to the Mossi monarchy in the capital, Ouagadougou, expressed especially through the rights of the landlords who had the correct ties to the system. At this point, Ouagadougou, the ancient seat of the Mossi, had been growing fast for twenty years. The patronage system and the French-created planning regimen were not very helpful in integrating rural migrants into the urban fabric. With the slogan of "one family, one roof," the regime hoped to engage poor urban residents to become involved in civic loyalty and improvements. *Comités révolutionnaires* were created as local developmental partners to the national state. Abolished in 1991, these *comités* were not ineffective. Jaglin argues that they introduced the vital concept of shared management to Burkina Faso. There was a joint recognition of the need for local initiative and central state intervention. The greatest successes were reached in terms of construction of clinics and schools and sports fields. There was less success, given

---

[9] Both Myllyllä and Tati are to be found in Arne Tostensen, Inge Tvedten & Mariken Vaa., eds., *Associational Life in African Cities* (Uppsala: Nordic Africa Institute, 2001).

the poverty of the country, in equipping these facilities properly. The availability of water was substantially improved, whereas electricity remained too expensive for most poor residents. Nonetheless she argues that this was the route towards integrating peripheral urban-ites into some kind of citizenship.

Of course, it is not so clear that CBOs, politically self-conscious agencies from below, and other beneficent activities on the ground are everywhere prevalent. If we return to Zambia, research does not really suggest much of a sense of effective local organisation. There is a striking monograph by Benetta Jules-Rosette (1981) on a particular Lusaka community with special potential in this regard, but it is a migrant community with a unique and remarkable religious history. Moreover, with regard to basic needs of the poor, as Jean-Luc Piermay reminds us in his analysis of Kinshasa, survivalism is not the same as building a real urban social fabric.

Nor are "communities" in Africa necessarily so welcoming or egal-itarian as the concept usually implies. In the bosom of self-help there lies also exploitation and growing forms of differentiation. It is, more-over, not only the poor who help themselves in situations where the state weakens. Particularly in those African cities with more substan-tial middle classes, the possibilities are greater both for new forms of accumulation through uncontrolled urban expansion and for yet greater problems in terms of achieving some kind of sustainable urban planning, as the North African literature indicates. The rich are far more unsustainable than the poor in a world of limited resources. Landlordism is an ideal means for the slightly better-off to accumu-late and stabilise their lives, but it can evolve into more unequal and exploitative relationships when absentees begin to own multiple prop-erties. A fine study based on Rabat, Morocco by Allain-el Mansouri demonstrates how an ancient culture based on providing water for cit-izens as a common good (public fountains, baths) synonymous with urbanity has recently given way to the idea of water as a market good in which access depends for quality and quantity on wealth.

The laissez-faire city may also help breed hostility to foreigners and those from distant regions. The major countries of West Africa – Nigeria, Senegal, the Ivory Coast, and Ghana – have all notably been the scene of large-scale expulsions of "outsiders" from neighbouring countries since independence, despite the obvious fact that such "out-siders" have been major contributors to wealth and prosperity in the past. Such expulsions are often tangled with the rivalries of neighbour-ing states. Urban Nigeria in particular continues to experience very bloody ethnic conflict in such varied urban communities as Kaduna, Jos, Warri, and Lagos. The "supertribal" identities that have been explored a bit in the previous chapter on the colonial city are traced in Brazzaville where politics became dominated, with the collapse of an authoritarian and superficially Marxist system, by regional loyalties. While the centre of Brazzaville lost much of its significance except to the large firms, the national professional elite, and foreigners, the east and west sections of the city became fortresses sustained by ethnic militias, and both have experienced devastating destruction in two major waves of violence in the 1990s. This has been a vicious fight in a zero-sum game over a fixed amount of wealth, and it obviates the construction of an economy that can grow with the aid of a supportive state.

Turning from the developmental to the cultural, the recent collection *Under Siege: Four African Cities* (2002) proposes, however, a counterpart to the post-modern approach of some development studies of African cities. For some of the contributors, the collapse of many features of urban life as developed over decades represents a cultural renascence, the genuine *Africanisation* of the African city. What has collapsed can be represented as a cultural Eurocentric imposition that is being, perhaps in some respects painfully, discarded. Over time many a proud but, for the mass of black Africans, forbidding and hostile urban core towards whose sustenance his or her labour had to be directed, has now fallen into neglect or decay.

The Francophone literature particularly – especially since Marc Vernière's influential work on Dakar and its now equivalently large "double," Pikine – is especially emphatic here. Dakar's official, planned world which does not serve the mass of people and its elite areas which use up massive resources are contrasted to Pikine, where the majority now live and interact and try to build a new life for themselves. This kind of contrast has been drawn by others for such cities as the Centrafrican capital of Bangui, the Nigerien capital of Niamey, and the great conurbation of Kinshasa. Making a living and securing a bit of land in Kinshasa is tough, but nonetheless statistics suggest a child born in Kinshasa still has a better chance for a longer life; the city has higher birth rates and lower death rates than elsewhere. This is why people stay here, not the links to the industrial and communications core of wealth to which they have very little access.

New forms of organisation are matched with new cultural forms; this is where new African music and art is coming from. In bookstalls in African cities, school texts have given way to themes dealing with the ideals and dilemmas of an urban reading public. *Kwani?*, a

FIGURE 13. Lagos 2000. Highway bridge and a world of small-scale production and commerce. *Source:* Edgar Cleijne; used by permission.

journal established by Kenyan intellectuals, aims at tapping into popular language and the tropes of everyday life: it highlights language that mixes Kiswahili, English, and other languages spoken in Kenya as the *sheng* argot spoken in Nairobi. As the *Under Siege* collection comes from the inspiration of the art world, it reflects the changing interest from a static and ethnographic African art based on tradition and the countryside to one looking for innovation, assertive protest, juxtaposition, and situation within a globalised world. The distinguished Dutch architect Rem Koolhaas, in getting to know Lagos, has come to know the city not (merely?) as a welter of disaster, chaos and crime but also as a place where massive traffic jams inspire equally massive numbers of informal sector traders to find their customers, and where the complex processes of waste disposal lead to the creation of vast numbers of jobs and to ingenious forms of recycling. Lagos "is a patchwork of self-organisation that has evaded the rigourous organisation of '70s planners."[10]

The condition of African cities today varies. Cities do not entirely change from one era to another. This book proposes that they have longer-term trajectories in Africa as elsewhere. The post-colonial

[10] Rem Koolhaas in *Under Siege*, 183.

decades have added another important layer to an existing and expanding history. Catastrophe and creativity, good governance versus effective government, these paradoxical approaches are part of a clash of ideas about where African cities are heading today. African cities generally are unable to progress according to the strictures of colonial planning and colonial values. Whether they are now moving in the direction of new and more realistic governance regimes is the question. Considering various trends alongside each other seems more useful than merely subjecting them to an all-purpose "Afropessimism" that obscures the variety of often contradictory movement and prevents us from grasping any sense of a way forward. In the following chapter, we shall conclude by looking at these issues in more detail.

Selected Readings

This chapter is almost entirely dependent on the work of social scientists rather than historians, albeit social scientists with a bent for interdisciplinary work. Historians are only beginning to look at the postindependence years as history. A good summary of the state of the art as it was understood in the first years of African independence

FIGURE 14. Lagos 2000. The traffic jam on the bridge and repair shops beneath. *Source:* Edgar Cleijne; used by permission.

can be found in W. J. & J. L. Hanna, *Urban Dynamics in Black Africa* (Chicago: Aldine-Atherton, 2nd edition, 1981). For a general perspective on the material in this topic, R. E. Stren and R. R.White, eds., *African Cities in Crisis: Managing Rapid Urban Growth* (Boulder, CO: Westview Press, 1989) was a volume that changed the approach of many readers. The overview in Akin Mabogunje, "Urban Planning and the Post-colonial State in Africa," *African Studies Review*, XXXIII, 1990, 121–203, is very useful. An excellent large reader, Carole Rakodi, ed., *The Urban Challenge in Africa: Growth and Management of its Large Cities* (New York/London/Tokyo: United Nations University Press, 1997) contains many outstanding contributions. For a single volume study, Margaret Peil, *African Urban Society* (Chichester: Wiley, 1984) is very handy.

Apart from Hake, *op. cit.*, there are a number of observant sources that traced the irrelevance and collapse of late colonial planning models: outstanding and early was Peter Marris, *Family and Social Change in an African City: A Study of Rehousing in Lagos* (Evanston: Northwestern University Press, 1961). But see also Janet Bujra, "Proletarianization and the Informal Sector: A Case Study from Nairobi," *African Urban Studies*, III, 1978/79, 47–66. Richard Stren, "Urban Research in Africa 1960–92," *Urban Studies*, XXXI, 4/5, 1994, 729–43; and Jaap van Velsen, "Urban Squatters-Problems or Solution" in David Parkin, ed., *Town and Countryside in Central and Eastern Africa* (London: Oxford University Press, 1975), 294–307. A French equivalent can be found in Marc Vernière, "A propos de la marginalité: réflexions illustreés par quelques enquêtes en milieu urbain et suburbain africain," *Cahiers d'études africaines*, 51, 1973, 587–605. A special issue of *Cahiers d'études africaines*, 81–83, published in 1981, as well as *Politique africaine*, 17, published in 1985, were also important markers of change.

For housing issues specifically, see P. Amis & P. Lloyd., eds., *Housing Africa's Poor* (Manchester: Manchester University Press, 1990). Also recommended are Philip Amis, "Squatters or Tenants? The Commercialisation of Unauthorised Housing in Nairobi," *World Development*, XII, 1984, 87–96; Seltene Seyoum, "Land Alienation and the Urban Growth of Bahir Dar 1935–74" in Anderson & Rathbone's previously cited historical volume; Carole Rakodi, "From a Settler History to an African Present: Housing Markets in Harare, Zimbabwe," *Society and Space*, XIII(1), 1995, 91–115; and M. Chebbi, "The Pirate Developer; A New Form of Development in Tunis," *International Journal of Urban and Regional Research*, XII, 1988. For inequality in water access, see

Béatrice Allain-El Mansouri, *L'eau et la ville au Maroc: Rabat-Salé et son périphérie* (Paris: L'Harmattan, 2001).

The political issues engaged were addressed in a striking way by Peter Gutkind in such articles as "From the Energy of Despair to the Anger of Despair: The Transition from Social Circulation to Political Consciousness among the Urban Poor," *Canadian Journal of African Studies*, VII, 1973. For an economist's perspective, see Vali Jamal & John Weeks, "The Vanishing Rural-Urban Gap in Sub-Saharan Africa," *International Labour Review*, CXXVII (3), 1988. On different aspects of urban politics, see Michael Chege, "A Tale of Two Slums; Electoral Politics in Mathare and Dagoretti," *Review of African Political Economy*, 20, 1981, 74–88 with reference to Kenya; Richard Jeffries, "Urban Popular Attitudes towards the Economic Recovery Programme," XCI, *African Affairs*, 1992, 207–26 on Ghana; and Jeremy Grest, "Urban Management, Local Government Reform and the Democratization Process in Mozambique: Maputo City 1975–90," *Journal of Southern African Studies*, XXI(1), 1995, 147–64 on Mozambique. How a city really works from the perspective of ordinary residents is the subject of Diane Sugarman, *Avenues of Participation* (Princeton: Princeton University Press, 1995). As with other subjects, titles from the previous chapter can be used very profitably here.

A partially postmodern collection with some striking illustrations of contemporary African cities can be found in *Under Siege: Four African Cities: Freetown, Johannesburg, Kinshasa, Lagos*, Documenta 11, Platform 4, Kassel Art Festival (Ostfildern-Ruit: Hatje Kantz, 2002) (managing editor Gerti Fietzek). On attempts to explore new ways of understanding and planning African cities, see Arne Tostensen, Inge Tvedten & Mariken Vaa, eds., *Associational Life in African Cities* (Uppsala: Nordic Africa Institute, 2001) and Karen Hansen & Mariken Vaa, eds., *Reconsidering Informality: Perspectives from Urban Africa* (Uppsala: Nordic Africa Institute, 2004). Mark Swilling, ed., *Governing Africa's Cities* (Johannesburg: University of the Witwatersrand Press, 1996) is also recommended.

On particular cities, there are a number of very substantial studies in French. For some important examples see Marc Pain, *Kinshasa: écologie et organisation urbaines* (Toulouse: Université le Mirail, 1979); Guy Mainet, *Douala: croissance et servitudes* (Paris: L'Harmattan, 1985); M. Samkale, L. V. Thomas & P. Fougeyrollas, *Dakar en devenir* (Paris: Présence Africaine, 1968); Marc Vernière, *Dakar et son Double: Dagoudane Pikine* (Paris: Bibliothèque Nationale, 1977) for Dakar and Pikine; Elisabeth Dorier-Aprill, Abel Kouvonama & Christophe Aprill, eds., *Vivre à Brazzaville: modernité et crise au quotidien* (Paris: Karthala, 1998) for Brazzaville; and Ali Hadjiedj, Claude Chaline & Jocelyne Dubois-Maury, eds., *Alger: les nouveaux défis de l'urbanisation* (Paris: L'Harmattan, 2003) for Algiers (also Benatia, *op. cit* in Chapter Three). The North African picture is briefly summarised in Janet Abu Lughod, "Developments in North African Urbanism: The Process of Decolonization" in B. J. L. Berry, ed., *Urbanization and Counter-urbanization* (Beverly Hills: Sage, 1976), 191–211; and one type of development is captured in Justin McGuiness, "Neighbourhood Notes: Texture and Streetscape in the Tunis Medina" in Susan Slyomovics, ed., *The Walled Arab City in Literature, Architecture and History* (London: Frank Cass, 2001), 97–120. Margaret Peil, *The City is the People* (Chichester: Wiley, 1991) provides a good description of Lagos. There is a good recent French work on Maputo and other Mozambican cities: Brigitte Lachartre, *Enjeux urbains au Mozambique* (Paris: Karthala, 2000). For Addis Ababa, Girma Kebbede, *Living with Urban Environmental Health Risks: The Case of Ethiopia* (Aldershot: Ashgate, 2004) provides a grim but valuable introduction.

James Ferguson's important study of the Copperbelt, *Expectations of Modernity*, was cited in the previous chapter; recommended also are Benetta Jules-Rosette, *Symbols of Change: Urban Transition in a Zambian Community* (Norwood, NJ: Ablex, 1981); Ann Schlyter, *Recycled Inequalities: Youth and Gender in George Compound, Zambia*, Nordic Africa Institute Research Report #114, Uppsala, 1999; and Karen Hansen, *Keeping House in Lusaka* (New York: Columbia University Press, 1997) and *Salaula* (Chicago: University of Chicago Press, 2000). Aili Tripp's perspective on Dar es Salaam can be found in her article "Women and the Changing Urban Household in Tanzania," *Journal of Modern African Studies*, XXVII, 1989, 601–23 and in *Changing the Rules: The Politics of Liberalization and the Urban Informal Economy in Tanzania* (Berkeley: University of California Press, 1997). The Burkinabe experiment in urban residential development is detailed in Sylvy Jaglin, *Gestion urbaine partagée à Ouagadougou: pouvoirs et peripheries* (Paris: Karthala/ORSTOM, 1995). There is a short version of her ideas in Sylvy Jaglin, "Why Mobilise Town Dwellers?," *Environment and Urbanization*, VI (2), 1994, 11–32.

Finally, some scattered drives: on the effort to plan the expansion of Cairo, Bénedicte Florin, "Six-Octobre; ville secondaire ou banlieue de Caire?," *Villes en parallèle*, 22, 1995, 179–200; and Henk

Knaupe & Ulrich Wurzel, *Aufbruch in der Wüste: Die Neuen Städte in Aegypten* (Frankfurt: Peter Lang, 1995). Cairo and its many problems and opportunities feature in an excellent series, *Cairo Papers in Social Science*, published by the American University in Cairo. The city comes to life in many of the novels of Egypt's Nobel Prize–winning novelist, Naguib Mahfouz. For urban agriculture, see Donald Freeman, *City of Farmers: Informal Urban Agriculture in the Open Spaces of Nairobi, Kenya* (Montreal: McGill University Press, 1991); Carole Rakodi, "Urban Agriculture: Research Questions and Zambian Evidence," *Journal of Modern African Studies*, XXVI, 1988; and Beacon Mbiba, *Urban Agriculture in Zimbabwe* (Aldershot: Avebury, 1995). On popular culture, an interesting exploration can be found in Sidney Lemelle, "Ni Wapi Tunakwenda? Hip Hop Culture and the Children of Arusha" in Dipa Basu & Sidney Lemelle, eds., *The Vinyl Ain't Final: Hip Hop and the Globalization of Black Culture* (London: Pluto Press, forthcoming). For *Kwani?* as well as other manifestations of East African popular culture, see *Africa Insight*, XXXV(2), [Pretoria], 2005.

CHAPTER 6

Globalisation and the African City:
Touba, Abidjan, Durban

Descriptions of African cities in desperate conditions are generally coupled with assumptions about globalisation, a term that became fashionable in the course of rapid international economic growth in the 1990s. Globalisation can work as a term if we posit that it represents a stage in international economic interactions. It has gone together with an intensive increase in networking through telecommunications and the large-scale use of computers, with the dominance of big multinational corporations that deploy investments, production, and other activities relatively freely to desirable corners of the globe. Linked to globalisation and given the end of the Cold War, there has come an allied emphasis on international governance intended to ease the flow of goods and currencies amongst other forms of regulation.

For the globalisation champions, Africa has fallen off the map of the civilised world. With its poor infrastructure, its chaotic politics, not infrequent episodes of natural disaster causing havoc, and its continued dependence on primary product sales as its only desirable exports, it has been marginalised in the networked world. Where urban sociologists and geographers consider the fate of "world cities" that compete with and integrate largely with each other as national boundaries become less important, what is left for the cities of Africa? How Africans survive, form human communities, and access necessities in these cities is part of the picture which we have already considered in the last chapter. In this chapter, which is in a sense a continuation of this theme, we shall look as well at aspects of globalisation which do not exactly fit the scary stories of the Afropessimists. The three following examples indicate that some Africans have responded creatively and originally to global economic changes, that some of the trends that are causing change in cities elsewhere in the world are taking place in Africa as well, and that the possibilities of counter-formation are not negligible in Africa. The first looks at an original example, the rise of a new post-colonial city in response to cultural and identity factors coming into play with successful responses to changes in international commerce. The second is a less happy story, that of a major city which is showing forms of differentiation that mirror the sharper class differences exhibited in wealthier urban centres in the world with striking spatial implications. Intensified reliance on identity as legitimacy worsens the chances of renewed prosperity. The third contrasts the laissez-faire consequences that go with the decline of state regulation to the advantage of the privileged with a counter-movement that has gone directly against the apparently dominant trends for particular reasons.

A Mouride Jerusalem

Touba is not a city that many outside Senegal know. Until the final quarter of the twentieth century, it was only a small town associated with the Mouride religious order established by the Senegalese Muslim teacher and organiser, Cheikh Ahmadou Bamba. However, it has become a good-sized city within recent years when its growth has frequently exceeded 15 percent per year. With a population counted at three hundred thousand in 1994, estimates a decade later ran to as much as five hundred thousand. It has certainly become the largest city in Senegal apart from the capital Dakar. This growth is the more striking by contrast with the relatively slow development of other provincial Senegalese towns.

Religious brotherhoods structure the world of Senegalese Muslims, and the Mourides (Muridiyya) are the best known of these born in Senegal. The Mourides have long fascinated scholars of Africa and are the subject of a number of celebrated studies. Thanks to the recent outstanding work of the Senegalese geographer Cheikh Guèye, who has termed Touba the Mouride Jerusalem, it is possible to follow the latest developments among the Mourides and, in particular, the rise of the city of Touba and the urbanisation of the Mouride order.

In the early colonial period, the French looked askance at the preaching of Bamba which they feared would take on an anti-French character, and he was exiled for many years to Gabon. However, as time wore on, a rapprochement was established and the Mourides gradually began to be seen as an element making for stability in Senegal. Bamba encouraged Senegalese men to volunteer for the French military in World War I. In return, after the war, he received permission to begin the construction of a great Mouride mosque in Touba in 1924 (completed only in 1963). The French consented to his burial in the town in 1927 and, to accommodate a growing annual pilgrimage to his tomb, allowed a spur of the railway to be extended to Touba in 1931. Nonetheless the growth of Touba was relatively modest; its core was (and is to a large extent) after all a monument to the dead. Its population was only 4,353 in 1960 at the time of independence, rising to 29,738 in 1976.

During the final generation of French colonial rule, and indeed well after, the Mourides acquired fame as the producers of a large part of Senegal's key export, the peanut. Indeed they tended towards growing peanuts as a monoculture and spread its cultivation deeper into the Senegalese interior into semi-arid areas of doubtful environmental sustainability, the so-called *Terres Neuves* (New Lands). This process went together with the hierarchial system whereby disciples or *taalibes* were considered to be under the discipline of their *marabouts* or religious leaders, themselves ultimately subordinate to the Khalifal order of Bamba's descendant-successors. Disciples were required to produce peanut crops in effect as part of their obligation in extending and sustaining the Mouride order, and they were heavily tithed. The Mourides were prominent backers of the politician Léopold Sedar Senghor, Senegal's first president (and himself a Christian). Amongst other things, they received in return the right to distribute land in and around Touba, which lay in the heart of Mouride country. The mosque and the railway line extension were in part the work of pious Mouride volunteers.

However, this kind of economy did not lend itself to any very substantial sort of urbanisation. Gradually, a growing number of Mourides did settle in Dakar and other urban communities, but, generally speaking, Mourides remained in rural areas and became the mainstay of the population of numerous small settlements. The *daara* was the name given to the pioneer settlement typical of this phase. The peanut export economy of Senegal reached its peak in the 1970s, however. Drought

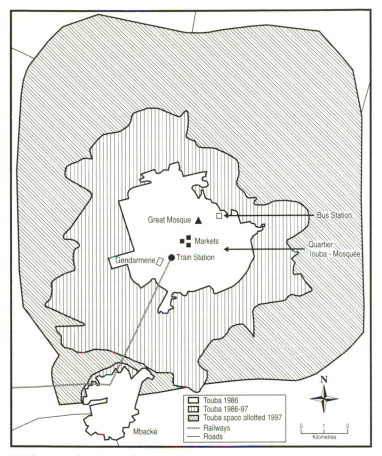

MAP 8. Touba, Senegal.

and declining international prices then brought about a marked decline and the Mourides in fact refused to sustain national efforts to rebuild the peanut economy to its peak.

Instead, they turned in growing numbers to commerce in a wide range of commodities as the order established impressive and far-flung economic networks. From 1980, very large numbers of Mourides began to be found not merely in West African cities such as Libreville and Abidjan but throughout Europe, North America, and further afield. This emigration has itself been organised and promoted by the leadership of the order. Within Senegal itself, the order has given its blessing to the explosive growth of a city of peace and order – holy Touba. The great mosque at the heart of Touba was completed in

1963 and now boasts the sixth biggest minaret in the world, eighty-seven metres high. The pilgrimage attracts hundreds of thousands of worshippers.

But in addition, large numbers of Mourides have also been persuaded to abandon their residences in west-central rural Senegal and move to Touba itself, which has quickly grown into a substantial city. Land in Touba has been in the gift of the order to distribute and theoretically cannot otherwise be bought or sold. Thus the *taalibe* acquires his share of urban life through his adhesion to a Mouride leader. If the core of the order consists of the male grandchildren of its founder, the quarters of the city were established through the Wolof matrilineages established by him and his sons. Bamba had himself twenty-nine wives, who included women from the families of both religious leaders and Wolof aristocrats of the pre-French era, and some of their descendants have established important neighbourhoods in Touba.

Guèye has provided us with a picture of the growing economic complexity of Touba. Apart from the benefits of religious activities, the city also contains merchants and speculators in local produce; with the decline of peanuts, as elsewhere in Africa, there is a growing commoditised trade in agricultural produce (with corresponding speculation) for local consumption. Perhaps one-third of households are primarily committed to farming, and their inhabitants are often elsewhere in agricultural villages where they maintain a livelihood. In the 1990s, a growing percentage of the Touba population has come to consist of women and children, indicating that it has become the principal family residence of most of these households.

More important is commerce. More than half of all Touba households are described as primarily active in commerce, and here imports, and a consumer economy tied to the outer world, is especially significant. International remittances account for a huge share of income while the importation and dispersal of industrially produced goods from the whole world have taken over the Senegalese economy, so weak in "internationally competitive" productive activity. Touba makes sense as a town only if one starts to take stock of one major aspect of globalisation – the large-scale temporary or permanent movement of Africans, notably West Africans, to all corners of the globe, together with the decline in productive local activity. For the Mouride hierarchy, the logic of the internal structure of the order is to collect funds in order to construct God's city of Touba. In this context, it is convenient and

FIGURE 15. Roof delivery: how Touba is being constructed.
Source: Dr. Cheikh Guèye; used by permission.

appropriate for economic as well as cultural reasons for large numbers
to collect in a dense location.

The markets play a key role in the town. They began to play an
important role in the Senegalese economy through the distribution of
untaxed goods arriving from the Gambia, a measure of the growing
inability of the Senegalese state to control its economic frontiers. Other
goods coming across borders have now supplemented and replaced this
initial source. Guèye stresses the complicated relationship of Touba to
the Senegalese state. In a sense, this is a city that has emerged directly
out of civil society and local forms of accumulation completely independent of the order of the colonial and post-colonial state. (Ironically,
the present president of Senegal, Abdoulaye Wade, is a Mouride.) It
benefits from the extent to which Mouride influence keeps the state at
bay and tries to substitute a religious way of life for a secular order. It
is a visible symbol of the eclipse of a political order in which the state
would be expected to be the principal bearer of the gospel and accoutrements of development. In holy Touba, smoking, drinking, and other
vices are all banned and there are virtually no resident non-Muslims.
Europeans are not supposed to live in much of the city. In theory, such
infrastructure as electricity and water are available at no cost; Touba
is tax-free.

In reality, however, the very material reality of a modern city has intruded in all too real a way on the Mouride Jerusalem despite these bans. The very rapid growth of the city has engendered the other leg of its economy, the sheer weight of the construction and building industry. Devolution of plot assignments from the religious leadership to the neighbourhood village chiefs has gone hand in hand with a more or less legal but very extensive and lucrative market in housing, justified by the need to partition estates on death, amongst other things. This certainly has the potential to subvert the spatial order of the city focussed on the control of key lineages and their access to land near the great mosque.

If religious-based associations (*dahira*) are founded sometimes to, for example, provide cemeteries or hospitals for the city, they are very inadequate.[1] In fact, the infrastructure, still not very developed, does require state intervention (telephone lines, water supply, road construction), even though this is difficult for Mourides to take into account in comprehending their city. There have been intense struggles over repayment of bills for services. In theory there are no squatter settlements in Touba, but in fact there are: squatter settlements (*khayma*) justified as homes-in-waiting for those not yet allotted plots of land.

The decline in recognised employment in Senegal and the burgeoning of the black market has led, even in Touba, to serious levels of crime, which the Islamic regime is unable to control. This includes alcohol, drugs, and a trade in arms. Many successful traders bring back a huge array of luxury durable items for their homes in Touba, again tempting criminal elements. Even in areas such as traffic control, the attempt to minimise the presence of the secular state by banning national police has created great problems. Touba lacks the most visible sign of the striking power of a state, an effective police force. As a result of some of these contradictions, the national state has been allowed to creep in the door with certain services. Here we have a considerable urban agglomeration which has arisen despite or against the state, in sympathy with the dynamism of globalisation to which Senegal's main successful response has been emigration, creating a new kind of social phenomenon. But in Touba the classic problems of a modern city are far from absent, but they are not the problems of decay or collapse. This is a new kind of city in so far as its growth has

---

[1] For *dahira* see Momar Coumba Diop, "Fonctions et activités des *dahira* mourides urbains (Sénégal)," *Cahiers d'Études Africaines*, 81–83, 1982, 79–91.

been quite autonomous from the colonial and post-colonial economic or administrative logic of the twentieth century.

The Pearl of the Lagoons

Surprisingly our second city, which we shall highlight in order to consider aspects of the globalisation of Africa and its urban landscape, is almost of an age with Touba. Abidjan was established by the French administration of the Ivory Coast, also in French West Africa, in 1920. At that point, its population consisted only of those inhabiting a couple of dozen Ebrié and other villages around a network of islands and peninsulas on a lagoon. The French goal was to establish the ideal site for a railway terminus that would evacuate useful tropical commercial products and could be connected easily to a seaport. They wanted to find a relatively healthy site and they meant to develop it as a territorial capital. Abidjan became the capital of the Ivory Coast only in 1934, and in 1950 a cut through the island of Petit Bassam brought deepwater ships directly through to the lagoon, confirming Abidjan's location as the core of colonial development not merely in the Ivory Coast but in French West Africa more generally.

By contrast with Touba, the growth of Abidjan was explosive in the later colonial period, and above all in the early independence period, the era of the so-called Ivorian miracle. In the decade after the Second World War, the Ivory Coast economy boomed as a source of coffee and then cocoa, grown in the forest hinterland of Abidjan. Initially produced by French planters who could dispose of unfree labour thanks to the colonial labour regime, real economic expansion came to depend on the initiative of small to medium growers using very little introduced technology. As was typical of colonial circumstances, Abidjan expanded dramatically as the headquarters of the administration and site of social, cultural, and economic institutions. Under self-government and then independence, it was the purpose of the long-lived Houphouet-Boigny administration to make Abidjan a splendid gateway to the prosperity of this unusually successful territory. The air-conditioned modern towers of the urban core, the Plateau, rose over shops that made available the full array of French consumerism to what was by West African standards a large affluent population. There were 46,000 inhabitants counted in 1945, 180,000 in 1960 at the time of independence, and some 1,269,000 by 1978.

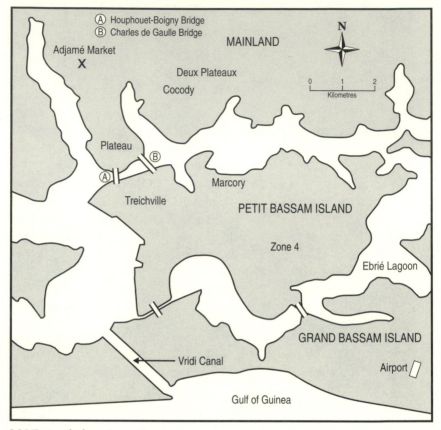

MAP 9. Abidjan, Ivory Coast.

To a casual visitor, a striking feature of Abidjan lay in the presence
of numerous French people and the apparent replication of a provincial French city. The wealthy districts seemed to be a West African
echo of the settler cities of East and South Africa. Indeed this was the
intention of early planners who did wish to minimise the African presence on the Plateau and create as salubrious and exclusive as possible
an atmosphere suitable for the capital of a colony intended to have a
significant white settler presence. This was how the residential district
of Cocody to the east of the Plateau was laid out.

However, for a variety of reasons, it was not possible to reproduce
southern African conditions in this sense in the Ivory Coast. Early
on, the French rewarded building workers on the harbour and elsewhere with *lotissements*, plots of land on which to build houses and

remain in Abidjan. The nature of the Ivorian economy was linked
to the growing intensification of markets, markets that brought tropical products to the port but also connected the whole territory in
time through the distribution of foodstuffs and a wide range of other
goods. Across the impressive *Pont Charles de Gaulle* from the Plateau
lies the great commercial hub of Treichville, an urban and always predominantly black neighbourhood, where the early Ivorian elite used
to gather to make plans for political change in the halcyon days of
nationalist activity after World War II. A second great market breathed
economic life into Adjamé, inland from the Plateau and the obvious connection point to the interior of the country. But indeed there
were markets everywhere. And the different neighbourhoods of Abidjan, streets thronged with people, were far less defined in class terms
than one found in southern Africa. Most of the spreading sections
of the city contained petty bourgeois elements, notably clerical and
other white-collar workers, living amongst the poorer population. The
richest parts of the city also hid squatter settlements full of those
employed in the building services, providing services, and so forth –
settlements which have been, as Alphonse Yapi Diahou has shown,
major sources of economic activity and stimulation themselves. In

FIGURE 16. "Abidjan des tours." Abidjan high-rise towers from the
lagoon, ca. 1980. *Source:* Alain Dubresson, Université de Paris-X; used by
permission.

the early independence period, there was a tendency to destroy such unsightly and unworthy settlements, but since the 1970s they have been tolerated and accepted, although their status remains somewhat precarious to the benefit of a patrimonial system based on bargaining and clientage.

In fact, in important ways, planners were never successful in creating a "rational" structure for Abidjan. While postwar governments constructed blocks of flats suitable for employees, the Ivorian people much preferred to live in compounds which would inevitably contain a varied range of relatives and clients as well as the core family. Indeed, over time, suburbia developed, which allowed for such compound life while the blocks of flats, often in deteriorating condition, were rented out and subdivided to poorer people. The city also contained other complexities: the French and, after independence, the Ivorians did not generally disrupt the original Ebrié settlements in and around Abidjan which were allowed considerable economic and planning autonomy in controlling their own development. On the whole, by the 1970s, Abidjan had evolved into a city that was taking on a distinctive cultural feeling based on its *maquis*-restaurants and cuisine, its distinctive French argot and its cosmopolitan character. This was despite the fact that the Houphouetian political machine defined everyone (apart from the Ebrié) as outsiders who had their real home – above all their political home – in some ethnic hinterland from where their roots could be identified.

Many observers would ascribe a very large part of the success of the city, and of the Ivory Coast, to its tolerance and its capacity to engage the energies of large numbers of outsiders. Not only were there many French residents, there were an even larger number of Lebanese who played a role in most aspects of the economy. The agricultural export economy was dependent on the migration of northern Ivorians into the originally lightly peopled south, but also on hundreds of thousands from the savanna countries, particularly Burkina Faso (Upper Volta), once joined as a colonial territory to the Ivory Coast, and Mali. There were also many migrants from neighbouring countries such as Dahomey (Bénin), Togo, Liberia, and Ghana, often also from forest zone environments. Immigrants were apparently able to own land and to find their way into the professions and civil service as well as the informal commercial sector while Ivorians exerted dominance in general in government work and in the formal working

FIGURE 17. Abidjan courtyards from the air, ca. 1980. *Source:* Alain Dubresson, Université de Paris-X; used by permission.

class. Up to a third of the population in 2000 could be defined as being of "foreign origin."[2]

Establishing a balance between different parts of the heterogenous Ivory Coast and between the natives and the outsiders was certainly the focal point of the system created by Félix Houphouet-Boigny, compared at an early stage to a big city political machine playing to a myriad of ethnic communities in the United States of America by the political scientist Aristide Zolberg. On the one hand, the final supremacy of the Ivorians who deserved the finest fruits of the harvest was to be sustained. But on the other, foreigners were to be welcomed and given their place in the pecking order. There were outbreaks of violence against foreigners at different points in time. Indeed the Ivory Coast government was critical in causing the break-up of the French West African federation in order to retain the rewards of regional success within the territory. Zolberg wrote already in 1964 of antiforeign prejudice as an Ivorian characteristic. But problems were inevitably

[2] By Pierre Janne in *Le Monde Diplomatique*, October 2000. In fact the most recent census figure given was 26 percent.

resolved in terms of firming up a political and social order which promoted the Ivorian miracle socially and politically, elegantly defined in
terms of the hospitality of the Ivorian people. The state fostered ethnic
identity, ruled the countryside through networks of ethnically defined
chiefs, and then established an expert and flexible balance that usually
worked, offering something to everyone.

Unfortunately, the miracle did not endure past 1980. From 1980 to
1995, GNP per capita fell by approximately one-third. Despite various initiatives, the Ivorian economy failed to branch out and diver-
sify very effectively. Indeed in the 1990s it tended to focus more
narrowly around cocoa. Globalisation promotes exports but not generally peasant crop production that can be produced in a wide range of
countries; prices fell and the indebtedness of the state mounted enormously. From 1990, Houphouet-Boigny, who had always bought out
and incorporated political opposition, was forced to accept a multi-
party system which threatened his machine's smooth running. When
he finally died in 1995, he was succeeded by a far less effective political operator, Henri Konan Bédié. Bédié was the promoter of what
was called *ivoirité* – a philosophy which exalted those who could prove
that they and their parents were indigenous Ivorians. This opened a
Pandora's Box. On the one hand, it took off as a popular slogan for
Ivorians who could identify with it in their frustration at a stagnant
or declining economy and blame it on outsiders or foreigners. On
the other, it was seen with mounting anger on the part of northern
and western Ivorians as a ploy by the Akan-speaking cocoa-belt forest
dwellers to retain state power for themselves. In 1990, foreigners lost
all residual rights to vote in the Ivory Coast while in 1999 they lost the
ability to own land and have since been obliged to formalise their status
as non-Ivorians by accepting a system of relatively costly identity cards.
A key state-commissioned report by the *Conseil Economique et Social*
asserted that the number of those of foreign origin in the Ivory Coast,
although no longer increasing, surpassed by far the limit which could
be found "tolerable." Konan Bédié's opponents demanded democracy, but they also wanted a sharper distinction between Ivorians
and foreigners.

All this happens in an environment of expanding unemployment
(according to statistics, considerably higher among Ivorian nationals
than foreigners) and AIDS, significant in Abidjan particularly. In the
good times, education, access to the civil service, the move to town,
and ultimately Abidjan was the golden road to success, to becoming

a real *patron* to one's friends, family, and ethnic group for more and more Ivorians; now the road was virtually cut off. The state offers less and less to the citizen. Good quality health and education increasingly means having the funds to revert to the private sector. No more public housing is erected. The economic environment is becoming notably harsher, especially in this city of more than two-and-a-half million inhabitants. The long stagnation of the 1980s was to a limited extent briefly reversed in the middle 1990s but only due to a rise in cocoa and coffee prices that has not been sustained in the long term. At times, crime waves have overwhelmed urban life.

If we turn from the national picture to the urban one, I will suggest that there are two scenarios which have emerged within this context that are threatening to change Abidjan substantially. The first represents a strategy of capital and of class. I am able to understand this strategy thanks to the work of my Ivorian colleagues in our mutual Three Cities Project but particularly am indebted to the ideas of Sylvie Bredeloup. Bredeloup has made a systematic analysis of commercial transformation in Abidjan. A noticeable shift lies in the growing decline of the popular market, maintained by the public authorities and used by everyone. Of course, the great Adjamé market continues, but it is concerned to a considerable degree with produce and with wholesale activity. Elsewhere markets have been the victims of questionable arson attacks. They are tending to be replaced by covered private markets which are far more closely linked than in the past to nearby shops. Moreover, Abidjan, and especially the up-market parts of Abidjan, has seen the creation of a considerable number of shopping malls and super-cum-hypermarkets. The most important locales are focussed on Cocody, the eastern end of the mainland of Abidjan and the newer suburbs beyond (above all Deux Plateaux which expands more and more into the interior), and on Marcory Zone 4, a desirable if far more crowded and environmentally problematic *quartier* on the island. The latter is near the industrial port but also near the airport and the Atlantic beaches beyond. Much of this recreation of commercial life owes itself to a small number of Lebanese and Indian firms which are acquiring dominance in this sector of the economy.

This shift in the market network can be seen as a gradual restructuring of the commercial arterial life of Abidjan putting paid to the old market structures of West Africa and creating new value for a bourgeoisie in touch with globalisation. Again, the accent is on imports and imported goods of an international character with a higher value, despite growing immiseration of large numbers of Abidjanais, some of whom return to the countryside but many of whom have no real option to do this. A signal feature of contemporary Abidjan is the decline of the once-splendid Plateau; most desirable commercial activity has departed from the historic centre of the city. One could point also to a certain decline in state intervention. The capital has been moved, if rather ineffectually, to Houphouet-Boigny's home town of Yamossoukro. The urban administration has been weakened through decentralisation into ten self-governing units which enjoy elections but have little in the way of revenues, forced as they are to find ways to tax itinerant traders and depend on the market rentals.

Bredeloup links this commercial shift to plans aimed at the construction of new bridges. This could create a new network for Abidjan traffic, linking up the two key elite residential areas to the commercially and industrially important parts of the island of *Petit Bassam* and the airport. It would bypass the old link between the Plateau and Treichville and confirm the decline of the Plateau, which would lose its sense of centrality. One aspect of new transport development, the modernisation of the airport, has in fact taken place.

But the new bridges haven't come into being. Instead, Abidjan has been plunged into prolonged waves of political crisis marked by considerable violence.[3] Konan Bédié was overthrown by the army in 1999, the first intervention of its kind in the Ivory Coast. This in turn led to an election result rejected by the army strongman General Robert Gueï. Gueï in turn was forced in a popular rising to give up power. One prominent aspect of the election was the attempt to freeze out former World Bank bureaucrat Alassane Ouattara, denounced as a Northern Muslim and foreigner, or son of foreign parents.[4] This financial specialist was reclothed by his enemies as an outsider to the code of *ivoirité* and demonised.

In a second phase of violence, elections were held (October 2000) and won by a southerner prepared to use this code himself, Laurent Gbagbo, a long-time "democrat" and opponent of the ruling regime. Killings, with bodies found in the lagoon and forest, accompanied this victory. In fact, this led to civil war in 2002, in which Gbagbo has held on to Abidjan while losing control of the north and west of the Ivory

---

[3] For a convenient guide to the first stages of the crisis through 2001, see Marc le Pape & Claudine Vidal, *Côte d'Ivoire, l'année terrible 1999–2000* (Paris: Karthala, 2002).

[4] In fact, the origins of the Ouattara are mentioned in Chapter One.

Coast. The French have played a leading role in trying to come up with some sort of compromise solution in order to bring back into place the old system or some reasonable substitute for it. Gueï was murdered in Abidjan in September 2002.

It may be that the uneasy truce of 2003 will lead to a stabler situation, but it has so far not marked the end of problems that threaten the cosmopolitan character of Abidjan. Violent youths have been the bearers of the chauvinist politics that is taking on unprecedented strengths. Tensions, curfews, and political murders have taken place in an environment where popular nightclubs feature singers who bemoan the illegitimate influence of foreigners. In the nightclub of Joël Tichi, former captain of the national soccer squad, Ivorians danced to "Libérez," and they meant liberate us – from the foreigners. One of the Ivory Coast's best-known comedians, a resident of Adjamé known to support Ouattara, was murdered, sparking violence in Adjamé amongst his supporters. Gangs set torch to informal settlements and tens of thousands of their inhabitants have made their way back to Liberia, Burkina Faso, and elsewhere. Burkinabe arriving back in Burkina Faso described themselves as "harassed, beaten and . . . arrested" in large numbers, as "treated like cocoa bags." Students burnt down the Burkinabe embassy in January 2003.[5]

Abidjan is too large and too complex a city to say that globalisation has finished it off; its capabilities remain large compared to almost any other West African city. But there is no question that this classic city of import substitution, of the strong state, of peasant export crops, and of the neo-colonial bargain of 1960 is reeling from the impact of a turn inwards. This turn inwards must be related to the decline and presently limited prospects of the previous economic system that created the Ivorian miracle. And, as Bredeloup has shown, initiatives at reconstruction on the basis of more modest forms of growth are really aimed at hardening class lines and creating a new and potentially less humane kind of urbanism in Abidjan where they have come on line; they are about identifying and privileging the minority still able to feed the circulation of money in a substantial way. Nor is there the sign of a new moral order such as the Mourides offer in Touba to create a rainbow on the horizon. Abidjan is not dying, but it is altering in the new environment in important ways.

---

[5] For Internet references to these events see *Hindustan Times*, 25.04.03; *Voice of America* online, 3.2.03; httw://afrol 25.1.03.

Durban: Umhlanga Rocks and Cato Manor Farm

The last example we shall examine is Durban, which, together with
Cape Town, is one of the two really large provincial cities in South
Africa. The population of the extended metropolitan region approaches three million, which makes it roughly equivalent in size to
Abidjan. Unlike Cape Town, Durban's growth is entirely tied up to the
emergence of gold mining and the rise of Johannesburg and the
complex of surrounding towns on the Witwatersrand some six hundred kilometres deeper in the interior. Durban is the port for this inland
urban complex, with a partly artificially opened harbour and a road-
rail-air network efficiently and impressively built up through the
twentieth century. By 1980 there were perhaps 180,000 industrial
workers in Durban, but the economic logic of this industry, little of
which produced anything for export, was based on the harbour and the
availability of imports.

Amongst South African cities, Durban can be noted for its successful development of a large community of professional urban managers and technical specialists following the English model. Over
time, despite the existence of a rate-payer-based elected Council,
which since it was racially exclusive, reflected the anxieties and desires
of the different strata within the white population, the bureaucracy
acquired considerable autonomy over urban planning and effective
power in the city. In the 1980s Durban was more financially secure
and had more capacity for urban development than any other South
African city.

As a built environment, numerous commentators have in recent
years emphasized an ideology of "modernity" as promoting a South
African city where residential and business areas were distinctly separate, where the newer suburbs extended themselves on garden city
lines and where the shabby, the indeterminate, and the irredeemably
poor tended to be entirely left out of the city plans. The growing dominance of big firms and multinationals dovetailed with this process.
However, the South African dimension to this meant that the class
dimension was subordinated to racial politics. Particularly following
the Group Areas Act of 1950, while Abidjan was losing any trace of
formal racialisation, Durban was being reconstructed on precisely this
basis. Security concerns were flagrantly emphasised in this segregatory planning phase which partitioned the residential part of the city

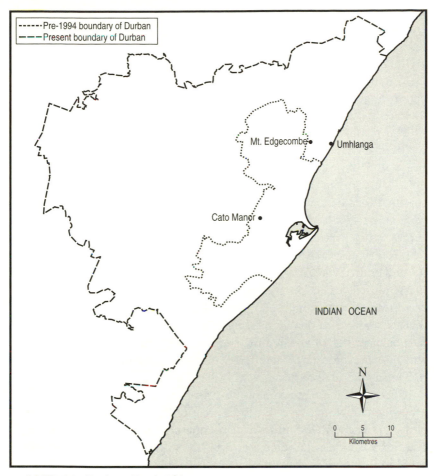

MAP 10. Durban, South Africa.

between white, Indian, Coloured, and African areas while making sure that in every sense the whites retained power over the core.

This created particular challenges for the new era which dawned from the late 1970s as this segregated structure began to manifest growing cracks in the wall. The city had carried out the construction of large family-orientated housing estates for African and Indian people, but these estates were poorly serviced with basic amenities, especially the African ones. Servicing required money, and after 1980 employment ceased to expand in the city, particularly for the working class, creating increasing tensions and politicising struggles over rent and payments for electricity and other basic services. There were few licit economic activities in the African townships, although market and even production activities gradually emerged, despite the planning laws, in some Indian areas. The centre of Durban witnessed the arrival of growing numbers of street traders, and the bad fit between the "modern" structuration of the 1960s and the actual needs of a city thronged with poor people looking for means of survival on their doorstep became apparent.

The townships witnessed violent struggles between two African political forces, the African National Congress and the Inkatha Freedom Party, of which the former was overwhelmingly stronger in inner Durban. On the edge of the city, in areas controlled by the patrimonial Inkatha government of the Kwa Zulu Bantustan,[6] squatters were able to settle in large numbers. In certain areas nearer the city centre, refugees from violence came to live in sordid conditions. The *apartheid* state began to waver in its ability to push them around; by the end of the 1980s, it was no longer possible to expel them. What the literature tells us about large cities with so-called Third World characteristics, unable to upgrade themselves to "world cities," suggests that they would be condemned to a downward spiral post 1980 and particularly after 1990 when the state effectively abandoned *apartheid* and agreed to negotiate a democratic future with representatives of the previously illegal opposition.

Thus we would seem to have an urban model which allowed for a city which grew impressively (the fastest of the bigger South African cities) in the era when South African mineral exports boomed, import substitution industrialisation appeared to work, and both helped to prop up the *apartheid* system. This model could be predicted to experience crisis in the post-*apartheid* era. In fact, Durban has experienced very significant deindustrialisation, especially in its consumer goods industries. The textile industry was a very large-scale employer of low-skill labour dependent on imported raw material and highly protected; it has experienced severe downturn, for instance. This has simultaneously meant a serious decline of the trade union movement, which had galvanised black workers during the 1980s when a number of the most important emerging trade unions had national headquarters for a time

---

[6] Bantustan is a commonly used sobriquet for the "homelands" created as part of the *apartheid* system intended to progress through decolonisation towards an independence that would not threaten the white South African core. In fact, the Kwa Zulu authorities never aimed at independence.

in Durban. Together with the impact of extraordinarily high degrees of unemployment, the city inherits an economic structure which makes it difficult for an "informal sector" to expand beyond the survivalist and the illicit and make a very significant contribution to productive activity. At the most positive we can talk about a clothing industry which has partly reinvented itself, with less social protection and lower wages in sweatshops located away from the traditional industrial districts and perhaps taking up most of the workers otherwise pushed into unemployment (when measured in numbers). Certain industries are far more successful (automobiles, chemicals, wood products, some metal goods), but based on stagnant or declining workforces. Moreover, Durban lies in the province of KwaZulu/Natal which has been considered the most highly affected part of South Africa by the HIV virus. And South Africa has the largest number of those living with HIV in the world. Very likely 20 percent of the population of Durban at the moment are condemned to die of AIDS within a few years – more than twice the proportion in Abidjan and several times that in holy Touba.

Yet only now is Durban experiencing another part of the modernist dream of the postwar era – the arrival of a national (and local) government committed to inclusive citizenship and determined to tackle poverty and lack of resources by the poor. As we shall soon see, there is a parallel to Abidjan in terms of attempts at physical restructuration to the benefit of the affluent. But the new government is committed to breaking down white power as it existed. From 1996, a new administration, presided over by more than forty previously extant and racially defined municipal structures, merged into a metropolitan council with submetropolitan bodies. This council was given the isiZulu name of Ethekweni in 2001 and restructured into a "Unicity" on a considerably more centralised basis that draws in a substantial rural periphery. This new structure is committed to equity in services, employment and other spheres as part of the making of the "new South Africa." Moreover, while the globalisation model predicts a growing dominance of ethnic and racial identity issues as the state is preempted by the dictates of capital, the ANC is committed to forging a new national identity, even while privileging the "previously disadvantaged," as they are termed, and with a strong bias towards centralised government dominating governance. In the remainder of this section of the chapter we shall look at a couple of parts of the Durban complex in evaluating these changes.

One visible index of the new Durban is the very rapid growth of the northern areas of Umhlanga Rocks/Umhlanga Ridge. In the postwar decades, this section of the city essentially consisted of sugar cane fields while a small settlement around a lighthouse and hotel attracted white tourists seeking an unspoilt seaside environment. From the 1970s, this settlement built up rapidly with flats and time-share units as the well-to-do in Johannesburg searched for an outlet to a warm place by the sea away from the traditional Durban beachfront, too easily reached by public transport and beginning to fade as leisure tastes changed. However, just inland the sugar fields remained, in good part owing to the tax regime which discouraged conversion from agriculture. One large company, Tongaat-Hulett, itself linked to the finance-mining giant Anglo-American, owned most of them.

However, as shifts towards economic liberalisation development planning began in the late 1980s, Tongaat-Hulett hired some of the best minds in the city to think about future spatial planning and has been a major actor in the growing environment of public-private partnership in Durban. In consequence of this, the company organised the sale of large amounts of cane land to create the foundation for what has been classically termed in the United States by Joel Garreau an "edge city." On the ridge overlooking the sea and the oceanside suburb of Umhlanga Rocks, one now finds hundreds of houses of the newly rich (no longer racially defined, of course), the largest shopping complex in South Africa modelled on activity-based U.S. shopping malls and a growing array of corporate service offices and headquarters. Meanwhile, further north, gloriously or hideously unplanned new beach suburbs on the so-called Dolphin Coast, much like Umhlanga Rocks, are expanding very rapidly to cater to the affluent retired and to executives seeking to recuperate from the pressures of life in Johannesburg or Pretoria; the most expensive developments are dubbed "eco-estates." Just inland, Mount Edgecombe sugar estate has been largely turned into a golf course and network of affluent gated suburbia. Further inland lies land designated for the less affluent and the site of what will be towards the end of the first decade of the twenty-first century a new international airport partly aimed at the tourist market. By contrast, the central business district of Durban, although still a centre of government and harbour-related business and still a thriving shopping district for the working poor and lower middle class, is now largely bereft of boutiques, entertainment facilities, and up-market office premises.

In more than one sense, Umhlanga symbolises the typical features associated with the globalised city: a sharp division between a cut-off and protected rich and growingly unwanted and irregularly supported poor, an obsession with security, and the hunger of capital for exploitation of new land for constructing houses and commercial property. The architectural models used are eclectic and international with little or no use of any South African indigenous building forms. While the expansion of Umhlanga serves to decentre Durban, as in many international examples, the gentrification option is however also present in the form of upgrading the wealthiest parts of the older inner suburbia of Durban. The stereotyped view of Africa assumes that the entire continent is simply cut out of these trends typical of richer nations and banished to some outer hell by globalisation. In reality, the example of Durban, even more than Abidjan – and increasingly less hesitantly – shows that these new divisions also form within Africa itself.

Up to a point there is one striking difference between Umhlanga and American edge cities. Umhlanga remains a part of Metro Durban. It does not and cannot escape the fiscal and political dictates of City Hall in the manner of U.S. suburbia. Tongaat-Hulett is also an important player in the attempt to create a new tourist mecca at the Point which marks the opening of the harbour right at the heart of the central city of Durban. However, this contrast should not be taken too far. The logic of capital is one that the ANC government is very unwilling to counter; there is complete acceptance of the need to accommodate and attract business through "competitiveness" as the key dictate in urban policy. Countering unplanned development (or better put, development planned purely in the interests of the affluent) is no longer considered a sensible way to conduct urban politics. And thus the continuing edge-city development of north Durban can be considered a certainty for the future.

Yet Durban's story is not this straightforward. A short account of Cato Manor development gives an interesting contrast to Umhlanga. Cato Manor is a large tract of hilly, relatively unstable land very close to and directly inland from the central business district of Durban. It was subdivided in large part and sold to Indian smallholders who were the main inhabitants of a lightly peopled district. During World War II, already notorious as a locale for illicit activity, especially the brewing and sale of alcohol to Africans, Cato Manor attracted some tens of thousands of poor African arrivals from the countryside to whom Indians rented land or shacks. In 1949 it was the scene of the infamous Cato Manor African-Indian "race riots" which were partly instigated by ambitious African would-be entrepreneurs. In the 1950s it became associated with pockets of militant antigovernment organisation and violent conflict between women beer-brewers and the police. Cato Manor was a zone that urban authorities could not control.

Before Group Areas, Durban had been largely segregated by race de facto. Now the state was determined to put segregation into force more thoroughly. Cato Manor was almost entirely uprooted and its Indian and African inhabitants forced to move into townships elsewhere in the early 1960s. It was proclaimed "white," but there was no commercial interest in developing the area for white suburbia and in effect this large central space languished for decades.

The post-*apartheid* authorities were anxious to use this space for large-scale greenfields housing, despite the cost of shoring up land in most sections. In effect, the new regime has defined shack dwelling as part of a "housing shortage" and put much effort into devising policy that would involve handing over new housing to large numbers of poor people – housing planned for secure building sites and fitted with indoor plumbing and electricity. Cato Manor posed a particularly serious challenge. Towards the end of the *apartheid* era, the state had proclaimed the area suitable for Indian housing, and some Indian families had returned to the area, purchasing new little bungalows from the middle 1980s. Indian claims for Cato Manor were strong; the compensation money doled out in the past was minimal and the sense of dispossession a burning part of the legacy of *apartheid*. Such dispossessed Indians formed a major part of the claimants asking for land from the new government. And yet in 1992, impatient Africans living nearby in crowded circumstances were so upset at the new Indian arrivals that they invaded the last lot of *apartheid* housing, seizing these properties for their own. Moreover, during the transition era, a considerable number of Africans, perhaps up to twenty thousand, had felt emboldened to build shacks in parts of Cato Manor. Many were refugees from violence, and here again there was some sense of wanting justice about the past. But equally pressing were the violent activities of shacklords and gangs dominated by so-called veterans of the liberation struggle who preyed upon the illegal shack dwellers.

Given this volatile context, the city was prepared to authorise the creation of the Cato Manor Development Agency in 1992 to administer and further the development of the area. This agency was staffed with committed ex-activists associated with alternative housing NGOs and foreign sympathisers, while there was a board of control with local representation. Circumstances meant that it was possible for these bureaucrats to operate free of political pressures. They were able to devote the first years of CMDA activity to knife-edge political negotiation at which they proved very skillful, gradually stabilising conditions. They also proved skillful at attracting outside funding, particularly from the European Union, to what was billed a model project.

This situation controverts neo-liberal wisdom in important ways: a strong central state eager to make centre-left interventions, a set of enlightened bureaucrats willing to dispense without overly much stakeholder intervention and large-scale extra funding with few or no strings attached. The results have been correspondingly positive in important ways. Housing, while proceeding somewhat slowly, has gone ahead and included some interesting experiments involving more quality and potential for community formation than is typical. Sites have generally been allocated as fairly as possible without patronage taken into account, thus creating citizens rather than patrimonial clients. The foundation for far more building has been laid. Indian ex-residents, uninterested in the end in returning to mixed neighbourhoods, have accepted compensation on a large scale for their previous losses. A few live in middle-class housing near the site of a large new specialised hospital. Others benefit from laying out commercial sites where they have been welcome to return as businessmen and women. The smaller post-1990 shack settlements have been destroyed and replaced by permanent housing. On the biggest site, where perhaps fifteen thousand people live, some upgrading has taken place, the shacklords' power has been broken, and there have at least been no successful further attempts at illegal settlement. A striking feature of the settled areas of Cato Manor has been the early provision of health facilities, schools, and community halls. Some green space has been left in many areas. A major road has been driven through Cato Manor, opening it up to easy access to key parts of the city and commercial and industrial properties have begun to develop alongside. A small number of African contractors (around one hundred) have been used locally, although, as is so typical of South Africa, construction remains overwhelmingly performed by public or corporate contractors with capacity.

The limitations of Cato Manor success need however equally to be spelt out. It is estimated (but still not studied definitively) that the residents suffer just as much from AIDS and just as much from unemployment as elsewhere in the city. The special features of the

CMDA from early in 2003 will be a thing of the past; the city has adjudged crisis conditions to be over and will start to administer Cato Manor like anywhere else. Patronage in the form of elected councillors and others will no doubt return, diluting the CMDA thrust on turning residents into pure citizens free of dubious forms of mediation.

Some of the housing in Cato Manor is pathetically tiny and basic and unsurprisingly gets sold illegally for less than the official value of the house (houses are supposed not to be legally sold for at least eight years). Given how rarely inhabitants are in steady employment, the private sector has effectively refused to involve itself with any signal assistance. South Africa lacks more or less totally small businessmen living on the margins and prepared to take such risks to fill this gap. There are beginning to be problems with non-payment of bills; an experimental densely settled rental area is refusing to pay rent. Why should they, after all, if houses have been made available to others for nothing? These issues highlight the basic contradictions in government policy generally. On the one hand, an urgent and intense desire exists to "make up for" *apartheid* by making available some funds for effectively free housing and infrastructure, but on the other, there is no capacity to intervene massively to create jobs and no desire to try to channel private funds forcibly in directions business does not seek. A thriving private sector has been adjudged to be the bedrock of any national future, and in the most cases this dramatically limits structured interventions by the state. And finally, Cato Manor is only very marginally "non-racial"; it is a black "community," in part because of the choice to create almost no middle-class housing (although the income mix is greater than in many other South African state-housing schemes).

Cato Manor is then a qualified success. What is successful goes against the grain of neo-liberal wisdom, and yet it is applauded within a global environment that supposedly allows for no alternatives. In practice, South Africa has been able to find some purchase on the new international economic environment. Its exports of fruit and wine and so-called non-traditional exports have shot up. It attracts far higher numbers of foreign tourists than in the past. By the end of the twentieth century, Durban harbour was choked with containers awaiting off-loading and badly in need of restructuring to accommodate larger business. The minerals and energy sector profited from growing international prices in the early twenty-first century, notably platinum and even gold. Moreover, there is a state anxious to retain nation-building prerogatives and to do something for its largely impoverished and often

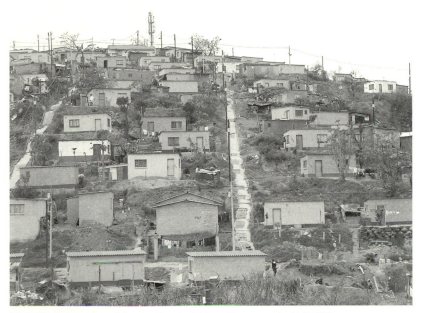

FIGURE 18. Cato Manor, South Africa. Post-*apartheid* 'RDP' state-subsidised housing. *Source:* Stéphane Vermeulin; used by permission.

marginalized supporters. However, globalisation and the prescribed ties it enforces with business tend to limit the possibility for state-led development and create constant pressure for further marginalisation, if no longer on racial grounds. At best Cato Manor is now another urban township with all the problems experienced by the others, no worse but not dramatically better either.

Three Cities

This chapter falls hard on its predecessor which contained some harsh scenes of urban life in contemporary Africa, scenes containing burgeoning cities struggling to cope with human needs. These cities seemed to tell a story where current trends in international political economy go right against desirable solutions. They undermine modernist plans of the late colonial era as well as the aspirations of the early independence period. This story seems to be one in which Africans figure largely as helpless victims. I have however tried to qualify this by suggesting aspects in which coping with these problems may contain

the seed of new kinds of urban forms and solutions. In this chapter, I
have tried to go a bit further and suggest that the script written above
at first was too simple. By way of conclusion it can be said that even
within Africa there is no simple formula for understanding the evolution of cities in the present phase.

The examples chosen here are not typical, although they are significant. Globalisation is not something that "affects" Africa from without; it also operates *within* Africa in ways that suggest patterns to come,
especially taken with some of the material in the preceding chapter.
The South African case perhaps suggests some of the limitations that
create boundaries for change today but also that possibilities for a
determined state to operate independently are by no means negligible. Outcomes are not predetermined; both the studies of Abidjan and
Touba also make it clear that they may be uncertain and contingent
on political and social developments. Some previous roads to development are now clearly cut off, but the alternatives people find to conduct
their lives, which will inevitably be in large part urban alternatives, are
more unpredictable. These very different examples, Touba, Abidjan,
Durban, draw a wider range of developmental thrusts. And even within
each the future is open-ended, uncertain, and not lacking in contradictions. The African city will continue to develop and expand; it will
continue to exhibit vitality and will more and more be the place where
African futures are decided.

Selected Readings

The pages on Touba are based on Cheikh Guèye, *Touba: la capitale
des mourides* (Paris: Karthala, 2002). A much shorter summary by the
same author entitled "Touba: les marabouts urbanisants" can be found
in Monique Bertrand & Alain Dubresson, ed., *Petites et moyennes ville
d'Afrique noire* (Paris: Karthala, 1997). There are a number of major
studies of the Mourides in French and English. A notable one is Donal
Cruise O'Brien, *The Mourides of Senegal* (London: Oxford University
Press, 1971). See also Cheikh Anta Babou, "Brotherhood Solidarity,
Education and Migration: The Role of the *Dahiras* among the Muslim
Community of New York," *African Affairs*, CI, 2002.

Most of the excellent scholarly literature available on Abidjan is in
French: Philippe Haeringer, "Vingt-cinq ans de politique urbaine à
Abidjan," *Politique africaine*, 17, 1985; Marc le Pape, "De l'espaces

des races à Abidjan entre 1903 et 1934," *Cahiers d'etudes africaines*, IC, 1985; Alain Dubresson, *Ville et industrie en Côte d'Ivoire: pour une géographie de l'accumulation urbaine* (Paris: Karthala, 1989), with a short summary of many of his ideas in the Rakodi collection cited in the previous chapter; Philippe Antoine et al., *Abidjan: "côté cours,"* (Paris: ORSTOM/Karthala, 1987); Alphonse Yapi Diahou, *Baraques et pouvoirs dans l'agglomération abidjanaise* (Paris: L'Harmattan, 2001) are a few of the most interesting contributions. See however Michael Cohen, "Urban Policy and Development Strategy" in I.William Zartman & Christopher Delgado, eds., *The Political Economy of the Ivory Coast* (New York: Praeger, 1984) and Aristide Zolberg, *One Party Government in the Ivory Coast* (Princeton: Princeton University Press, 1964).

For Durban, the two most important studies of the past are Leo Kuper et al., *Durban: A Study in Racial Ecology* (London: Jonathan Cape, 1958) and Paul Maylam & Iain Edwards, eds., *The People's City: African Life in Twentieth Century Durban* (Pietermaritzburg: University of Natal Press, 1996). See also the collection on contemporary Durban that I edited with Vishnu Padayachee: *The D(urban) Vortex: A South African City in Transition* (Pietermaritzburg: University of Natal Press, 2002). I have also made an earlier comparative study with Abidjan much more historically based: "Contrasts in Urban Segregation: A Tale of Two African Cities, Durban and Abidjan," *Journal of Southern African Studies*, XXVII (1), 2001, 527–46. Comparable studies of Johannesburg and other South African cities in the post-*apartheid* era are Jo Beall, Owen Crankshaw & Susan Parnell, *Uniting a Divided City; Governance and Social Exclusion in Johannesburg* (London & Sterling VA: Earthscan, 2002); Richard Tomlinson, Robert Beauregard, Lindsay Bremner & Xolela Mangcu, eds., *Emerging Johannesburg: Perspectives on the Postapartheid City* (London & New York: Routledge, 2003); and Philip Harrison, Marie Huchzermeyer & Mzwanele Mayekiso, eds., *Housing and Urban Development in a Democratising Society* (Cape Town: University of Cape Town Press, 2003).

Index